AFTER BARBARA

₰ ₰ ₰

JOSEPH J. BAKEWELL

©2002 Joseph Bakewell

ISBN 0-9718701-0-1

All rights reserved. No part of this book may be reproduced or transmitted in any form by any means, electronic, mechanical, photocopying, recording, or otherwise without the prior written permission of the publisher.

Unabooks
P.O. Box 322
Boxford, MA 01921

Printed and bound in the United States of America

DEDICATION

To my family

"Family's the beginning and the end of everything. Isn't it?"

a quote from the book.

❧ ❧ ❧

CHAPTER ONE

It happened on a clear cool day in September, the kind of day that the people of Woodcliff Lake, New Jersey celebrate at the end of summer's heat and humidity. Barbara and Tom Brogan went for a bicycle ride. As they neared home, Barbara dawdled behind. Tom went on ahead and was putting his bike in the garage when he heard it — the squeal of tires, a loud thump, a crunching sound, a car racing off. In the first instant, he tried simply to wonder what it was. He started to walk down the driveway; then he began to run, and then to run faster. Entering the street, he saw nothing, then some neighbors hurrying along and across the street. A man knelt down; a woman turned away covering her face. He looked at the expressions as he approached. And then, he saw her, lying alongside her twisted bicycle, one leg folded under at an awkward angle, arms splayed out, mouth open. He knelt close, looking for any sign of life. He reached out.

Someone said, "Harry's gone to call an ambulance."

A policeman stopped the car less than a mile away when he spotted its broken windshield. The driver was drunk, and his license had been revoked. Tom wanted to hate him — hate him enough to kill. Then he learned that the young driver had a wife and three small children. Sometime later, he would pray for them all.

The days that followed the accident were nothing but a blur. John and Helene, his adult children, took care of everything, and somehow he got through. Jerry and Alice Healey flew up from Washington for the wake and the funeral. That meant something; a United States senator from New Jersey drops everything to be there.

Three weeks later, he called Jerry to tell him that he had been fired from his job as general manager of Newcomer and Company, a Wall Street investment firm.

"They wanted me out of the way. The dopey bastards want to do mergers and acquisitions with a company that's set up to manage pension funds."

"Man, you're really taking some lumps," Jerry said.

"I should have quit last year like Barbara wanted. We could have had that time."

"Yeah, I guess it's pretty hard not to look back." He paused. "I've got an idea."

"You won't blame me if I don't jump on it."

"How would you like to go to Ireland? You've been there a few times. I know that you like it."

"I've only been there with Barbara."

"You wouldn't be going to the same places. It's a trade mission. You'll travel with a group, visiting shopping centers and industrial estates. You'll listen to proposals for investments. When you get back, you write a simple report, and that's it. You're good at that financial stuff; you might find it interesting."

Tom was intrigued; some involvement in the world of investments would be a healthy distraction, but he did not fool himself about Barbara. He went to Ireland, and she was everywhere: at Shannon Airport; in the scenery; in the lilt of Irish voices; and especially in the hotel rooms at night.

During a reception near the end of the trip, two young men approached Tom. Kevin McBride and his cousin, Vincent Kelly, were from County Leitrim. They heard that his ancestors came from there. They told him of a European Union subsidy for raising trees in Ireland. Their enthusiasm impressed him, and he soon found himself in Country Leitrim negotiating to buy a farm. The cousins were to own a small percentage.

❧ ❧ ❧

All that was in the fall — months ago. Now, he was in New York for the first time since then to have lunch with Jerry. He paid the cab fare and turned to walk under the blue awning, which extended from the curb to the restaurant door, held open by a uniformed doorman. Inside, the lighting was subdued and sounds hushed by dark-green carpeting and antique–gold drapery. He gave his hat and coat to an attractive young woman with upswept blond hair wearing a svelte black cocktail dress and then followed the maître d' to a secluded table.

Jerry was waiting. They exchanged pleasantries, and then the conversation turned serious.

"You can tell me that it's none of my business," Jerry said, "but are you sure about making all these changes in your life?"

"I didn't make the *big* changes, Jerry. They happened *to* me."

"God knows, you got more than your share. But a tree farm in Ireland? Jesus!"

"I need to do something different. This tree farm business looks pretty good to me."

"What do John and Helene say about it? They must think you've flipped your lid."

Tom had picked up his menu and was trying to make a decision. "My god! And I thought the prices downtown were steep."

"I'm buying," Jerry said, picking up his own menu.

"You can afford this on a senator's salary?"

Jerry lowered his menu just enough to make eye contact. "Senators do all right. Not in your league, but not bad."

Tom smiled and put his menu down. "You asked about the kids. John's okay with it, he's preoccupied with his job and my first grandchild, but Helene's upset. Wants me to stay home."

"She misses Barbara?"

"Big time. They were getting to be real buddies."

"And this Ireland thing is your way of dealing with it?"

Tom nodded. "That's part of it."

"And the other part?"

Tom sat back, softly biting his lower lip. "The other part? I don't want to depend on my kids for a life. I don't want to be a 'has been' that comes to visit." His eyes fixed on Jerry. "I want to be interesting."

Their waiter came in a starched white jacket and black bow tie; his dark mustache only slightly distracted the eye from his badly pockmarked cheeks. He took their orders and left. Neither man spoke. Tom gazed out across the room, idly watching the comings and goings of waiters and patrons. He turned back to his friend. How long had it been now since they had roomed together in prep school? Over thirty years? Remaining friends as Jerry became ever more the consummate Irish-American politician. They were the same height, each a little over six feet and athletically built. They had the same Irish-blue eyes, but Jerry's seemed a deeper blue because of his black hair and the way his eyebrows drooped down at the sides, giving him a sad-eyed, basset hound, look. A look that seemed to work wonders with girls when they had been out on the prowl together—all those years ago.

Tom said, "Clever, the way they use plants to create privacy without taking up much space."

"Yeah, pretty neat." Jerry leaned forward. "Listen, Tom, as long as you're determined to do this tree farm thing anyway, I've got a favor to ask."

"Ah, now the government's buying my lunch."

"Funny. You'll be in County Leitrim, right?"

"That's right. The farm's a little northwest of Carrick-on-Shannon."

"Near the border with Northern Ireland?"

Tom shrugged. "It's not far."

Their waiter arrived to set a tray down nearby. He rearranged everything on their table to make room for more dishes than seemed necessary for what they had ordered. When things were settled and the waiter gone, Tom asked, "What did you have in mind?"

"You know, the Irish-American vote is pretty big in New Jersey. Ted Kennedy and the Democrats have got everyone convinced that they are the only ones that know anything about Ireland. Particularly, Northern Ireland. We Republicans look like a bunch of dimwits. All we can do is rubber stamp whatever they come up with. Even if it's the right thing to do — and it may not be — we look like we don't care."

"And do you?"

"Care? Yes, we care. I care. I really do, and I want to be better informed. The whole thing is such a can of worms."

"It sure is. And, I don't know that much about it."

"But you can find out."

"You want *me* to figure out what's going on in Northern Ireland?"

"I'm not asking you to solve the problems. Just come up with a report on them."

"Just like that?"

"I've got some money in my budget for consulting. It's not much, but it would pay your expenses to go up there and ask questions. I can arrange letters of introduction. Talk to people, get your own sense of how things are."

Tom leaned back and put his hand up behind his neck. *God, doesn't he ever relax?*

Jerry continued. "You wouldn't have to make long trips. I have always valued your judgment, Tom. And, you'd be surprised at how much misinformation we get in Washington."

"Sounds like it's my patriotic duty to provide a shaft of light in the darkness."

Jerry grimaced. "I get the pun. I know you're not a big fan of Washington politics, but shaft, or no shaft, this would be a real help."

"When do you need it?"

"Well before the elections. Say, the end of August?"

"It figures," Tom said, his mind struggling for a way out — a way to slip the noose being put around his neck. And yet, he did not have that many friends, and Jerry wasn't always being the politician. He had dropped everything to be at Barbara's wake and her funeral, and he would surely make an effort to be at Helene's graduation from Princeton. A good friend.

"I'm full up with the farm and getting trees planted — at least until after Helene's graduation."

"Do what you can. Whatever I get will be more than I have now."

The waiter came to refill their water glasses and to ask if everything was satisfactory. Jerry nodded to him, and then turned back to Tom.

"What are you going to do about Helene?"

"I don't know." His eyes followed their waiter, now talking to an elegantly dressed woman at another table. She wore a small hat. He could remember that — when women wore hats. Barbara had several, but he could not recall what they looked like. He listened to the murmuring voices and the soft sounds of clinking china before turning back. "She's a mature young woman. She'll understand, even if it takes a while. She'll be starting her career soon."

"She's a beautiful woman — takes after Barbara."

Tom stared at his plate; a vision of Barbara and then Helene flashed through his mind. He waited a moment, and took a breath before answering.

"She does take after her, in many ways."

CHAPTER TWO

It rained the day before as it often did during early spring in Ireland. But not on this day. Tom went to Carrick-on Shannon to close the deal on his new farm and then headed back to his B&B in the village of Drumshanbo, situated at the southern tip of Lough Allen, not far from the farm. As he drove, many shades of green assaulted his eyes; greens throbbing in the bright sunshine; greens so varied and strong that one could never put them completely out of mind. A great day for a walk. He parked just inside the village.

The houses, the church, and the stores had almost all been built years ago. With a few exceptions, they were in good repair. The stores were typical of Irish towns; twenty or so feet wide, two or three stories high; built to house the family as well as the business. Each was unique in structure and color, and yet all the pastels and shapes blended together creating an effect as pleasing to the eye as an old fashioned quilt. As he passed people on the street, each acknowledged his presence, the women with a nod of the head and the men with a nod, or a touch to the cap. Everyone murmured a soft "good morning". Near the center, he crossed over a bridge, as much a part of the town as any building; he paused to lean on the railing and watch the busy water below. For how many centuries have the cheerful sounds of this brook lifted spirits in this town? As he stepped back, a young girl nearly ran into him on her bicycle. "Sorry," she yelled over her shoulder, never missing a stroke. A young boy had been chasing her, probably her brother. He stopped near Tom and yelled after her, "eedjit." He glanced at Tom, as if to say, "That'll fix her." and strode off.

On the main street, which was at most a hundred yards long, he spotted a store with a collection of trophies in the window. He read the inscriptions. They were for marching band competitions, two recent ones for first place in the All Ireland competition. Looking past the trophies, he saw that the store sold candy, ice cream, sodas, and newspapers. He went in to buy some newspapers. There was no one in the store, but an open door connected the store to the pub right next to it. There was a woman behind the bar washing glasses. She dried her hands and came into the little candy store. Tom selected a couple of papers, and was getting his money out. "Is this all one establishment?" he asked, pointing at the connecting door.

"It is," she said, "including the play hall in the back. I'm Mary Donohue, my husband, Frank, is the proprietor."

"I'll be back to meet him," Tom said. "Does he know any building contractors?"

"You'd have to ask him that yourself."

"I will. By the way, my name is Tom Brogan. I'm buying the Cochran farm."

"I thought that would be you. You're from America?"

Tom shook his head and then turned to leave. God! I just got here. He went back to his car, and drove to his B&B, The Shannonside, to read his papers and use the phone.

After supper, that evening, he went back to the pub, and immediately noticed the acrid pungent smell of peat burning in the fireplace. It was a smell that never failed to bring images into his head: images of ancestors gathered to tell stories of bygone heroes; or of a little starving family huddled together in a pitiful shack, craving a bit of warmth to ease the pain in their stomachs.

Two other patrons, older men, sat together at the long side of the bar. They were watching the television set, mounted high up at the far end of the bar, just above an opening into the play hall at the back, where teenagers played video games, ping pong, darts and snooker while consuming generous amounts of Coke. Tom sat at the front, around the bend of the bar. The barman come up to him, his shirt sleeves rolled up to just below the elbow; a short wiry man, dark eyed with black curly hair sprinkled with individual, decidedly white, flecks. His hands seemed too large for his wrists and forearms.

"Are you Frank?" Tom asked.

"Aye."

"I'm Tom Brogan." He held out his hand. "I was in this afternoon. I met your wife."

Donohue's grip was gentle, his hand cool and hard. "You'll be taking over the Cochran farm?"

"Yeah. Or vice versa."

Donohue smiled and wiped the bar in front of Tom. The two old men had turned slightly to check Tom out. He smiled, and waved to them. They both nodded and turned back to the television.

"Will you be having anything?"

"A Guinness, please."

Donohue went over to the tap and began the slow process of drawing a pint. "Do you like the Guinness?" he asked.

"Yes. I can't drink much of it, but I like it."

When the pint was finally ready, Donohue brought it over and carefully set it on a coaster in front of Tom. He moved aside and wiped the bartop nearby. "Mary said that you were asking about contractors?"

"Yes. I want to renovate the Cochran house. But, I want to do it with modern materials and techniques."

"Ahh," Donohue nodded as he moved back to the tap. He finished drawing two more pints for the other patrons, and then came back over to Tom. "There's not going to be many contractors around here that can help you."

"Yeah. It's going to be tough. I have an architect coming up from Galway next week. I'll see what he has to say."

"If he's a good man, there might be fellas here that can do the work. He'd have to show them what to do."

"We'll see what he says."

"Have you met any of your new neighbors?" Donohue asked.

"Not yet."

"Do you like horses? I've not much use for them myself."

"I don't mind them."

"Your nearest neighbors, Philip and Meagan Clark, keep horses. You might want to learn to ride them yourself."

"Are they nice? Not the horses, the Clarks?"

"Nice enough, I'm told. I've never met them, but I'm sure that you will. Some of the fellas have had some things to say about them — the woman especially — but I'm sure you'd rather meet them for yourself."

"Yeah, it's probably better that way."

Tom finished his pint. He said good night to Donohue, the two old men, and left, ending his first visit with Frank.

≥❧ ≥❧ ≥❧

In late April, with the house nearly finished, Tom ate supper in the dining room for the first time. Most of the furniture had been delivered, and he planned to leave his B&B to move in when his bed arrived later in the week. He looked around at the freshly painted white walls and at the new windows, including the picture window, which still had smudges of putty on the glass. *It's going to be cheerful, especially when they get the molding up and some kind of curtains. What's wrong with me? I should be happy. Is it all crazy?* His thoughts wandered off into visions of Barbara. *What fun they had in that first dingy little apartment in Jersey City — painting and cleaning together. That first weekend when they discovered that they did not own an ironing board, or a corkscrew. Can it ever be like that again? Am I too old to have that sense of adventure? That feeling of completeness that Barbara gave me?*

Brid, his housekeeper, came in and broke his train of thought. "Did you know that Ireland has too many sheep?"

"No, I didn't know that."

In early March, he had hired Brid Greenan and her husband, Sean, as housekeeper and caretaker. They were both in their sixties. Brid was of medium height, stocky and talkative while Sean was quiet, tall and thin, with the body and hands of a man who had worked hard all his life. He had a shock of bright gray hair, parts of which were always conspicuously out of place. They worked hard and seemed to have a real sense of ownership for the house and farm. Tom began to think of them as extended family.

Brid set his glass of beer on the table. "Yes," she said, "the butcher says that they'll be paying the farmers to get rid of them."

"That sounds familiar."

"Can you imagine Ireland with too much food?" she said.

"Amazing."

"Oh, and I met a woman I know from years ago. She works for the neighbors, just over the hill."

"The Clarks?"

"Yes, she's the housekeeper, Sarah Gallagher. I'm invited to visit."

"Oh, good. I've been negligent; I should have gone over and introduced myself."

"I'll ask when would be a good time," she said.

The next evening, Brid filled Tom in on her visit to the Clarks' house. "They're not married, you know. It's a brother and a sister. He's a writer. He's there most of the time. She's not. She teaches in Galway and comes home weekends. She has a little boy, Jimmy. He's a darling."

"Is she a widow?"

"Divorced. She lived in the North. They're Protestants."

Tom laughed. "That's okay with me."

"Sarah says they're grand, just grand. They have horses, you know."

"Yes, I knew about the horses. I guess I should go over this weekend?"

"I'm sure that would be fine. You should know that there's a problem."

"With the weekend?"

"No. With the fence."

"The fence?"

"There was a bridle path that they use. It goes across the back corner of this farm and down to the Lough. You've got a fence there now."

"Great. Just what I needed." Tom got up from the kitchen chair, and walked over to gaze out the window. He turned back toward Brid and curled in his lower lip, gently biting while he thought. "I wish I'd known. I can probably use something else back there to keep the sheep out." After supper, he called Kevin, the young man who had helped him buy the farm and restore the house, and who had recommended Brid and Sean, his aunt and uncle, to Tom.

Kevin said, "It won't be a problem, Tom. We can make some openings in the fence. We can put up one of those gates that riders can open and close without getting off their horses."

Early in the afternoon on the next day, Tom paid a call on the Clarks. He drove up to the front of the house. As he got out of the car, he could see the barn out back, and the paddock next to it. The barn door was open, and there was a small yellow bicycle just inside. He paused to stare at the bike. It would be a big step to start riding again — a healthy one.

The large wooden house had two stories and was painted a dark brown. There were porches on both the front and back — unusual for Ireland. He went up the steps. A man came to the door, and Tom introduced himself.

"Come in. Come in," the man said. "I'm Philip. I'm the only one here. My sister, Meagan, won't be home until Friday, and the housekeeper's gone to fetch my nephew from school." Philip's pale skin appeared to be slightly translucent, displaying traces of blue veins around his temples. He was thin and appeared to be about forty. He had reddish brown hair, and his pale blue eyes hinted at the dreamy wisdom of an esthetic writer.

"I can come back another time," Tom said.

"No, no. Let me fix a pot of tea. It's the limit of my domestic skills, but it generally comes out just fine." Philip led Tom into the living room. "Have a seat," he said. "I'll be back in a minute."

Tom sat on a couch near the fireplace. It was an antique French style couch, covered in an off-white and light-green striped satin fabric. He looked around at the wallpaper, a soft floral design, and at the ornate picture frames. There were large area rugs over a polished hardwood floor. It reminded him of rooms he had seen in colonial houses in the States — currently museums. Philip returned with a pot of tea, cups, cream, sugar, and some biscuits — all on a silver tray. "I've been so wanting to meet you," he said. "I understand that you're going to grow trees over there."

"That's the idea. I'm trying a new kind of hardwood tree. It's supposed to mature in ten years."

"That would be something. Most of our wood is imported now."

"I hope to remedy that," Tom said. "This is a nice house. How long have you lived here?"

"Thank you. It's been in the family for years. I've lived here all my life. Meagan lived in the North for a time." Philip sat in a chair across a low table from Tom. He served the tea, and offered Tom some biscuits.

Tom took one. "I wanted to meet you," he said. "But, I also came to apologize."

"Whatever for?"

"For the fence across the bridle path. I'm having it fixed tomorrow. You'll be able to ride through there by Friday."

"That's very generous, Tom. We certainly appreciate your consideration. Meagan will just be delighted."

"I hope so. I'll have to get over and meet her sometime after I get settled in."

Tom stayed for another twenty minutes and enjoyed his conversation with Philip. As he got up to leave, he noticed a picture on the mantle. He went over for a closer look. "Is that Meagan?"

"Yes, it is."

"A recent picture?"

"Oh, yes. You must come and meet her."

CHAPTER THREE

Saturday morning; Tom finished his breakfast, poured more coffee into his cup and carried it out onto the back porch. What a day! He filled his lungs with fresh clean air and scanned the sky. Not a cloud. His eyes fell across the barn. Should start cleaning it out. Nah, too nice a day. Next he looked at the porch railing and convinced himself that it needed to be painted on a day like this. In less than half an hour, he was busy scraping, sanding and painting. By noon, he was more than half finished and thinking about going in for lunch. A crunching sound caught his attention, and he looked up to see a woman riding into the yard on a gray spotted horse. It was Meagan.

He left the porch and went out to greet her. What kind of impression was he going to make in his baggy pants and paint stained old shirt? He wiped his hands on a rag as he walked. When he got close, he looked up. She was wearing blue jeans, a loose fitting denim jacket and a riding helmet, which virtually matched her black hair. He stood and waited for her to stop. What was he supposed to do? Hold the horse? Help her down? Her eyes fixed on him. He felt clumsy, leaden and nervous. He stood still.

"Hello," she said, "I hope I'm not stopping at a bad time?"

He shook his head. She smiled and slipped off her horse. In one motion, she removed the glove from her right hand and holding the glove, her riding crop and the reins in her left, she held out her hand. "I'm Meagan Clark."

He was surprised at how tall she was. At least five foot ten. He wiped his hand one last time before gently taking hers. "Yes. I recognized you from your picture. Didn't expect to meet you so soon."

"I couldn't wait to thank you for fixing the fence and clearing out some of the brush too. The path is easier than ever."

"You're more than welcome. I should have known better in the first place. Would you like to come in for a minute?"

She moved back to the side of her horse. Her eyes fixed back on his face. God! What color are they? Blue? Green? Why do they look like there are lights inside?

"The house looks marvelous," she said. "I'd love to go in and see what you've done, but I have to get back." She swung up onto her horse. "Can you come to tea, tomorrow?" she asked.

"What time?"

"Four," she said, starting to ride off. "And you won't be obligated to drink tea."

"I'm learning to like it," he said.

She turned to look back over her shoulder and wave. He watched her leave and then looked down at his feet; he had not moved since they shook hands.

Tom looked in his closet at the meager wardrobe he had brought to Ireland. There was no decision to make; he took out the sport jacket. The one custom made of Donegal tweed he had bought years earlier while on vacation in Ireland. He added a pair of tropical worsted trousers and a cotton button-down shirt. That's it. At least I'll look better than I did yesterday. He got dressed and checked the results in the long mirror attached to the closet door. "Like I said, better than yesterday." He went into the bathroom and gargled with some mouthwash. He spit out, and as he straightened up, caught himself in the mirror. "What are you doing, Tom? It's just a visit to the neighbors. That's all. It just happens that beautiful neighbors are more interesting than ugly ones. Don't get carried away."

He went down and got into his car. Silly, driving less than a half-mile, but it keeps the mud off. Meagan met him at the door. "You're right on time," she said, "and all cleaned up."

He laughed and stepped inside. A black Labrador came up to greet him.

"You didn't meet Kiki the other day. She was out picking up Jimmy from school. Weren't you, Kiki?" Kiki agreed with that. Tom bent over to pat her and then straightened to hand Meagan the gift he had brought. It was wrapped in white paper. "Fancy cookies," he said.

"I'll have Sarah set some out," she said. "Come inside."

He followed her down the hall, keenly aware of how his eyes locked onto her. She wore a simple rose-pink cotton dress, belted at the waist. It was not form fitting, but it didn't need to be. As they entered the living room, Philip got up to shake his hand. There was a boy off to one side. Tom moved to take Philip's hand and winked at the boy, saying to Philip, "I didn't think I'd be back so soon."

Philip motioned him to take a seat on the couch and offered him a drink. Tom requested a weak Irish and water. His eyes flashed around the room, still familiar from his earlier visit when its elegance reminded him of a museum. He glanced at Meagan, and it all made sense, the harmony of woman and room. She sat down across from him and called Jimmy over. "Come and meet Mister Brogan."

Jimmy, dressed in freshly pressed shirt and pants, came up to Tom. He stood straight looking confident as he held out his hand. His face was slightly freckled, his hair dark brown, tinged with red, and his eyes the same radiating blue of his mother's. A shy smile revealed still-new front teeth, only half grown.

"I'm pleased to meet you, Jimmy. How old are you?"

"I'll be eight — when school starts again." Jimmy sat down next to Tom.

"You're just getting old enough to read some really great books," Tom said.

"I have a book about King Arthur," Jimmy said, "but I can't read it all by myself yet."

"Does it have good pictures?"

"Yes! Would you like to see it?"

"Yes, I would."

Jimmy started off to get his book. Meagan reached out a hand to stop him for a moment. "Jimmy, after this, Mister Brogan will want to talk with the adults. All right?" Jimmy nodded and continued to go after his book.

"I do love some of those pictures," Tom said.

"They certainly are imaginative," she said.

"Very. I sometimes wonder what it was *really* like in those days. No sanitation, no heat in the castles. History can give such a rosy glow to almost anything."

"Are you interested in history?"

"Yes. Not very knowledgeable, but interested."

Jimmy returned with his book, and Tom spent the next few minutes admiring the pictures and asking Jimmy questions. Philip set Tom's drink on the low table in front of him. Tom nodded his thanks. After about five minutes, Meagan interrupted and sent Jimmy and Kiki out for some exercise. Tom watched the two of them leave the room. "He's a nice boy," he said. "Whatever you're doing, keep it up."

Meagan looked pleased. Philip sat down in a chair near her, facing Tom.

She said, "King Arthur is my way of getting him interested in history. He loves to go visit castles."

Tom grinned. "I'm his soul mate on that. I love to visit castles."

Sarah came in with a tray of sandwiches. And then with the tea. Tom stood up to be introduced to her and then helped himself to a sandwich. He watched to see how Meagan and Philip went about the process of eating sandwiches, drinking tea and conversing. He tried to do the same. Sarah came back with a tray of sweets; she set them on the sideboard. When Jimmy returned with Kiki, he walked slowly past the treats, giving them a close examination. He was obliged to eat a sandwich and drink some milk before he was allowed to take one.

"Jimmy," Philip said. "Mister Brogan is very interested in castles,"

Jimmy, who was seated on the couch with Tom, turned to him. "Have you been to Dunmore Castle?"

"I don't believe I have."

"We're going on Saturday. Do you want to come?"

"It's very kind of you to ask me," Tom said. "But your mother doesn't have you to herself that often." He smiled at Meagan and held out his hands in a gesture of helplessness.

She looked at Jimmy and then back at Tom. "You're more than welcome to come," she said. "It might actually be a help; Jimmy likes to climb on things."

Tom hesitated, non-coherent thoughts racing through his head. What am I doing? I'm still dying over Barbara — Can this be right? Maybe if it's just neighbors. Finally he said, "Let me just check to be sure that I don't have anything scheduled that I can't get out of."

The rest of the visit passed surprisingly fast, Tom learned that Philip was an expert on ancient music and that he had published two textbooks on the subject. Meagan taught European History, but Irish History was her personal passion. Tom spoke briefly about his life before coming to Ireland. It was a light once-over; he could never talk seriously about it without dwelling on Barbara, and he was not comfortable displaying those feelings with anyone except his children.

Getting ready for bed that night, he fussed more than usual, his eyes straying often to Barbara's picture on the nightstand next to his bed. He sat on the edge of the bed, picked up the picture and kissed it before lying down. He snapped off the light and lay there staring into blackness. As his eyes acclimated to the darkness, the faint light of a night sky slipped through the window and allowed him to discern the outlines of the ceiling overhead. He liked to admire how the old ceilings followed a soft curve to the cornices at the top of the walls, but on this night, his mind was elsewhere.

He heaved a deep breath with the realization that this would not be one of his better nights. What am I getting into? What's she doing to me? Shithead, it's not her; it's you. He flipped onto his side. If she were just ordinary, there would be no question; I would just be a good neighbor. Maybe, it will wear off; she's not *that* good looking.

On Wednesday, he called Philip to say that he would go to Dunmore Castle.

❧ ❧ ❧

This castle has an interesting history," Meagan said. "It was occupied as late as the nineteenth century."

Tom looked up at the high walls. "It's in pretty good shape."

They stood in a small courtyard. He tried to imagine having come in over a drawbridge spanning the now filled-in moat, the sounds of horses' hooves echoing from the wooden bridge and rebounding against the sullen, weathered gray walls. He turned; empty doors and windows led to dark rooms and corridors. There was a cold forbidding feeling to the place.

"You can see that there have been many repairs and alterations," she said.

Jimmy began to move off on his own. She turned to him. "Jimmy, before you go climbing on anything, I want to know exactly where you are."

Jimmy nodded and trotted off. She turned to Tom. "Help me keep an eye on him, will you?"

"Sure. Why don't we just follow him around?" They walked after Jimmy. The sound of gravel crunching under their feet made him feel closer to her. It was a warm feeling, a kind of subliminal bonding. Above the walls, now multi hues of gray from years of patching and filling, high clouds stood still in the distance.

"It's a mixed bag," Tom said. "I love the places that haven't been touched since the thirteenth century. But this place probably wouldn't be here at all, if it hadn't been occupied all those years."

"That's true. Although, there are still many castles that are in good condition, and they haven't been touched, except for some shoring up in spots."

"The ones that break my heart are the ones that Cromwell blasted apart."

"What about the monasteries?" she said. "He really did a job on virtually every one of them."

They walked about talking mostly about Irish history, its import to western civilization, and its connection to current culture in both Ireland and the United States. Jimmy was in his own world, content to be left entirely out of the conversation. Tom could not resist climbing up to join him on one of the parapets. "Jimmy, isn't it amazing to think that six hundred years ago, soldiers climbed these very same steps."

"And they shot their arrows out through here," Jimmy said.

"Some probably died right about where you're standing."

Jimmy looked around by his feet. What could he be looking for?

"It's only their ghosts that are here now, Jimmy. Everything else has been washed away by thousands of rainstorms."

"Do you believe in ghosts?" Jimmy asked.

"Don't you?" Tom put his arm around Jimmy's shoulder and pointed out through the wall. "Can't you just see them, men in armor, shields, swords and helmets, all clanking and banging as they come to attack?"

Jimmy leaned forward for a better look.

Tom whispered in his ear. "They're there, Jimmy. They're all around us. It just takes a little imagination."

Jimmy kept staring. "I think I see them," he whispered.

Tom returned to Meagan.

"What were you two talking about up there?"

He raised his eyelids. "*Ghosts,*" he said.

"Grand. If he doesn't sleep tonight, I know who to blame."

"Hey, don't knock it. The kid's got a great imagination."

Meagan laughed. "That's true. He was fascinated by that story you told him in the car. All about cowboys and Indians. All true, I imagine."

"Absolutely. The Gospel — every word."

"Now *that's* validation," she said. "The Gospel, according to Saint Thomas."

Meagan looked up to check on Jimmy, still climbing around, looking into every crevice. Tom liked it when she was distracted by Jimmy, or when she was pointing out some artifact of the castle; it gave him a chance to look at her without embarrassment. It was the first time he had been with a woman, in a companionable situation, since Barbara's death. Until this day, it hadn't sunk in. He missed women. It wasn't just sex. It wasn't romance. It was something less obvious, well below the surface, a need, a craving for that completeness, that energizing companionship that can only come from being with a woman. He looked at her again. Beautiful. Why did I have to start with her? Why Meagan? Why not someone older? Plainer? Anything?

Jimmy rejoined them. He stood politely, waiting to be noticed.

"Let me guess," Meagan said to him, "you're getting hungry?"

"I'll buy," Tom said. "How much can he eat?"

"*I'm* the one you have to worry about," she said. "I'm starving."

They found a small storefront restaurant with some open tables and settled in. The place resembled an American luncheonette, but as with most Irish restaurants, there were pleasing differences. More light came through the front window; pictures of country scenes hung on the walls. There were fewer tables, and more emphasis on cleanliness and neatness. Tablecloths were draped uniformly, chairs placed just so and condiments organized. Best of all, was the quiet; everyone spoke in hushed tones, and the staff avoided unnecessary noise.

Tom picked up the menu. "Great, they've got real coffee."

"I thought you liked tea?" she said.

"Yeah, well — when in Rome." He continued to look at the menu. "Hey, Jimmy. It looks like they've got some real cowboy food here — meat and vegetables."

"I thought that cowboys ate beans?" Jimmy said.

"Not when they're in town."

Jimmy looked dubious.

"More Gospel?" Meagan said.

Tom shrugged. "Okay, you do it."

Meagan explained the allowable options to Jimmy. He selected a hamburger dish. Tom and Meagan ordered salmon salads and biscuits for themselves. The conversation drifted back to history.

"There are some megalithic tombs up in Sligo that date back to 2,500 BC," she said. "They've been excavated. You can enter some of them."

"That's impressive. I'd like to see that."

"You can visit Mohill on your way."

"What's that?"

"It's the birthplace of Turlough O'Carolan. He was a blind harpist, the last of the Celtic bards. He died in the eighteenth century. His music was used for your own national anthem: The Star Spangled Banner."

"Amazing. I wonder how many Americans know that ."

Later, Jimmy enjoyed a dish of ice cream while Meagan finished her tea and Tom had a cup of coffee. "How does Bewley's compare with American coffee?" she asked.

"It's not up to Starbucks, but it's pretty good."

"What's Starbucks?"

"It's a company that serves and sells gourmet coffees. It started in Seattle. There's lots of rain there; they need good coffee to keep them from going nuts."

"They should come to Ireland."

"It's too late, the Irish are already nuts."

"I'm tempted to ask if you feel at home here."

"I do right now," he said. "You're good company."

"Thank you," she said, "I'm glad you came along."

They stood on Meagan's front porch. The shadows were long, and clouds were moving to hide the sun's last act. It was noticeably cooler. Jimmy shook hands with Tom and said, "Thank you," before he went inside to find Kiki.

Meagan asked, "Would you like to come in for tea, or a drink?"

"Thanks," he said, "I really should get going."

"You're sure?"

"Yeah." He bit his lower lip. "I had a great day. Jimmy's a fun kid. He's really smart, isn't he?"

She smiled. "I hope he's smart enough not to take you seriously. At least not completely."

"I don't suppose we could, uh — do it again sometime?"

"I could."

"Me too."

He could almost feel her eyes on his back as he went down the steps and got into his car. He concentrated on starting the car and drove off. At the top of the driveway, he stopped and opened his window. Meagan stood silhouetted against the darkening sky, its giant clouds helping to carry the night forward. He waved and then tried to focus his entire mind on the business of driving.

CHAPTER FOUR

Meagan stepped inside and sat on the bench to remove her shoes and put on a pair of slippers.

Down the hall, Philip stood in the light coming through the library door; he wore an old gray sweater, baggy pants, and slippers. "I want to hear about your day," he said.

"I'll be there as soon as I've taken care of Jimmy."

A few minutes later, she entered the library and sat down in one of the large leather wingback chairs, which half faced the fireplace. Philip handed her a drink. He went back to pick up his own drink and then sat in the other chair. They often did this: sat talking while staring into the fire. The room was of medium size, but it felt small and intimate. In addition to the chairs, it contained two large worktables, covered with newspapers and books of interest to Philip. Some of the books lay open, others were stacked up; all had many bookmarks — slips of paper sticking out. The walls, except for where the sideboard stood, were lined with books. Few of the covers matched.

Philip settled in. "So?" he said.

"He's very nice."

"Nice?"

"Philip. I've only just met the man."

"I know that. He's also the first man you've shown any interest in since God knows when."

"If you saw the type that I've had to contend with, you wouldn't wonder at that."

"There's more to it than that."

She turned her head toward him and thought about what he said. "You're right. I've been trying to think it through. He is having an effect on me that I do not entirely understand. I like the way he treats you, and he seems genuinely fond of Jimmy. He seems comfortable with himself; he's not pushing. I've just slipped into being relaxed and enjoying his company."

"You have a lot of wisdom about you, Meagan, and a great deal of self discipline, but don't be afraid to go with your heart. We humans all need that complementary someone, the one that fills in our sense of self. Most of us never find that person."

"Oh, Philip." She reached out her hand, and he grasped it for a moment.

"And we're talking about you and Tom here. He's obviously interested in you."

"He misses his wife."

They both took sips of their drinks.

Philip said, "I gathered that from what little he said last week."

"He hasn't said much, but I get the feeling that he's still seriously grieving."

"Is that an impediment?"

"I think it might be," she said. "Probably not a good foundation for a relationship."

"Will you see him again?"

"Yes. I'll play it by ear. Jimmy likes him. You should hear some of the stories he told him. Unbelievable!"

"As bad as the Irish?"

"Worse."

"Not possible," he said. "Anyway, I like him. I wish you all the best."

They raised their glasses in a little toast.

"At the least," she said, "he'll be a good neighbor."

☙ ☙ ☙

When Tom got up on Sunday morning, Brid and Sean had already left to attend Mass. He started the coffee and tried to decide what to eat. He looked at the new appliances. Neither the Mix Master nor the food processor appeared to have been used, and he had his doubts about whether Brid had deciphered the microwave oven yet. Pancakes, that's it. With chopped apples and syrup warmed in the microwave, he could use them all.

He finished breakfast and was loading everything into the dishwasher when he heard the car pull up to the back porch. It was ten o'clock. Did Meagan go to church, he wondered? He put on his jacket and met Sean at the back door. "There's plenty of coffee left, if you're interested." He drove down to get the paper. It was too early for a Guinness, but he killed some time sitting at the empty bar with Frank, while some of the Donohue kids and their friends ran in and out. When he got back to the house, he put the paper aside without reading it. I wonder what Meagan's doing? I should call her. He looked at his watch. It's too early. He went back and picked up the paper, but he did not sit down. I should get some exercise. He went to the window and peered at the sky, trying to assess the probability of rain. The clouds were low and moving slowly against a gray background and there was a suggestion of mist in the air. A good day for a hike. He selected a guidebook from the bookcase.

He found the directions to an abandoned coal mine on nearby Corry Mountain. The "mountain" was only 1400 feet high. It sounded interesting; he put on his hiking boots, his waterproof jacket, and set off. Two hours later he was surrounded by the remains of what had been a working mine as late as 1990. In his mind's eye, he conjured up the past. He saw the miners with their blackened faces and lantern helmets, the coal cars being pushed and pulled. He heard the clanking of overhead conveyors and the roar of trucks. He imagined men's voices, shouting in an effort to be heard above the din.

Old industrial sites all seem to share the characteristic of having been abandoned on a single afternoon. They always look as if the workers had just picked up their lunch buckets and left with the intention of returning the following day. Machines and equipment stand, silently waiting. Time, weather and vegetation take their toll, but slowly, very slowly. He wandered about letting his imagination run along with his eyes. Here were buildings, a tramway, tracks leading to a mineshaft now blocked off. Coal cars, everything but coal and miners. What a sense of history these places convey. Reminders every one, of industries, of ways of life once thought permanent; now abandoned, gone in less than a generation. He found a spot from which he could look back at Lough Allen. He could see his house. But not Meagan's. Funny, it's not Clarks' now; it's Meagan's.

It was after four when he got back. Maybe she'll be home. He phoned. "I just wanted to thank you again for yesterday," he said. "I really enjoyed it."

"Not at all. We all had a good time."

"I was wondering if there might be another excursion, of some sort, next weekend?" He was sitting close to the phone; he wiped his sweating palm on his trousers.

"Next weekend is quite busy," she said. "Jimmy's in a horse show at Manor Hamilton on Saturday, and he's invited to a birthday party in Boyle after Services on Sunday."

"Well. Sounds as if you'll have your hands full."

"Yes. We might be able to plan something for the following weekend."

"I'll be in New Jersey for my daughter's graduation, and then I've got some business in New York."

"Oh. You will get in touch when you get back?"

"Yes, I will. Definitely."

"Good. Well — I hope your trip goes well."

"Thanks."

Tom hung up and sat quietly, trying to assess his own emotions and the situation with Meagan. Maybe it's better this way. Just neighbors. By the time I get back — Who knows? I might feel differently about the whole thing. It will have passed over, and I can relax. He reached for the paper.

The paper did not do it. He went in and flipped on the television. He tried every station; nothing looked interesting. He turned the television off and went back to the paper. The phone rang. It was Meagan. "I was thinking," she said. "Since we won't be seeing you for a while, would you like to come for supper on Saturday? We won't be home until around five, but we can eat around half six."

"Yes!" It jumped out. He did not recognize his own voice. He tried again, "Yes. That would be very nice. Should I come at six?"

They agreed. He hung up and breezed into the kitchen to see how Brid was doing with supper.

"You must have had quite a breakfast," she said.

"Yes, I played with all the new toys."

She laughed. "I'll have to try that, myself."

The last of the trees were planted on Wednesday. By Friday, Tom had finished most of the preparations for his trip including the purchase of some presents. Time passed slowly. Tree farming was certainly not going to be a full time occupation. At least, not until he expanded to a much larger operation.

On Saturday afternoon, he drove up to Manor Hamilton, a town named after the large estate which once occupied the area. It was a neighborly thing to do, and it would be fun to see Jimmy and whatever kids do at these things.

He asked directions and found the farm where the horse show was being held. He parked on the grass next to several cars, which appeared to have been simply stopped at random places rather than parked. He walked along a gravel path, past the horse trailers to a place where people stood around in groups or sat on folding chairs. The day was overcast and cold; the grass still wet from rain that morning. The judges sat at a table near the edge of the field; one of them used a megaphone to direct events on the field. Someone, it looked like a young girl, moved her horse around, or over, a series of obstacles. The jumps were modest, less than two feet high, and the horse appeared to be having less difficulty than the rider. He stopped where he could watch without obstructing anyone's view.

"I thought you'd be playing golf." Her voice — right at his shoulder. He turned. God! She was close. She looked at his face. "I shouldn't get so close," she said. "I probably smell of 'eau de cheval.'"

"I wouldn't mind," he said.

She took his forearm. "We have some chairs over here. Philip is helping Jimmy get ready for his round." She pointed to a group of horses and people at the far end of the field. "Jimmy says I make him nervous."

"I'm glad I got here in time to see him."

"There's not much to these things," she said. "Each rider performs for a few minutes. We all clap politely. They give out some ribbons, and we go home."

They sat on two folding chairs. He looked up at the sky; rain appeared imminent. "Still. It's a confidence builder for the kids. Isn't it?" he asked.

"It is. And they keep going if it rains."

He smiled. "So do golfers."

"You don't golf?"

"It's like bowling. I'll take it up when I'm eighty."

"Oh, dear. I love golf."

"You do?"

"I'm teasing. Jimmy will be so pleased that you came."

Jimmy came on to the field, and they stood up to watch him. Meagan moved her hands, as if she could help him, and spoke to him softly with words of encouragement, as if he could hear. It didn't help. He made several mistakes, but he stuck with it to complete his round.

"Don't worry," Meagan said, "they give some kind of little prize to everyone."

"He should get one for guts," Tom said.

The rain held off. Jimmy was surprised and delighted to see Tom. He got a ribbon and Tom helped them prepare for the ride home.

"Thank you for coming, Tom," Philip said. "We're all very pleased."

Promptly at six, Tom knocked on the door, and Meagan welcomed him in. He had brought two presents: a bottle of wine and, for Jimmy, a copy of Treasure Island, illustrated by N. C. Wyeth. Jimmy opened it to look at the dramatic full color illustrations. He was hooked. Tom glanced over his shoulder at the once familiar picture of Blind Pew. For an instant, Pew came to life once more, with his flared black cape, and his menacing cane, tapping the road ahead as he moved toward the reader, leaving that ghostly house in the background.

"I don't know how much of it you can read yourself, Jimmy," Tom said. "It's about a boy, much like you. His name is Jim Hawkins. He has to deal with some pretty mean pirates."

Jimmy thanked him and took the book over to a chair at the side of the room where he could continue to look it over while Philip served drinks for the adults. They sat in the living room where peat burned in the fireplace. The room was becoming familiar, and the faint scent of the peat fire added to Tom's sense of being welcome. The lighting was much softer than during his earlier visits, making the ornate picture frames and wallpaper give off a warm glow. The atmosphere stirred something in him, a feeling of being uplifted. Meagan's face seemed like something out of a dream.

"I understand that you're going back to the States for a visit?" Philip said.

"Yes. There's some business that needs to be taken care of, but it's mostly a family visit. My daughter, Helene, is graduating from college and I'll be seeing my son, John, his wife and my granddaughter."

"You don't look old enough to be a grandfather," Philip said.

"That's what I said, but they did it anyway."

"I'm sure that you'll have a marvelous time."

"I'm looking forward to it," Tom said. "I may also meet with a friend about a report on Northern Ireland that I'll be working on."

"Northern Ireland?" Meagan said. "Now, *there's* a subject."

"A complicated one from what I can see," Tom said. "I was up there a few years ago with my wife. She wanted to leave. Didn't like all the soldiers and the police with automatic weapons. We did like Derry, though."

"You mean *Londonderry?*" Meagan said.

"Now, Meagan. Don't start on that," Philip said. "Tom has nothing to do with it."

"I was being facetious," she said, "but you're right. Let's talk about something else."

Sarah came in to say that supper was almost ready. Meagan put down her drink and went in to help her. Jimmy put his book aside and followed Meagan. Tom and Philip stayed, waiting to be called in.

"Meagan went to school in Belfast," Philip said. "After graduation she got involved in Unionist politics. She wound up marrying a party functionary. I sometimes wonder if she's gotten it all out of her system."

"Is she pro Unionist?"

"I don't know just where she stands these days, but that 'Londonderry' business was just a joke; I'm sure she agrees that the people who live there can call it whatever they like. I'm afraid I don't care for politics."

They went into supper. Tom offered to open the bottle of wine that he had brought. He went to the sideboard where he found the bottle and a corkscrew waiting. He held the bottle out with its label toward Philip. "I brought a few bottles of American wine with me. I thought that you might be interested in tasting one." He proceeded to cut off the foil and pull the cork with a noisy pop. They sat on four sides of the table, with Tom directly across from Jimmy. He waited to see if Meagan would offer Jimmy a taste of the wine. She did not. Conversation was light.

"How's your lamb, Tom?" Philip asked. "Not too rare?"

"It's just right." Tom said. "Did you know that Ireland has too many sheep?"

Philip laughed. Meagan said, "Ireland has too much of many things. Except trees of course."

"I'll drink to that," Tom said, raising his glass. Later, he spoke to Jimmy. "Jimmy, you could never pass for an American kid."

Jimmy waited for the explanation

"Your table manners are too good."

Jimmy looked at his mother.

"It's a compliment," she said. "If you ever go to America, you'll do just fine."

"He will," Tom said. "I'd love to show him around."

As the meal continued, Philip became quiet, and as Sarah began to take the plates away, he excused himself. "I'm feeling a bit light headed," he said. "I think I'd better get up and get to bed."

Tom and Meagan expressed their concerns.

"I'm sure it's not serious," Philip said. And then, to Meagan, "I'll be able to drive you back to Galway tomorrow night. I'm sure."

"It won't be a problem, if you're not up to it," she said. She explained to Tom, "My car is in the shop for repairs."

Philip left them, and then Meagan sent Jimmy up to get ready for bed and church the next day. "I'll be right along," she said.

Tom wanted to stay, and would have done so if Philip had not gone upstairs, but he felt that it was appropriate for him to leave. He got up and said that he'd be going. "It's been another great day," he said. "I really enjoy being with you people."

Meagan walked him to the door.

He hesitated before leaving. He said, "If Philip's not feeling well tomorrow, I'd love to drive you down to Galway."

She paused and looked away for a moment, and then she turned back. "That's very kind. It won't be a problem. I can always take Philip's car, and Philip and Sarah can use mine when it's ready."

"I wouldn't feel right about that."

"We'll see," she said. "Thanks for the offer. Good night."

❧ ❧ ❧

Tom occupied himself with preparations for his trip. He did some packing and reviewed correspondence regarding the final disposition of Barbara's estate. It all seemed so cold and clinical. Fresh in his mind was the warmth of the previous evening with Meagan. Was it wrong, hypocritical, to want to see her one last time before leaving?

What time would the birthday party be over? Three-thirty? Four? She would be home by five. He called, "How is Philip feeling?"

"He's doing better. I'm afraid yesterday was a bit of a strain."

"I have a confession to make."

"Oh my; what could that be about?"

"I want to drive you to Galway, even if Philip is just fine."

"Well now. That puts me under a bit of pressure."

"No. Please don't feel that way. That's not my intention. It's just that I'll be gone for a while and — Well, I do enjoy your company."

"And, I yours."

"Let's do it."

"It would be helpful."

"What time?"

"If we leave at half seven, you'll be home at a decent hour."

It was raining gently but still light out when Tom picked her up. It had been raining all afternoon, one of those rainy days in

Ireland, which are noticeable to Americans principally because the Irish seem not to notice them at all. Earlier, he had enjoyed the rain himself; it gave a cozy feeling to the house and enhanced his anticipation of being with Meagan. She came to the door wearing a tan summer raincoat and hat. He took her small bag and opened the car door for her. He put her bag in the back seat and got in. She had removed her hat.

"This is a first," she said, shaking her hair out.

"How's that?"

"We've not been alone before."

"Is that right?"

"You hadn't noticed?"

He grinned at her. She smiled back.

"I'm planning to head down through Castlerea," he said.

"That's fine."

Tom turned the windshield wipers on as he left the driveway. Swish-flup, swish-flup. The one on Meagan's side did a poor job of clearing the windshield. "It's not critical for you to be able to see," he said.

"I don't mind," she said. "You won't be here when I get back?"

"Right. I'm leaving on Thursday."

"And you've not set a return date yet?"

"No. But I probably won't be gone more than two weeks."

A truck passed in the opposite direction, throwing up a quantity of water, which made a loud thrashing sound against the side of the car. Tom switched the wipers to high and then back to medium.

"You must be lonesome for your family?" she said.

"Yes. I get lonesome."

She looked out her window, and nothing was said for a short time. She turned back. "How do your children feel about your being over here?"

"They don't like it. My son, John, understands it — at least better than my daughter does."

"Will you go back after you get things established here?"

He did not answer right away.

"I shouldn't ask such personal questions," she said.

"I'm flattered by your interest," he said. "I just don't know the answer to that one. It will depend on a number of things."

"I can understand that."

They rode in silence for a while, listening to the rhythmic swish-flup, swish-flup of the windshield wipers. She stared absently out her window. He studied the road ahead with brief glances at her profile.

"How about you?" he asked.

"Me?"

"Yeah. Do you get lonesome?"

"Oh, yes."

"It's hard for me to imagine."

"Why?"

"Any guy in Galway, who has got any juices flowing, would like to take you out."

She let out a light sigh and turned to gaze out her window. "Even if that were true," she said, "it wouldn't solve anything."

He glanced over at her, and she looked back at him.

"No. I guess it wouldn't," he said.

Again, silence for several minutes.

"I do have some men friends," she said. "And the occasional date."

He nodded. "Of course"

More silence. This time she continued to look at him. Another truck passed casting a loud torrent of water, forcing Tom to work the windshield wipers.

"There's no one special," she said.

He smiled and glanced over at her. "I won't make believe that I'm sorry to hear that."

She said nothing. A minute passed.

"Could there be?" he asked. He could almost feel her eyes on the side of his face.

"Be what?"

"Someone special."

"Oh," she laughed, "yes — he would have to be someone I can respect."

"Uh-huh."

"And he would have to respect me."

"Right."

"And, of course, he'd have to be good for Jimmy."

"And get along with Philip," he said.

She looked at him. "And get along with Philip."

A little later, she said, "I don't know where I'd be without Philip."

"Has he ever been married?"

"No."

"How old is he?"

"Forty-two."

"And no plans to get married?"

"No."

He waited for her to elaborate. He glanced over. She was looking down.

"He's a real gentleman," Tom said. "You seem to all love each other. It's very nice."

"Yes," she said. "They're my family."

Time passed. They were entering Castlerea.

He said, "If you'd like to stop for coffee, or anything, just let me know."

"I'm fine," she said. "You'll be getting home late as it is."

"I'm in no hurry."

They passed through the town. Tom squinted to read the signs. "Okay. Tuam, next stop."

"You have a nice family," she said.

"Yes. We've been very close."

"From what little you've said, I can tell that you loved your wife, deeply."

Tom nodded slowly before speaking. "I did and I do. I felt eviscerated when it sunk in that she was gone. Without my kids, I don't know how I could have endured."

"It takes time."

"Yes," he said. He cleared his throat. "Some guys aren't meant to be alone. I think I'm one of them."

She reached over and briefly put her hand on his shoulder. "Will you be staying at your old house in New Jersey?"

"Yes, but my son and his family will be there. I won't be going into an empty house."

"That's good."

"Yeah. Nothing like a baby to really change things."

"How well I know."

"Did Jimmy change things?"

"I grew up very fast after Jimmy's arrival."

He glanced over at her. "He seems to have been a good influence."

When they got to Galway, she directed him to her apartment. It was raining harder and had gotten dark, lights reflected from silvery wet streets, and beads of water on the car windows and hood captured dim lights and turned them into twinkles which quickly moved on. Tom shut off the ignition and sat for a moment looking at Meagan before reaching into the back for an umbrella. They walked slowly to the door of her apartment; he getting more wet than necessary. He put her bag down on a dry spot next to the door. They stood sheltered from the rain by an overhang.

"I'll be on my way," he said. "I'm really glad we had this time together."

"It was good to talk. Have a safe trip." She offered her hand.

He took it and held it. "I'll send Jimmy some postcards."

"He'll love that."

"And to you too."

She smiled.

"Good night," he said. He let go of her hand.

CHAPTER FIVE

He arrived at Kennedy Airport and took local transportation to Fort Lee, New Jersey, where Helene picked him up for the drive to Woodcliff Lake.

"You look tired," she said.

"Yeah, I didn't get much sleep at the airport hotel last night."

"John and Anne won't be at the house until tomorrow afternoon. I thought we'd eat out tonight."

"That's okay." Tom looked out his window. "God! Can you believe all this development? Where do they find enough customers for all these stores?"

"Beats me," she said.

"How's the house?" he asked

"Fine. Tony Amalfi has been taking care of the yard. I've run your car a few times. Everything's fine."

A big truck went whipping past, its draft clearly felt in Helene's car. "I hate trucks," she said.

He smiled. "I plan to sleep in the guest room."

She turned to look at him. "Are you sure?"

"Yeah. John and Anne will need the big room, and I'll probably sleep better."

When they arrived at the house Tom got out and stretched his limbs. He looked around the yard. "Tony has been doing a nice job." He walked around the front yard. The sun was bright, bringing a slight haze and heaviness to the air. Summer was further along here than in County Leitrim. He took deep breaths and noticed the humidity, the flower buds, and freshly cut grass — a sure sign of hot days to come. Those days that seem made for iced tea on the patio. Days when he and Barbara would work in the yard until it got too hot; then they would shower and sit in the shade talking about the kids, or some far-fetched philosophical subject, until it was time to decide about dinner. He strolled around to the back; the cedar and cast iron lawn furniture was still there, waiting for someone in a freshly ironed summer dress to sit down, pour some iced tea, and smile at him. He got his bag and followed Helene into the house. "I'll just put this upstairs," he said. "You haven't told me much about your new job."

"I'll tell you later," she said. "Why don't you lie down for a while before we go out."

"I'm okay," he said, "I'll just take a shower and then we can go."

Tom went up and put his bag on the bed in the guestroom. He went to the master bedroom to get some of his clothes. He took some underwear and socks out of the dresser and, as he straightened up, he looked into the mirror at the bed behind him. He turned around. How many times did I get into that bed and not touch her? Not kiss her? Not caress her hair, her cheek? How many times did I roll over and touch her accidentally? And then, been comforted by the knowing of her warm body next to me? How many times did we make love in that bed?

He dropped a pair of socks. He whispered to himself, "Come on, Tom. Take your shower."

Later in the restaurant, Helene said, "You're pretty quiet tonight."

"Yes," he said, "but I still want to hear about your job."

They sat in a curved booth against the wall. The seat and back were covered with tufted, dark red Naugahyde. The lighting was turned down to a yellowish glow; the candle flickered inside its ruby-red vase casting shadows on the white tablecloth. Vivaldi's The Seasons played softly in the background complementing the sounds of tinkling glass and gentle laughter of the other patrons.

"As I told you in my letter," she said, "it's with Eicogen. They're a biotechnology company. I'll be working in marketing."

"Where are they located?"

"Englewood. I will be living at the house. At least for a while."

"That's great."

The dinner passed easily. Helene did most of the talking. She filled Tom in on the schedule for the weekend and told him more about her job. Finally, she said, "You haven't told me anything about Ireland."

"There's not that much to tell. The house is finished. The trees are in."

"When do you have to go back?"

"I left it open. There's no need to rush. Maybe in a week."

"What do you have to do there?"

"Well, the trees need to be watched very closely, and I've got to get going on the barn. Also, there's that report I've committed to do for Jerry."

"It doesn't sound too exciting. Do you have any friends there?"

"There are some people I'm getting to know."

John, Anne and baby Catherine arrived on Friday afternoon. Tom helped John carry things into the house. "Jesus. All this stuff for one kid," he said. "You've got enough here for a small army."

"Don't let Anne hear you say that. She wanted to bring more. We ran out of room."

"Mum's the word. I want to stay on the right side of my daughter-in-law."

"Good idea. And no stories about how you were too poor to afford these things, and I had to sleep in a box."

"In a box? We weren't *that* poor."

"You can lay it on pretty thick sometimes."

Later, Anne and Helene fixed supper while Tom and John played with Catherine on the back porch. John spoke of his job. He was excited about a new software package his company was introducing. Tom gave him an update on Ireland, including a few horror stories from the house renovation. "I came in one day and found this fellow putting up dry wall before the pipes and wiring were in. I asked if he could be making a mistake. He said, 'Oh no, that's the way we do it here.' Sure enough, a few days later, they were in, drilling holes and making a hell of a mess to get the pipes and wiring in."

There was one rough spot after dinner. Anne had taken Catherine upstairs. Tom, John and Helene sat together in the living room having coffee. Helene said, "This is the first time we've been together in this house since Mother died." She began to cry. John hung his head.

Tom nodded. "Strange, isn't it?" he said. "In some ways, it seems like a long time ago and, at the same time, it can seem like only yesterday."

"She never saw Catherine," Helene said.

John raised his head. His eyes were moist. "She would have been a super grandmother," he said.

"She certainly looked forward to it," Tom said. He tightened his jaw and swallowed hard.

They sat quietly, the only sound Helene's gentle sniffing. Anne came back down; she tiptoed into the room and sat down without a word. Tom turned to her. "She asleep?"

"She'll fuss for a while," Anne said.

ɜ ɜ ɜ

The weather held up for the rest of the weekend. Catherine provided a focus for everyone's attention. She was a big hit with Helene's friends at the graduation. Jerry sent his regrets along with an elegant fountain pen. Helene had made reservations at a local restaurant for after the ceremony. She invited her friend, Sheila, and Sheila's Dad to join them. It was a nice little party and everyone was ready for bed by the time they got home to Woodcliff Lake.

Sunday was more difficult for Tom; John and Anne left after breakfast, and Helene left later to join Sheila and some friends for a few days at the shore. Sunday night he was alone. One week earlier, he had been with Meagan. Nine months earlier, he had been married. Married to the woman of this house. How could he even think of Meagan? How can I think of her here?

Monday he kept busy packing things to ship to Ireland: clothes, his computer. He made special arrangements to ship his skeet shooting equipment. He disassembled his bicycle for shipping. It was the first time he had touched it since Barbara's death. It was important to move ahead. He kept any implications of what he was doing out of his head. He could always ship things back. No need to dwell on each item. No need to make any long term decisions. Just pack anything that might be needed.

On Tuesday, he drove down to Summit to meet Jerry. They went out to lunch. Jerry was very interested in the details of Tom's new venture; the European Union aspect of it fascinated him. He also wanted to know the details of Tom's life in Ireland, particularly his relationships with local people.

"What's your life like in Ireland, Tom? Any interesting friends?"

"Things are going okay with the farm. Friends — that's a little confusing."

Jerry waited.

"I met a woman. She's my next door neighbor. I had to meet her."

"She must be pretty nice, or you wouldn't mention it."

"Yeah, you're right. She's pretty nice. There's nothing — I mean we've only just met."

Jerry nodded.

"She has a seven year old son; she's divorced. We went on a little excursion, the three of us. I went to see the kid in a horse show. I had dinner at the house. Things seemed to be just friendly."

"But?"

"Yeah. There's always a 'but'. Isn't there? I'm attracted to her, Jerry. More than attracted."

"It's been a while, Tom."

"Not *that* long."

"There's nothing to be ashamed of."

"I'm not ashamed. It's not shame. Coming back here. Staying at the house. It's really brought me back to my senses."

A busboy showed up to clear their dishes, and then the waiter took their orders for coffee.

"What are you going to do, Tom?"

"I don't know. I don't know what I'm going to tell her when I get back."

"How old is she?"

"Mid thirties."

"Intelligent?"

"Quite. She teaches history at the University."

Jerry took his time putting sugar and cream into his coffee, stirring it slowly. "Don't do anything that you might regret later," he said.

"What do you mean?"

"Look at it this way," Jerry said. "Nobody can ever take Barbara's place; we both know that. But this woman sounds like she might be the next best thing that's happened to you. Why don't you buy some time?"

"Time?"

"Yeah. Tell her how you feel. Tell her what you told me. Ask her to wait."

"Ask her to wait?"

"Yeah. One month. Six months. When you feel better about it."

"I don't know, Jerry. I don't want to lose her, but I can't handle the guilt. Maybe things will start to look different again when I get back to Ireland."

"Just tell her how you feel."

"Christ! I wish I knew, myself, how I feel."

"Just tell her. You'll do fine."

When they got to the subject of Northern Ireland, Jerry produced an envelope from his pocket. "Here are copies of the letters I've sent to the leaders of all those political parties they've got in Northern Ireland," he said. "You can refer to them when you're setting up interviews."

"Great. I'll get moving on it right after I get back."

❧ ❧ ❧

On Thursday morning in New York, Tom met with the Newcomer brothers, principal owners of his old firm. His good friend, and former subordinate, Ed Riley, met him in the lobby and ushered him in. Ed was dressed in his customary slightly rumpled suit with overly long pants, outdated yellow tie and scuffed Sears Roebuck shoes. Not much was said; they were going to have lunch together after the meeting. On his way to the conference room, he stopped to shake hands with employees. Marsha, his secretary for seven years, rose to greet him. He stopped to give her a quick hug and to leave a small present of fancily wrapped Irish teacakes on her desk. Ed left him at the conference room door. He would meet with just the two brothers.

Tom had always considered the Newcomer brothers to be somewhat irresponsible — a couple of loose cannons in a business that relied on predictability, but they had always been exceedingly polite. Even on the day that they had fired him, they were deferential to a fault.

Sid, the older brother, was slender with sharp features including a hawkish nose. He had dark hair and eyes. He wore rimless glasses and favored expensive dark suits, which never seemed to fit properly. Alan was the more laid back of the two. He was overweight but not fat. He almost always wore sports jackets and pastel shirts. They fit him well. His ties did not look nearly as expensive as Sid's

There was some polite small talk for a few minutes and then Sid came to the point. He explained that they had made a few bad investments, and that some of the older clients had gotten wind of it. They were worried about Newcomer & Co.'s ability to continue managing their accounts, many of which were retirement funds.

"To put it in a nutshell, we'd like you to come back," Alan said.

"On your own terms," Sid added.

Tom was not surprised. He had kept track of things during his absence, and the brothers' request for a meeting was almost expected. "I'm not prepared to do that," he said, "but I think I can help you." He outlined a proposal that consisted of putting Ed Riley in charge of the old accounts, giving him investment authority and getting him out to visit and reassure the clients. Tom would provide some consulting support. "First," he said, "you need to invest a few bucks on getting him dressed for the part."

The brothers looked at each other.

"When could you spend some time here?" Sid asked.

"In the fall."

They nodded.

ta ta ta

Helene returned the next day and she and Tom enjoyed each other's company for two days before she started her new job, and he went back to Ireland. They went into the City, to the Metropolitan Museum of Art, dinner and to a Broadway show — <u>Chicago</u>. They drove up Route 9 to Newburgh and walked the grounds at West Point.

At one point she said, "I hate to admit it, but I think Ireland has been good for you."

"How's that?"

"You can talk about Mother sometimes, in a cheerful way."

"Yes. I am beginning to be able to see through the grief. And, you know what? The memories are all good ones."

CHAPTER SIX

It was Friday night; Meagan was home for the weekend. She had just put Jimmy to bed after reading part of Treasure Island to him. She joined Philip in the library.

"I didn't know that there were cowboys in New Jersey," Philip said.

"Neither did I," Meagan said. "I don't know where Tom could have gotten that card, but it certainly was a hit with Jimmy."

"He must have had it all along," he said.

"I suppose. You're looking well, Philip. Better than last weekend."

"Oh, yes. Much better."

"You weren't faking it, were you?"

"No. But, it was nice of Tom to drive you back. What did you two talk about?"

"Oh — lots of things. Family. His and mine."

"Ye — s?"

"He misses his family. He misses his wife, terribly."

"I gathered that from the few times he's mentioned her. When is he coming back?"

"It's not clear. A week or two. He has some business matters to take care of."

"Is there any chance that he'll be moving back to the States? He could sell the tree farm to investors and sell the house separately"

Meagan settled back into her chair and looked away. "The thought has crossed my mind. There's more to hold him there than here."

"Except for one thing."

"And that is?"

"You, my dear."

"You're sweet, Philip. But I don't know how deep his interest goes."

❧ ❧ ❧

Late on the following Monday night, Tom got back to the farm. A welcoming note from Brid told him that he would find a sandwich in the refrigerator. He opened a beer and sat in the kitchen to eat his sandwich before going to bed.

Brid was waiting when he came down the next morning. She served him coffee, which she had made in the new coffeemaker and then an omelet with cheese and peppers. All of this came with homemade bread and muffins. "We used everything," she said. "Every day, Sean and myself read one of the instruction books and then we made something. That food processor is very handy."

"Wonderful. You cut up the cheese and peppers in the food processor. You made the bread and muffins in the mixer. How about the microwave and the dishwasher?"

"I'm using them all," she said. "It does seem a waste sometimes."

"You'll get used to it," he said. "These muffins are great."

After breakfast, Tom went into the office to check his mail. He flipped through, sorting it out. He had to go through twice; things kept getting flipped onto the wrong pile. *She probably won't be home until Friday. Maybe I should drive down to Galway. Get it over with.*

He went outside and walked up the hill, toward Meagan's house. *I'll just check and see if her car's there.* The wind bent the grass to one side. Some wild flowers were just starting to bud. Scaling upwards in layers, the clouds reached for heaven, one, two, three layers, the highest clouds on the verge of escaping from earth altogether. He got to the top of the hill. There was the tree: a large oak with thick trunk and widespread branches, a lone sentinel, standing guard, master of all in sight. He looked down. No car. I'll call the house. I told her I'd call when I got back.

Philip answered the phone. "She'll be home late on Wednesday, Tom. It's the start of school vacation."

"I'll call on Thursday. Thanks, Philip."

On Thursday after breakfast, he went to his office, closed the door and called Meagan. As he waited for her to come to the phone, his left hand twiddled with some keys in his pocket. He heard a motion at the other end and took a deep breath before speaking. "Hi. I brought some Starbucks back with me. Would you like to try it?"

"I can't wait."

"I'll meet you at the top of the hill. We can walk back together."

Tom reached the top of the hill before Meagan. He watched her come toward him, through the windblown grass, her black hair streaming out to one side, her light blue dress pressing against her legs. It was a moment he wanted to suspend; a videotape he wanted to save, to play over and over in his mind. His mouth was dry. She came up to him and smiled. They turned to walk back to his house before either spoke.

"What will you do with your vacation?" he asked.

"Oh. I've got lots to do. There is a new course to be prepared for next year. There's gardening, horses, Jimmy. And whatever else comes up. What will you be up to?"

"There'll be more work with the trees; watering, drainage, fertilizing; I've got to do something with the barn. Also, I've really got to get going on that Northern Ireland report for my friend."

They talked easily about Tom's trip, his family, the weather while he was away. At the house, Tom served Meagan her first Starbucks in the dining room.

"It's a little darker and stronger than most coffees. If it's not to your taste, I'll fix you some tea." He disappeared, and came back with a plate of muffins and some marmalade. "Be sure and make a fuss over these muffins," he said. "Brid has been using all the new appliances. I want to encourage her."

Meagan took a small bite of one. "They're good. I'll be sure to mention it."

Their conversation continued as before. Meagan finished her coffee but refused a second cup. "I'm sure that I could learn to love it," she said.

They had been in the house for almost an hour when Tom said, "I'll walk you back."

She got up and he followed her out the door. Almost nothing was said until they neared the top of the hill.

"I'm having my bicycle shipped over," he said.

"That sounds as if you're settling in."

"I may have to go back for a while in the fall."

"Oh?"

They reached the tree at the top of the hill. They stopped. Tom put his hand up to lean on one of the branches. "My trip back to the States," he said. "It brought some things together. Put some things in perspective." He looked at her. She listened attentively and waited. "I thought I could handle it," he said.

She nodded.

He continued, "The guilt — It wouldn't be a problem, if..."

"Yes. If?"

"If I wasn't as attracted to you as I am."

"I see."

"I just wasn't — I'm not prepared for how I feel about you."

"That's understandable."

He brought his hand down and looked down at his hands, touching each other just in front of his belt. "I need some time.

I need time to get my head, and my heart, and my gut together. I need to get them all going in the same direction." He looked into her eyes.

She reached out and put her hand on his forearm. "Take as much time as you need. I'll be here," she said. "There's just one thing."

"Name it."

"If you decide to leave, I want you to tell me right away."

"I will," he said. He felt his throat starting to close off. "Do you want me to walk you down?"

"No," she said, "it's best if we part here. I have to.." She shrugged. "...adjust myself before I go into the house."

"Try to explain to Jimmy. I'll miss him," he said. "And Philip too."

He forced the words out. She nodded, gave him a little wave and started down. His throat was burning now; he blinked hard to try to keep her in focus. He stood and watched until she entered the house. He could feel the door closing.

It was the same day that Brid told him of her son, Brendan's, coming visit.

ಜಾ ಜಾ ಜಾ

He sat in his study trying to think of some worthwhile activity to absorb his mind. He flipped on the computer to check his email, but when it failed to connect, he simply turned it off. He picked up a stack of bills and account statements; he checked the due dates. Nothing in the stack required immediate attention. He put it back into a cubbyhole in the roll-top desk that he had bought in Dublin and turned to look out the window at the rows of seedling trees quivering in the wind. He gazed at Barbara's picture and then at Helene's and John's. What am I doing here?

A soft rustling sound came to his ears. He turned.

"Mister Brogan, I've a favor to ask." Brid stood in the doorway with her hands wrapped in her apron and an anxious look about her.

"Come in, Brid. What is it?" He was never comfortable dealing with the Irish when they were being obsequious. He had been doing it all his life it seemed, but it was more prevalent here in Ireland than back home, one of the less endearing traits of the Irish. He was never sure what role he should take.

"It's my son, Brendan. He's down from the North. It's a bit of a surprise."

"Well, that sounds very nice. Bring him in I'd love to meet him."

"You needn't be taking time from your work now, sir. It's just we were wondering would it be all right for him to stay a few days, sir?"

God. This 'Mr. Brogan', and 'Sir' shit drives me nuts. "Of course. Have him stay as long as you like. And feed him well, so he'll come back soon."

"Thank you, sir. It'll be no bother to you. He'll sleep in one of the rooms in the barn."

"As you like." With a vague promise to himself to look up Brendan later, he let his mind wander off in other directions, finally settling on writing some letters. He wrote to John, Helene and Jerry. His letter to Jerry was the only one in which he mentioned Meagan, giving him the gist of what had transpired.

At supper, he told Brid that he would look up Brendan in the morning. He went to the pub and stayed later than usual, but when he got to bed, it still took a long time before he nodded off. His last thought being that it might have been better to hold onto Meagan and live with the guilt.

☙ ☙ ☙

CRACK!, CRACK! "Holy Christ! What's that!?" It was one o'clock in the morning. Tom jerked out of a sound sleep. Right off, he knew, and at the same time, he found it hard to believe, that it was gunfire, the sound of an automatic weapon. He leaped from bed and ran downstairs. The house was dark; there was just enough moonlight to see where he was going. At the bottom of the stairs, he found a distraught Brid Greenan, cowering on the floor against a wall in the hallway. "They're after my Brendan!" she cried.

"Who? What the hell is going on?" He dropped to his knees and crawled toward her.

"They're after him," was all she could manage.

"Who? For Christ's sake!" he shouted in her face.

She was crying, barely coherent. "It's the IRA! They're after my Brendan."

"My God!"

He raced into his office and called the guardai.

"We have a car nearby; it's on its way," the sergeant said.

He went back to Brid, took her hand and noticed that the shooting had ceased. They remained frozen, looking at each other, listening. They heard the sound of a car door slamming. A car started, tires squealed. Silence again. And then, the sweetest sound: a siren. The guardai had arrived. It could have been a bugle and the U.S. Cavalry. Slowly, he brought Brid to her feet.

The rest of the night was spent answering questions and traveling back and forth between the hospital, where Brendan had gone with a leg wound, the Guardai station, and home. From Sean he got most of the story of how he and Brendan took turns on watch, how they had spotted the IRA people and fought them off. Brendan had been wounded, but it was not too serious.

"He'll be able to recuperate at home," Sean said, looking at Tom with a worried expression.

Tom didn't react. He wanted time to think about what he had gotten himself into.

He did not try to get any more sleep that night. He went into his office and sat there, thinking about the night's events and what had led up to them. Brid and Sean, they were getting to be family, my friends. Not just a housekeeper and caretaker. Why did they have to lie to me? I should have suspected something when she said that Brendan would sleep in the barn. There's more than enough room in this house. Kid's in trouble with the IRA — that's for sure. But, an informer? I better keep him the hell out of here.

As the sky lightened in the east, Tom reached across his desk to turn out the lamp. His left hand pressed against the folder on his desk. It was empty, but he had written on it "Northern Ireland Report." With the light off, he leaned back. "Well, Jerry, old buddy, it looks as if your report is going to be a little more interesting than we had in mind."

Later, Tom phoned the Clarks, and spoke to Philip. They had undoubtedly heard the shooting, and he wanted to assure them that he would take steps to see that there would not be any more incidents.

During the day following the shooting, Brid and Sean avoided Tom in subtle ways. When paths crossed there were a few polite words, followed by withdrawal. They feel guilty as hell, and they should. Just a visit home, they said — some visit. Why don't they say something? Talk to me?

That evening, as Brid set out his supper, she avoided eye contact, and he noticed a slight trembling in her hands. When she finished serving, she stepped back but did not leave. He wanted to say something, something to reassure her, to tell her that he was not going to lash out at her and Sean, that he was a parent too and understood.

She stayed, near the table, wringing her hands in her apron. "Sean and me — we want to apologize."

Tom picked up his water glass. He held it and looked at her. "Why didn't you tell me he was in trouble?"

Brid avoided his eyes. "We were afraid you'd send him away. We didn't know what else to do."

Here was a situation as primal as they get: Two humans facing each other, one a supplicant, the other with power — power he did not want. He set his glass down.

"Ah Brid, it's over. Let's think about how to get Brendan to a safe place."

"You'll help us?"

"Yes, but no more surprises. And, by the way," he said, "what did Brendan do to merit this extraordinary attention from the IRA?"

"He was in a pub. He'd taken a bit too much drink. There were some girls. He tried to impress them." She nodded her head. "The next day, the British raided a house, got some weapons, made some arrests. They think it was Brendan, that let the information slip." She took an audible breath.

"He's not an informer?"

Brid hesitated. "I pray to God, he's not."

Tom paused a moment and then said, "We'll get him out."

She nodded rapidly then turned and almost ran out of the room, calling for Sean.

After supper, Tom drove down to Donohue's pub. Frank would know all about the shooting and probably some related details as yet unknown to Tom. *Maybe I can get him to open up, give me some ideas on how to deal with this mess. Who knows, maybe he has connections to the IRA. Why not, he's connected to just about everything else in County Leitrim.* He parked in the car park around the corner from Donohue's and sat there, thinking a minute more, before making his way to the pub. *Yeah, it will be interesting to see what he has to say about this IRA fiasco.*

He squared his cap and pulled the hood of his parka up over it before stepping out into the rain. At this time of year, it would not be dark in Ireland for another two hours, but it was raining hard enough so that even the Irish were indoors. Hands jammed in his pockets and shoulders hunched up, he quickstepped his way around the puddles and along the sidewalk to push open the door and go inside to the familiar surroundings of Donohue's pub. He stomped his feet and shook his parka before hanging it on a hook alongside his cap. What a simple place; the bar, a few shelves holding a limited selection of whiskies, a couple of posters (God knows how old.) extolling the benefits of Guinness and the tradition of Paddy's Whiskey.

"Tom, it's good to see you." Frank Donohue greeted him as he took a seat at the bar. "Guinness is it?"

"Yes, Frank, a pint, please."

"A pint it is. You remember Brian?" Frank nodded his head in the direction of the only other patron in the pub while continuing to draw Tom's pint.

Tom waved to Brian, a young man with reddish blonde hair, seated a few stools away with a half-empty pint of dark ale on the bar in front of him. " How's the garage going? Keeping busy?"

"Oh, it's doing right well," Brian replied, smiling warmly at Tom.

Tom had talked with Brian a number of times in the pub. He was shy but he always welcomed Tom's attention and liked to talk once he got going. It did not suit Tom's purpose to enter into a conversation with Brian right then. He really needed to talk with Frank and hoped for a slow night with that purpose in mind. Irish manners however, called for him to continue talking with Brian for at least a few more minutes before trying to talk privately with Frank.

"Is your oldest still in the band?" Tom asked.

"Oh yes, she'll be in it for a few more years now."

"Weren't they supposed to be in some kind of a contest about now? In Cork?" Tom remembered making a contribution to the travel fund a month earlier.

"Aye, the 'All Ireland.' They'll be going next week." Brian turned now to fully face towards Tom

"Wow, another trophy for Frank's window." Tom raised his pint.

Brian nodded his head and laughed in appreciation of Tom's little joke. Tom turned to Frank, "Frank, I need some advice," and then to Brian, "Brian, please excuse me for a few minutes, I need to talk to my consultant."

Brian raised his hand, and then turned his attention towards the television set which featured a snooker match.

Tom never ceased to be amazed at some of the stuff they put on prime time television in this country. It reminded him of some of his early dates when he would go over to some girl's house, ostensibly to watch television. Of course, it really did not matter what was on, which was just as well given the caliber of some of those early shows.

"Been busy?" Frank asked. He set Tom's pint on the bar and began wiping up around it.

"Yeah, I'm sure you know about part of it." Tom could not conceive of how Frank got all his information. He seemed to be clued into everything that happened, or that mattered, in this and the surrounding counties. For a while Tom had made a game out of trying to come up with some piece of information, even trivia, that Frank had not heard about. He rarely succeeded. He took a drink of his Guinness and then wiped the foam from his upper lip.

"Bit of a fracas," Frank commented.

"Scared the shit out of me, I'll tell you. I want to get your advice on how to get things back to normal."

Frank gave a little laugh raising his eyebrows and waggling his head as if to say, "That'll be the day."

The Irish sure do a lot of talking with head wagging and nods; I'll have to learn a bit of that myself.

Frank put down his bar towel and moved a stool over to sit directly across from Tom. "Something to do with Brendan is it?"

By now, Tom had gotten used to Frank's ability to anticipate his next thought, he even enjoyed it. Very efficient. "Yeah.... I need to talk to someone in the IRA."

More head nods, this time from side to side with his eyebrows raised. Then Frank leaned forward and lowering his voice said, "I know that you're aware, they don't go around advertising."

Now Tom leaned forward, "Yeah I know, it's all a big secret, but if the Brits can find one to talk to when they feel the need, I sure as hell ought to be able to." Tom suspected that Frank could put him in touch with the IRA directly if he chose to. He had not been in town very long when someone had told him of the time when IRA weapons had been found in one of the adjacent empty buildings, which happened to be owned by Frank. More likely Frank would find some indirect way to help him. Tom guessed that this would be the case based on the fact that Frank was always so careful and tight-lipped whenever subjects touching on the IRA came up in conversations at the pub. He waited for Frank to speak.

"You might try talking to Sinn Fein." Frank said this with a facial expression, which implied that this was more than a casual suggestion.

"I thought they made a big deal out of having nothing to do with the IRA?"

"That's what they say." Frank let his statement hang there. He was looking directly into Tom's eyes.

"So what do I do, just call them up and tell them I want to talk to the IRA?"

"They have offices in Derry. There may be one closer like in Armagh or Strabane. People stop in looking for help with all kinds of problems. Remember they're a political party. Being an American won't hurt; that's where they get most of their money."

Tom rubbed his chin while he considered this. "Okay, I'll give it a whirl. And don't worry, I won't tell them you sent me."

Frank's expression almost said, "I'm glad to see that we understand each other." Then he got up from his stool and moved away.

Tom turned his attention back to Brian. He also made a sign to Frank indicating that he'd like to buy the young man a drink.

Tom said, "So, Brian, are you going to make the trip down to Cork?"

"No, her mother's going. I'll be home taking care of the wee uns."

"You can bring them in here. What's a few more running around, right Frank?"

When Tom left the pub, the rain had almost stopped; he slowly made his way back to his car. Good advice. I'll start with Sinn Fein. If they can get Brendan off the hook with the IRA, he can stay in Ireland, be near his folks. Smart man, Frank.

He decided to try to talk to someone in Sinn Fein as soon as possible. He consulted a map to decide where to go. He picked Derry. He had spent several days there on a vacation trip with Barbara and had pleasant memories of the city. It was these memories really, more than the driving time involved, which determined his choice.

ِ ِ ِ

It was over nine months since Barbara's death. The mourning process continued but had undergone some subtle changes. The tears still came but most of the time thinking of her was a pleasant experience in that it was as close to being with her as he could get. Going to Derry would bring back a flood of memories; he knew that, but rather than shrinking back from the prospect, he sought it out as a kind of spiritual experience, a cleansing that somehow he expected to at least partially free him from his deep sense of loss and from the guilt attached to any serious thoughts of Meagan.

He packed a small bag, in the event that he needed to stay overnight, and set off early the next morning. After eating lunch in Omagh he drove on through Strabane and into Derry on the A 5. He knew that he could get directions and a good map at the tourist office, so he entered the city center and parked at the top of Bishop Street. As expected, the tourist people provided him with a map and clear directions to the Sinn Fein office in the Bogside.

The day was gray and overcast with occasional showers, but he decided to walk over to the Bogside anyway. It was so much simpler than negotiating all those one-way streets and queer intersections that he remembered from last time. As he left the walled city center behind him and headed down the hill, the Bogside stretched out below him. God! It sure has changed from the pictures we saw twenty years ago. Not affluent but neat. On his earlier visit to Derry with Barbara, the Bogside had already been largely reconstructed as part of a political solution to what they referred to as the "Troubles" that started in the late nineteen sixties. Large areas of slums had been razed and replaced with two-story housing estates and wide streets.

That earlier visit with Barbara was part of a three-day excursion into the North during a two-week vacation in Ireland. They had been close to the border on previous vacations and had seen some evidence of military activity; they were curious as to what it would be like in Northern Ireland itself. They enjoyed their time in Derry, staying pretty much in the city center. They did not visit the Bogside. In spite of the obvious military presence, things had seemed fairly relaxed and congenial to Tom. Barbara didn't agree.

"Tom, we should get out of here. I'm scared," she said.

She was concerned by the daytime presence of the Royal Ulster Constabulary, the RUC, wearing bulletproof vests and carrying automatic weapons. She was very upset when the British troops, peering over the high sides of armored cars, rolled out onto the streets, as they did every day at five o'clock to take up strategic positions throughout the city.

She said, "They look so mean, like they'd shoot you without blinking an eye."

"They're just kids. They're trained to look mean. It's part of the show," he said.

"Kids can be dangerous. I want to go back to the South."

One thing Tom had noticed so far on his current visit was the absence of British troops and patrols. There were still RUC officers around, armed with automatic weapons, but security measures had definitely been toned down.

He reached the Bogside and was looking for Cable Street where Sinn Fein was located. He spotted a school crossing guard, an old man dressed in a yellow rain slicker and a uniform cap with a yellow stripe.

"Can you tell me were I'll find Cable Street?"

The old man looked him over, an obvious stranger. "Isn't it a fine day?" he asked. "Have you come far?"

"Lovely day," Tom said. "What's a little rain?"

The old man said nothing; he just nodded gently and waited for more.

"I'm just up from Leitrim today," Tom said.

The man continued to nod at him.

"Do you know where it is?" Tom asked.

"Cable Street?"

"Yes."

The old man looked around as if thinking about how to direct Tom and then said, "Oh, it's right over there," pointing to a nearby street, not ten yards away. Then as an afterthought he added, "That's where I live."

Tom walked off chuckling, then turned and waved, saying, "Thank you."

He walked down the street of row houses and found the one that Sinn Fein occupied. He had the feeling that everyone in the neighborhood was aware of his presence. He arrived at the door at the same time as a young woman carrying boxes of some kind of literature. He offered to help and soon found himself helping to empty her car and listening to the detailed instructions she gave to the woman behind the desk inside. All this stuff was to be distributed in time for some local election. When the task was completed, he seemed to be automatically accepted as belonging there. He was told to have a seat and that a counselor would be with him in a few minutes. He sat in the tiny cramped reception office and surveyed his surroundings. The room was not well lit and everything was old and beaten up, especially the furniture which consisted of just a few old chairs, no two of a kind, and what looked like a desk under piles of papers. There was a faint odor of dampness and the distinct smell of stale tobacco. The walls were covered with political posters and notices. Some of both had been there for a long time; they were discolored and curling at the corners.

A woman, apparently a housewife, sat in the other visitor's chair next to Tom. She engaged in conversation with the woman behind the desk, who also looked like a housewife, working there part time. Most of what they said was ordinary gossip, but there was something having to do with streetlights being out that the woman behind the desk promised to attend to. She took notice of Tom looking hard at one poster, people running in the street, mouths open, as if screaming.

"Bloody Sunday," she said. "The British paratroopers had a fine time that day, killing innocent people."

"That was a while ago," he said, "1972?"

"Yes, 1972."

Her tone of voice and expression said all he needed to know about how little time had passed by Irish standards since 1972.

He noticed the security system, which seemed to be for emergency purposes only. It consisted of a locked front door, which could be unlocked with a buzzer from the desk in front of him. There was also a TV camera connected to a monitor in this same office so that someone sitting at the desk could see who wanted to get in. People, some of whom had keys, were coming and going with such rapidity that the buzzer seldom came into use. Tom himself had walked in without so much as giving his name.

63

After he sat there watching all the coming and going for about twenty minutes, a woman of between thirty and forty years of age came out and introduced herself. "Hello, I'm Eileen Traynor. Sorry to keep you waiting, we've been so busy."

"That's all right, it's been fun watching all this activity."

He followed her down a narrow hall, out of force of habit, taking note of her figure. She was a little overweight but otherwise quite attractive with dark hair, blue eyes and a winning smile. She had on a simple dark blue sweater and dark gray slacks. She wore no makeup and projected an air of nervous energy, as if she were engaged in work of great importance. She made some comment about having just come from a very important meeting

"We can talk in here," she said, leading him into an office — no bigger than the first. She sat behind the small desk, and he sat in a simple orange plastic and chrome "cafeteria" chair facing her. This office was a little less cluttered but otherwise much like the first with battered furniture and posters on the walls.

"May I have your name again please?" she asked, taking a pad from a drawer and making ready to take notes.

"Tom Brogan, I'm an American, as you may already have gathered, but I'm living in Ireland now. I've bought some property in County Leitrim and I intend to raise trees for sale in the EU."

She gazed directly at him. Her eyes and expression held that delicate balance between observation and flirtation. "You've come a ways to see us, Mr. Brogan, and we're always happy to see Americans." She was smiling now while continuing to fix on him with deep blue eyes. He began to feel a little self-conscious. He knew this game; the Irish women were so good at it. They hold you with those eyes and charm you with the lilt in their voices; always ready with a sharp tongue if they catch you out. He was determined to concentrate on the business at hand.

"It's Tom, please. I've come because I need a favor, and I was told that you people can help me." He looked at her directly but then quickly away.

"If it's in our power, Mr. Bro..,Tom, we'll certainly do that." She still had that soft smile.

"I need to talk to someone, in a position of authority in the IRA."

She glanced at him and then looked down. She took a moment before answering. "Well, Tom. I hope that you haven't been misinformed. You see, Sinn Fein and the IRA have nothing whatever to do with each other." Her expression was now more serious.

"Is that right? I had been given to understand that Sinn Fein was the political wing of the IRA?" Tom said this as a soft query, not a challenge. He was the one now gazing full on at her.

She averted his eyes. "That's a very popular misconception. In fact, they are two distinctly separate organizations. Sinn Fein is strictly a political party, and the IRA is an army, a secret army. We have nothing to do with them." She waited.

Tom sat there feeling irritated with himself for not having gotten more specific information on this point. He knew that there was a connection; perhaps they deliberately kept it ambiguous. He tried to recover. "I understand, but aren't there at least some common objectives?"

"We both want the British out of Ireland. If that's what you mean." Her manner was clearly a bit cooler now. She sat well back in her chair.

Tom leaned forward trying to reestablish some undefined contact. "Yes, and while I understand that the organizations are separate and distinct, there must be an informal contact here and there?"

"If there is I don't know about it, and no one else is going to be talking about it."

Tom felt a bit frustrated and he could not figure out what he was doing wrong. But he knew that Sinn Fein must be connected to the IRA in some way or people like Frank Donohue would not have encouraged him to make this contact. He changed his tack. "Listen...May I call you Eileen?"

"Certainly," she said with a slight smile. She was still sitting back with her hands folded on her lap.

Now it was Tom who maintained eye contact, looking at her almost plaintively. "Eileen, I realize that I'm a stranger, just in off the street, but, as you say, Sinn Fein is a political party and that means all kinds of contacts. I need this favor badly; someone's life may depend on it. If you could just give me some guidance. Just the next step."

"Be assured, Tom, we want to help in any way we can. Let me think..." The soft smile returned, she leaned forward placing an elbow on her desk and her hand to her chin. Tom looked at her with an air of hope in his eyes, knowing that his silence would exert pressure on her to come up with something.

"I do know some *former* IRA people. They were prisoners of the British, now they're free to talk about the past. I don't know if they'll talk to you, or if they can help."

"It would be a start," he said. "There's some urgency to this. I came prepared to stay the night if it would be possible to talk to someone tomorrow."

"Oh, I don't know if we can do anything that fast," she laughed. " I'll try, you call me at eleven in the morning. Now, you say that you've bought some land in County Leitrim. Where exactly would that be?" Eileen went on asking Tom questions about himself and noting down his answers. It was obvious that she wanted to be able to show her superiors that she had done her homework. Also, someone might want to be checking up on him; he tried to give as much information as he could, including a few names of people who might be able to vouch for him, like Frank Donohue. The interview over, Eileen escorted Tom back to the front door, she held out her hand. He took it and glanced up at her eyes. She held onto his hand just a bit longer than was necessary and returned his gaze. He took his leave, promising to call the following morning.

Outside, Tom noted that the clouds were less threatening than earlier. No hint of sunshine, but at least he wouldn't get soaked on the walk back up to Derry center. The time was four-thirty, or half-four, as the locals would say. Time to see about a place to stay. He crossed Lecky Road and started on the path up the hill. Turning to look back at the Bogside, he noted the "wall" which was just that, a plain wall built in the middle of a traffic island. Painted on the wall was a sign saying, "Welcome to Free Ireland." Turning again to climb the hill he looked up at the gray stone walls surrounding the center of Derry and tried to imagine how forbidding they must have looked in the seventeenth century to the few Catholic workers allowed to live in what was then really a bog. He went directly to his car; he wanted to be out of the city before any five o'clock security measures were in force

He booked a room at a nearby B&B. When he arrived he asked his hostess to recommend a restaurant and went there for an early dinner. While enjoying a pre-dinner Jameson's, he began to think over his meeting with Eileen and its implications. He had thought that Sinn Fein might see some political advantage in getting the IRA to lay off Brendan, but now the party line seemed to be to deny any connection whatever. At best, they would get him in contact with some IRA commander, and thereafter he would be on his own. How do you deal with a bunch like that? Mad bombers, fanatics willing to kill one of their own, a kid, for a slip of the tongue. What can I offer? All through dinner, he continued trying to come up with a plausible strategy.

The following morning after breakfast and checking out of his B&B, he headed for the city center. It was a much brighter day than the day before and on the way in he took note of the sky. He and Barbara had always considered the sky to be one of Ireland's strongest attributes. Combined with beautiful landscapes that seemed to be everywhere in Ireland, the clouds, with their shapes and towering heights, created a sense of drama. A drama that lifted the spirits and let one's imagination run. One of his first impressions of Ireland was an understanding of how his forebears, under these skies, could conjure up such creatures as fairies and leprechauns.

At eleven o'clock, he called Eileen. She had made arrangements for him to talk to someone else in Sinn Fein at another location: Daniel O'Coyle. From what he gathered O'Coyle was a high-ranking member of the party and might be able to make a critical contact for him. She gave him the address and advised him to take a taxi since the directions were complicated.

O'Coyle did not expect him until after one o'clock; so, Tom sought out a little restaurant in a back alley where he remembered eating with Barbara. He ordered quiche, salad, a scone and coffee, just what he had probably eaten years before. Then he sat down where he could look out the window. How easily she came back to him now, Barbara. He could almost see her coming up the pedestrian walkway, stopping to compliment a young mother's baby, coming to sit down across the table, telling him excitedly about the wonderful fabric store she discovered while he was busy elsewhere. He got a little misty eyed and was startled when the waitress brought his meal.

Sure would be handy to have Barbara along on this deal. She could read these people better than I can. He was always amazed and sometimes angry when after what he thought had been an objective, factual discussion and agreement with someone, Barbara would take him aside and try to explain what the other person had *really* meant! He could never understand why people did not just come out and say what they meant in the first place.

Taking Eileen's advice, he left his car and got a taxi for a short but complicated ride to what appeared to be the industrial section of Derry. He got out in front of what looked like a temporary building left over from the Second World War. It was one story with a flat roof and was painted a light gray. Man, these guys operate with low overhead. They should see some of the digs on Wall Street. He went inside and noted that the place had been done by the same interior decorator that they had used in the Bogside. The rooms were a little bit bigger and brighter, thanks to the presence of more windows. There was the same buzz buzz of activity, people coming and going, phone calls and communicating from room to room with raised voices. Tom took a seat and watched all the goings-on until O'Coyle finished some previous business.

O'Coyle came out and greeted him in a very pleasant and friendly way. He mentioned something to his secretary/receptionist and ushered Tom into his small office, closing the door. Tom sat down, looking around. There was the now familiar collection of posters and news photos from the "Troubles" on the walls; a window covered with a partially closed venetian blind and papers stacked everywhere. There was not a single item of strong color anywhere in the room.

Noting the remnants of O'Coyle's just finished lunch on his desk, Tom started by saying, "I really appreciate your giving me your time on such short notice."

"Not at all. We certainly want to accommodate our friends from America."

O'Coyle was younger than Tom. Probably around forty, Tom guessed. A fairly good-looking man with a full head of strong black hair, a bit overweight but otherwise in good condition. He was wearing a white shirt open at the neck and a beige cardigan sweater.

"It is very busy here," Tom said. "What do you do besides get ready for the next election?"

"Ah well, elections are the least of it." O'Coyle sat forward in his chair, hands together, forearms resting on his desk. "Mostly we're here to help people with problems. Housing unit repairs, a part time job, relief payments. We can't always help, but we try. I understand that you yourself have a problem."

"Yes, I don't know how much Eileen told you of my situation, but...." Tom went on to describe the events which had brought him there. O'Coyle listened intently without interrupting until

Tom wound up by saying, "And so I'd like to intercede on the kid's behalf, and for his parents."

O'Coyle, obviously in thought, took an audible breath, before asking Tom, "What makes you think that anyone in the IRA would be interested in talking to you?"

This, of course, was the very question that Tom had been struggling with since Eileen emphatically denied any connection between Sinn Fein and the IRA.

"Well," Tom said, gripping his hands together, "it seems to me that the IRA has what we'd call in the States an 'image problem.' Most people seem to think of them as a bunch of irresponsible terrorists with no sense of morals or compassion. If that image is of any concern to them, maybe they'd like to modify it a bit by showing some common sense and some mercy toward this kid." Tom surprised himself at the intensity with which he spoke.

O'Coyle now sat back in his chair, his arms folded on his midriff. He studied Tom and then asked, "And from where do you get your information on the IRA?"

Tom recognized this immediately as a polite Irish way to disagree, to almost say, "You don't know much, do you?" He needed O'Coyle on his side, so he proceeded with caution. "To be honest, I don't know an awful lot about the IRA and whatever their rationale is for what they do. So, I see this issue as an outsider. I'm just hoping that they care what outsiders think. Is that unreasonable?"

"It might be. There are a few things that it might be helpful for you to know, if you're going to pursue this matter."

"I'll be grateful for any help you can give me."

O'Coyle leaned forward. "The Irish Republican Army is just that, an army. A disciplined military organization with an objective of getting an occupying army, the British, to withdraw from our native soil as the vast majority of Irish people so strongly desire."

Tom was puzzled by this last statement in that he knew that the majority of people in Northern Ireland were Protestant, and it was unlikely that they wanted the British to go home. He sat back and did not interrupt.

O'Coyle continued, "As in any army there's a discipline that must be enforced. No one would be safe without it." O'Coyle used his hands for emphasis.

Tom interrupted. "But he's just a kid."

"It's an all volunteer army. There's a thorough indoctrination before they're allowed to take the oath. Nobody gets in without knowing what the rules are. And they do not take children."

Again, Tom interrupted. "But doesn't an army need to represent some legitimate government? Where's the legitimate government behind the IRA?"

"Even a casual look at Irish history shows that the only legitimate Irish government we've had since the sixteenth century is that which we forced the British to accept. The twenty-six counties in the south would be under British rule today if it had not been made too costly for them to stay. You need to remember, we're dealing with a people that have an 'Empire' mentality. They never took their dirty fingers off any country without being forced to, your own country being a case in point." O'Coyle straightened up a little and nodded his head for emphasis

Tom choked a bit on this last point. He knew that the withdrawal from India was no love feast, but he thought that England's relationships with Canada, Australia and others were, at least in recent years, fairly progressive. He refrained from interrupting again because he could see O'Coyle warming to his subject, speaking with increasing fervor. Sinn Fein doesn't have anything to do with the IRA, heh. Bullshit! this guy might be one of them! "So you see the British as a foreign army?" Tom said. "One that just happens to have been here for four or five hundred years?"

"That's it. They've never been welcome. It's only by force that they've been here."

"Surely, nobody expects the IRA to push them into the Irish Sea."

"Certainly not. They'll leave when it's too costly for them to stay."

"You mean that the English taxpayers will get tired of paying the tab for keeping troops here?" Tom now sat upright with one arm across his front and the other holding his hand up to his chin.

"Aye, that's part of it but more important to the British is world opinion," O'Coyle said. "They make a big 'to do' of their special relationship with America. It's one of the things that they hold on to for dear life, so they can pretend to still be a world power."

"You expect the U.S. to get them out?" Tom said this opening up his hands with a note of true incredulity.

O'Coyle nodded and continued. "We have many friends in America, including those in high places who've come out and voiced strong support. Did you know that there are forty million Americans of Irish descent?"

"Really? That many?" Tom needed time to think. He was getting sucked into a debate with O'Coyle and, while all Irishmen love to debate, it was not his purpose for being there. He let his eyes wander to the ceiling near the window. A leak had stained the paint and caused some flaking. How many years ago? He returned to the problem at hand. He could see that O'Coyle was at least an ardent closet supporter of the IRA and might be in a position to do some good. He needed to cultivate the man. "Look, Mr. O'Coyle.."

"It's Dan. My friends call me Dan."

"Okay and I'm Tom. Dan, it's obvious that I don't know nearly as much as I should about this whole subject, but the clock's ticking. I need to find some way to help this kid. He's a nice kid and I've become very attached to his mother and father."

"I understand, and I wish I could offer some encouragement, but people in the IRA will be inclined to look at things quite differently."

Tom shrugged to indicate his question on this last point.

O'Coyle continued, his eyes holding Tom. "They have to think about the example, about the precedent this might set. They can't have everyone with a mother free to break the rules."

"Granted, but Brendan didn't do anything deliberately, he just had a little too much to drink and got careless."

"It's not my place to judge," O'Coyle said. "Why don't you just sneak him out of the country?" O'Coyle made a waving gesture with one hand as if to say, "And let that be the end of it." Was O'Coyle trying to tell him something, sub rosa?

"That's an alternative," Tom said. "I'm not sure we could do it with sufficient secrecy, and besides, he could never come back to see his mother and his friends."

"Tom," O'Coyle was shaking his head, "if I had a pound for every Irishman who has had to leave Ireland and never return, I wouldn't be sitting here."

" I know, I know, but at least they didn't have to worry for the rest of their lives about being shot."

"I'll do what I can, Tom, but it would be a rare thing indeed if anything can be changed."

Tom got up and held out his hand. "I know you'll do your best, and I appreciate it. Please, let me know right away if there's anything I can do."

O'Coyle got up and began to see Tom out. "I will, Tom, I will, but it would be my advice to think about getting him out."

"Yeah, I'll do that. Can I call you in a couple of days to see if anything's happening?"

"Do that, here's my card. And all the best to you, Tom." He shook Tom's hand and said this in a very friendly way.

ða ða ða

Tom barely noticed the taxi ride back to his car. His head was filled with the implications of his meeting with O'Coyle. So far, his thoughts were disjointed, skipping around from one part of the problem to another. This was always the case when he was confronted with a lot of complex input. At first, he would try to wrestle with the whole problem, and then gradually to break it down into elements that he could handle. Elements that he could manage with the logical, objective mind that was his strength. For the moment, he was content to let his thoughts ramble. He would not be able to concentrate until he was in his own car on the main road towards home.

On his way out of Derry, he thought of Barbara. I didn't moon over her as much as I thought I would. Interesting. And then briefly of Meagan. I wonder if she'd be of any help in talking through this situation? He had been thinking of Meagan with a frequency that surprised him, even now he was looking forward to the next time he would see her and wondering when he would be able to handle it. A twinge of guilt, and the thought died. He still did not feel free to give himself over to these new feelings, afraid that, somehow, it meant letting go of Barbara.

He brought himself back to the meeting with O'Coyle. Starting to pull it apart, to look for the elements. Most important, of course, was what to do about Brendan. Got to get serious about getting him out. Whom can I trust to help? Maybe I should just take a straightforward approach, hire a couple of bodyguards and ship him to the States. He certainly should qualify for asylum; Jerry could help with that.

It was late afternoon, he could stop somewhere for a bite and still make it home at a reasonable hour. Soon it would be twilight, his favorite time of day. Should be a spectacular sunset. God! Look at those clouds. Thoughts of Barbara returned. Wherever they traveled together, they enjoyed the sunsets.

She always said the same thing. "Tom, if we cut down some trees in our yard, we could have a sunset at home too," and he would reply, "When I was a kid I could only dream about having a house with trees some day."

He knew that she wasn't serious about cutting down the trees; she loved them too. It was just a little game. It ended when one of them would say, "The next house we get is going to have a sunset."

The sunsets in Ireland were often dramatic and these unfailingly reminded him of her. He remembered occasions when they had been driving along and would stop the car to get out and view a sunset. With luck, they would be at the top of a hill where they could see a long distance. They would stand there pointing out to each other the many little spots of particular beauty or interest. Often there would be a ray of sunshine piercing through the now darkening and back-lit clouds to highlight some farm buildings or a lake, just as in some of those corny paintings you see for sale at county fairs back in the States. Only here it was real and thrilling to see. On other occasions, they would be driving along and see the last rays of sunshine just hitting the hilltops with a reddish alpenglow. And there, on a hilltop, would be a stately mansion, or better yet, a castle, bathed in this golden reddish light while all else slipped into darkness.

CHAPTER SEVEN

"Why can't Tom come with us tomorrow?" Jimmy asked.

"He's very busy with some work," Meagan said.

She looked over at Philip who sat in his usual chair in the library with a book on his lap — a finger holding his place. Philip shrugged. It was Friday night, and Jimmy was getting ready for bed. He stood, just inside the door in his blue pajamas and white terrycloth bathrobe. Meagan planned to take him to a castle near Sligo on Saturday.

"When will he be finished?"

"I don't know, dear. It could take a long time."

"Can't he even come for just a visit?"

She held her arms out to him and motioned him to come to her. He came over to where she was sitting, and she put an arm around him.

"I can't explain it completely, Jimmy, but I think Tom needs to concentrate on what he's doing. So, he doesn't have time for other people right now."

Jimmy said, "He's not mad at us?"

"No, dear. He's not mad at us."

"Jimmy," Philip said.

Jimmy looked at him.

"Tom is very sad right now. He wants to be alone."

Jimmy turned to look at his mother, and then, back to Philip.

"You see," Philip said, "not long ago, his wife died. When he was away to America, he realized how much he misses her. And now, he does not want to be with other adults for a while. I know that's hard for you to understand. And, of course, he has some work that he has to get finished." Philip looked at Meagan. She nodded her approval.

"All right, Jimmy," she said, "it's time for us to go upstairs."

Fifteen minutes later, Meagan returned and sat down. Philip put down his book and removed his glasses. "He really dotes on Tom. Doesn't he?"

"Yes. They have fun together," she said.

"Tom seems to have a real affection for him. Maybe Jimmy should go over for a visit."

"Philip, please. Things are complicated enough."

"I was thinking that it's only a matter of time. A little more, or a little less."

"I don't think so."

"I think I detect a note of anger. Or is it frustration?"

Meagan got up and walked over to the mantel. She looked up and then turned to Philip. "I don't know what it is. I just think he should have known better."

"He got a little ahead of himself?"

"You could say that. After all, I didn't pursue *him*. I would have been content with just being neighbors."

"And he had other ideas?"

"He gave me that impression."

"From what you told me, he hasn't changed his mind."

"Maybe he hasn't," she said.

She walked back to her chair, sat down and gestured with her hands, palms out. "What am I supposed to do? Put my emotions in cold storage?"

"You're free to do whatever you like."

"Right, and what I've got to do is make sure that Mister Brogan doesn't take me for a roller-coaster ride."

"What will you do if he calls?"

"That will depend on *when* he calls, and how I feel by then."

"Ah well. It's entirely up to you of course. I hope it works out."

"We'll see."

ও ও ও

It was dark when Tom reached Omagh. He stopped for a meal, no Jameson's tonight, he was anxious to get home, to see if anything had happened on the farm and to sleep in his own bed. During the ride, he had continued to think about his meetings with Eileen Traynor and O'Coyle. He had gotten the strong impression that somehow they expected part of the solution to Northern Ireland's problems to come from the United States. That America would lean on the British and cause them to withdraw! Thinking about this gave him a strange sensation. He was drawn between a mild amusement at their naiveté and a sympathy for people passionately committed to a cause against overwhelming odds.

He reached home shortly after eleven. Both Brid and Sean Greenan were waiting to greet him with anxious faces. He told them right off that it would be a few more days, at least, before he knew if he was making any progress. After ascertaining that things had remained quiet in his absence, he went to bed.

On the following day, Tom met with Brid and Sean. They agreed that it was unlikely that the IRA would launch another attack on the farm, but they decided to send Brendan to stay with a relative in Sligo. A relative that would be unknown to the IRA. After that, Tom busied himself with some correspondence and looking around the farm until it was late enough to call the States. He managed to get through to Jerry Healey's personal secretary.

"This is Estelle Adams. May I help you?"

"Yes, I'm Tom Brogan, a former schoolmate and a personal friend of the senator's. I'm calling from Ireland because I need a favor." He went on to give her the particulars about Brendan and told her he needed to find a way to get him into the States

"Mister Brogan, when the senator comes in tomorrow, I'll tell him you called and I will get back to you."

Tom had the distinct feeling that if it were up to Miss Adams what he would get would be one of those bureaucratic Dear Johns. He had faith in Jerry. He knew that if Jerry got his message, he'd get a serious reply. He would wait a few days before trying again, and that was all he could do for the now.

Time for a walk. He went out the back door to check on the weather. It was misty and chilly; he turned to go back in for a jacket and his eyes cast over the hill that separated his farm from Meagan's. There was the tree at the top where they had parted. God! That was less than a month ago. I wonder what she'd make out of this Brendan business? Probably think I'm crazy for having anything to do with it.

A day later, he phoned O'Coyle.

"Tom, in all honesty, I can't say that anything is different from when you were here, but I think it would be worth your while to come up to Derry as soon as you can."

"Is Monday afternoon good enough?"

"I'll be waiting to see you Tom. And God bless."

He set out early; the forecast was for a clear day, but the sun was not high enough yet to confirm this. The route was familiar now; he did not need to read the signs, and the day opened up to display a few high clouds catching the sun and lifting his spirits. Surely, this is a day when good things will happen. He found his own way to O'Coyle's office where he was warmly welcomed. He sat in the same chair and waited for O'Coyle to finish some other business on the phone. He made a little game of checking the various piles of papers to see if he could notice any difference at all from his last visit. He found none and was amused to note that several piles had a single sheet of paper, somewhere deep in the pile, that had slipped about a third of the way out of the pile and had gathered enough dust to turn a distinct shade of gray. After finishing his phone conversation, O'Coyle brought Tom up to date. "Tom, I've made certain inquiries. Along the lines that we discussed."

O'Coyle paused; Tom waited.

"It's pretty much what I would have expected," O'Coyle said, and again he paused. "They won't make any concessions. They claim it's strictly a military matter, and that the lad will have to stand for a court martial."

Tom moved around in his chair, all the while watching O'Coyle's face. "You brought me all the way up here to tell me that?"

"No, Tom, it's just that it's not an easy thing."

"I understood that quite clearly last time."

"Yes, Tom, I know. There's more I wanted to say, if you'll just hear me out."

Tom sat back and gestured with his hands for O'Coyle to go ahead.

"Would you like a spot of tea, Tom?"

Before Tom could say no, O'Coyle was out of his chair calling, "Fiona", from the outer office. Fiona came in, using two hands to lift her horn-rimmed glasses from her chest, where they hung by a white string taped to the ear-pieces with cellophane tape; she adjusted them up onto her nose.

"Fiona," O'Coyle said, "could you find a clean cup for our guest and make us some tea."

O'Coyle handed his cup to her. She left, and O'Coyle sat down.

"What I was about to say, Tom, is this. It seems that you're a man of some importance."

Tom smiled. "I am?"

"Yes, we've learned that you're on personal terms with a United States Senator, and that you're to make some kind of an assessment on Northern Ireland for him. Is that right?"

Tom thought before answering. He leaned forward. "Yes, it is. But I want it to be clear that my report is in no way connected to getting Brendan off the hook with the IRA."

"No, of course not, Tom, and I wouldn't want to suggest otherwise."

Fiona reentered, a cup of tea in each hand. She set O'Coyle's on the corner of his desk and then came round to hand the other cup to Tom "Would you be wanting milk or sugar?" she asked.

"No thank you," Tom said.

As she left, he looked into his cup. The tea looked so strong that he regretted turning down her offer of milk and sugar. O'Coyle noticed him looking into his cup.

"Will it be all right?"

"Oh, yes."

O'Coyle returned to his subject. "You remember what you said last time? You said the IRA has an image problem."

Tom nodded and took a small sip of his tea.

O'Coyle also drank. He continued to hold his cup in his hand and used it to make small gesturing movements as he spoke. "It's clear to me that they want their position fairly represented in America, especially to people in government."

Tom held his cup in both hands and looked down into it while gathering his thoughts. For an instant, tea leaves distracted him, floating around in the bottom; he remembered his Nana who would tell his fortune from leaves like those as they clung together in mysterious patterns inside his empty cup. Invariably, she saw visions of great deeds to be accomplished by Tom when he got older. He slowly raised his head to make full eye contact when he began to speak. "Regardless of what happens to Brendan, one way or the other, I intend to make an impartial report."

"Tom, I wouldn't even hint that you should do otherwise."

"Why bring it up then?"

O'Coyle put down his cup. He clasped his hands together, tightly. It looked as if he were about to offer some kind of prayer. "I want Sinn Fein to be fairly and fully represented. That's only natural. I'm only trying to say that, whatever outsiders think of the IRA, they are not completely demented." He waited to see if Tom would object. He continued, "I'm in no position to negotiate anything. And I wouldn't, but it only makes sense that the IRA wouldn't tell you one thing and then turn around and put their foot in it."

"Let's make sure we understand each other," Tom said. "I try to fairly represent both sides of the argument here in Northern Ireland, including the IRA, and *in your opinion* they will act reasonably with respect to this kid?"

"That's it, exactly," O'Coyle said. "And Tom, in fairness I should tell you, I think that they now believe that it was someone else who informed the British. He may be off the hook, as you say — anyway."

Tom laughed. "I can't wait to talk to these people."

"Ah, now that's another matter," O'Coyle said, "they never talk to anybody."

Tom just stared at O'Coyle

"It won't be as bad as it sounds," O'Coyle said.

The meeting ended shortly after, and Tom left feeling somewhat bemused, wondering what might come next.

Back at the farm, Tom found that Jerry had tried to reach him during his absence. He connected with Jerry the following afternoon. "This has nothing to do with the report. It's personal," Tom said. Jerry offered to listen, and Tom summarized the situation concerning Brendan.

"I'll be happy to help out," Jerry said. "But I can't help but get the feeling that you're getting sucked into the quagmire up there in Northern Ireland."

"I'm convinced that I can handle it," Tom replied. "In fact, I think I can get some insights this way that would be impossible otherwise."

"Okay, I'll bow to your judgment on that. Maybe we should get this kid out right away. Make it a non-issue. And you can go from there."

"Any ideas?" Tom asked.

"Yeah, let's do it real simple. Send him to New York on a tourist visa. I'll have somebody meet him. He can stay at my sister's. We'll take it from there; I'll see that he's safe. We'll get him set up with a Green Card and a job. Just call when you've got the flight info."

"Great, I'll do it. And don't worry about the report."

"I won't. It would be nice if you got some insights on the Unionist side. If you know what I mean."

"I get it. I won't get sucked in. And thanks for Brendan."

Tom lost no time in making the arrangements to get Brendan to New York. Brid was apprehensive.

"He'll be safe. Don't worry," Tom said.

"Yes, but will he be back," she asked, "once he's seen America and has a job?"

Tom patted her shoulder. "If he doesn't come back, we'll go visit him."

Brid gave him a skeptical look, and went off about her business.

When the arrangements were complete, Tom loaned his car to Sean to take Brendan down to Shannon Airport. That done, he got busy catching up on work around the farm, and finally, at the end of the day, he sat down to think seriously about working on the report. *I've sure got a flying start on the Catholics, or Nationalists, or whatever they call themselves. Time to think about the Unionists.*

He got up from his desk to pace around, and found himself looking out the window. There was the hill, partly shadowed by a passing cloud. *Didn't Meagan say that her ex-husband was a Unionist? I don't think I want to go down that path. She* might know a lot about the Unionists herself though. If I call her, she'll think I'm a hypocrite. And I am. God, I miss her. And Jimmy too.

When he learned that Brendan had arrived safely and was in good hands, he felt doubly obligated to get working on the Northern Ireland report for Jerry. A call from Daniel O'Coyle gave him a place to start.

"Tom, I've got a fellow who is willing to talk with you. He's a former IRA member. He spent two years in Long Kesh Prison, as a guest of the British."

"That's nice, Dan. I'll be happy to talk with him, but I don't want to start there. I'd much rather explore the general political situation first."

"Very sensible, Tom. Very sensible. How can I help you with that?"

"How about I come up the day after tomorrow and take you out to lunch?"

"Ah, now, that's not necessary. We can talk in my office."

"We can do that too. I'll get there around eleven thirty."

"That's Thursday then, at half-eleven?"

Tom drove to Derry, arriving just before noon. O'Coyle directed him to a small restaurant just outside of Derry. Tom pulled into the gravel-covered parking lot, to the sound of small stones crunching under the tires and popping up against the car, and immediately noted that the place was a bit run down. There were weeds growing around the edges of the lot and along the lower edge of the restaurant's stucco walls. The walls had been painted white, years earlier; the paint now looked sooty and was chipped off in spots. Only the sign looked new — Paddy's Pub & Lunch. The architecture was nondescript, showing only a hint of Irish country-cottage styling.

Inside was a different story; things were simple but clean and neat. The tables were square and made of dark-stained wood. Each place had a simple white paper mat, a folded paper napkin, silverware and water glass. The condiments were grouped in the center along with a small vase containing two white flowers. The floor was dark slate, set in mortise. The barman and owner, Paddy, greeted O'Coyle enthusiastically and came out from behind the bar to show him to a table right by the window. Although the table looked clean, he wiped it off as they sat down, and he chatted briefly with O'Coyle about the local football team. He left to get them a couple of pints.

"One is definitely my limit," Tom said.

"Mine too," O'Coyle said. "Paddy's a distant cousin. He's only had this place for a little over a year. He and Mary, his wife, work so hard. They deserve to make it."

"He's friendly enough," Tom said. "And the place looks neat and clean inside."

The two continued to make small talk until Paddy returned with their pints and took their lunch orders. When he left, O'Coyle said, "Tom, you said that you wanted to start with the political situation in Northern Ireland. Does this mean that you want to hear Sinn Fein's position first?"

"Yes, I've already learned some things from our earlier meetings. You want the British out of Northern Ireland. I hear that loud and clear. I'm sure there's more to it than that."

"Indeed there is. But we don't want to leave the British too quickly; that would cause a great deal of difficulty in explaining our situation. The British are at the heart of everything that's wrong in this country." O'Coyle leaned forward, gesturing with his hands. He had not touched his pint.

"I can't believe that if the British left, all the other problems would disappear," Tom said.

"No indeed, but their presence here is what makes the problems and prevents their solutions."

Mary, the owner's wife, brought their lunches. O'Coyle broke off to greet her. He introduced Tom as his American friend and then engaged her in a short conversation. When she left them, he turned back to Tom. "Do you know how Northern Ireland came about, in the first place?"

"You mean the partition in 1922 that was part of the deal when Ireland won independence from England?"

"Yes. Did you know, for example, that the Unionists in the north formed heavily armed militia groups years before that? That they got their weapons from the British Army? And that they threatened a civil war and genocide against the Catholics? There was no IRA at the time."

"No, I always thought that it all started with the partition."

"It started five hundred years ago, but I won't take you through all of that. Not this time, at least."

"Thanks."

"The British caved in to the Unionists in 1922. They let them take their pick of the nine counties of Ulster. They picked the six with the best land, and those where they could maintain a majority."

"Very sensible," Tom said.

"Yes, you could say that. But the whole thing was artificial. Ireland was never meant to be two countries." O'Coyle paused to take a bite of his ham and cheese sandwich and a first drink from his pint. Tom, who had been eating a bowl of lamb stew while O'Coyle talked, looked around the pub. "Looks like Paddy has a good luncheon trade," he said.

O'Coyle looked around while continuing to chew. He nodded in agreement.

"Dan, the British weren't here before 1971," Tom said, "Northern Ireland was governing itself before then. Wasn't it?"

"That wasn't government. That was British condoned subjugation. The Catholics had no jobs, only the most primitive unsanitary housing and no representation in government." O'Coyle ripped a piece of sandwich into his mouth and chewed fast. Tom felt that he should say something. "Dan, I'm not trying to challenge your position on these things. I just learn better when I can ask questions."

O'Coyle slowed down, emptied his mouth and took a drink. "It's not you, Tom. It's just when you've been living with injustice all your life, it's hard not to have strong feelings."

"I can understand that. You say that there was no representation?"

"Not even in areas where Catholics were in the majority," O'Coyle said. "Right here in Derry, with a sixty percent Catholic majority, the Unionists had all the council seats."

"Wow," Tom said. "How did they do that?"

"Like they did it everywhere," O'Coyle said. "They drew the voting lines so that they maintained control."

"Gerrymandering, is what we call it," Tom said. "Is Derry still like that?"

"No, we've gotten control here, but it's bad everywhere else. They won't let us have 'one man-one vote.'"

They stopped talking for a while and finished their lunches. When the pints were almost empty, Tom suggested that they order coffee or tea. O'Coyle agreed. Tom hesitated before asking his next question because he suspected that the answer was obvious and he did not want to appear ignorant. "Dan, at the risk of sounding stupid, I need to clarify a couple of things," he said.

"I'll not make the mistake of thinking you're stupid, Tom."

"Well, okay. What keeps the Catholics from just saying that they're Protestants, so that they can get jobs and housing? I can't see any difference in the people?"

O'Coyle sat back with a broad smile on his face. "You know, Tom, I've only been to America once for a visit," he said, "but I know that there are many things that Americans take for granted that we don't have here. To answer your question, all anybody needs to know is where you went to school or where you live."

"So all the Catholic kids go to Catholic schools and all the Protestants to Protestant schools?"

"Yes, many of them don't even meet someone of the opposite persuasion until they go to university."

Tom sat back in his chair and watched as Mary served their coffee. He asked for the bill and she went off. "My God!" Tom said. "If you can't get the kids together..."

"Exactly," O'Coyle said. "And that's just the tip of the iceberg."

Tom shook his head and then remembered his other question. "There's another point that confuses me. You've been using the terms 'Catholics' and 'Unionists.' Why not 'Catholics' and 'Protestants'?"

"Ah, sorry about that. You see, not all Protestants are Unionists; some wouldn't mind seeing Ireland reunified, and many are sympathetic to the rights of Catholics."

"So 'Unionist' means that they want to remain part of England?"

"Yes"

"What about other terms like 'Republicans,' 'Nationalists,' 'Provos' and 'Ulster Defense Forces'? I feel like I need a dictionary."

"I think Tom, you'll find that the terms change depending on who's talking and whom they think they're talking to. In general, 'Republicans,' 'Nationalists' and 'Provos' would be Catholics and the others, like 'Unionists' and 'Loyalists' would be Protestants."

Tom paid the bill, and they got up to leave, O'Coyle stopping at several tables to exchange a few words and to introduce Tom.

Outside, the two men walked slowly towards Tom's car. The gravel made a soft sound underfoot; some birds hopped about pecking for seeds or crumbs amongst the small stones. Some of Tom's earlier impression of the place softened; having met Paddy and Mary washed away some of the seediness and replaced it with a quaint charm.

"I imagine you'll be wanting me to explain Sinn Fein's role in all this," O'Coyle said.

"Yes," Tom said. "But first, tell me about yourself. Do you have a family?"

"There's not much to tell. I'm not married, although I've got a girl friend. I live here in Derry with my mother. My father died five years ago. I'm a university graduate, qualified to teach at that level, but of course, there are no jobs so I'm on the dole."

"Sinn Fein doesn't pay you?"

"We're mostly volunteers. I get a little money here and there when the party can afford it."

They got into the car, and Tom started the engine.

O'Coyle continued, "You know, unemployment in the Catholic areas here is over forty percent."

"Whew, that's worse than during the Depression in our country."

"It's a way of life here, being on the dole."

On the ride back to O'Coyle's office the conversation continued on a personal level. Tom spoke of his family and especially about Barbara. "It was an accident. We were out for a bike ride; she dawdled behind. I was home, putting my bicycle in the garage when I heard the sound. It's all engraved in my mind. I keep thinking that I should have stayed with her. Maybe it would have made a difference."

"Ah, now Tom. It's natural to think that, but accidents will happen, no matter what we do. You mustn't carry that kind of guilt. Certainly, she would never have wanted it."

"I would never have imagined how much it was going to hurt," Tom said. "I'm really just starting to come out of it."

"Family's the beginning and the end of everything. Isn't it?" O'Coyle said. "In Ireland it's often emigration that brings the parting. But nowadays with jet planes, it not as final as it used to be. My sister left years ago. She lives in New York, has three kids. We see her every two years or so, when she comes for a visit."

"Is that why you went to the States, to visit her?"

"Yes, it is. I miss my Da, my father, most. How we used to talk. I could tell him things..."

"Yeah, it's family. And good friends too," Tom said.

When they got back to the office O'Coyle invited Tom inside. Tom went in but only long enough for O'Coyle to give him some literature on Sinn Fein.

"Here, you can read it at your leisure rather than have me just talking at you. You'll see that Sinn Fein is the leading party in fighting for the rights of Catholics and of women."

Tom took the literature, and they shook hands. This time the handshake was a little bit more than a simple formality. As he got back into his car for the drive back to Leitrim, Tom turned to the question of impartiality in his work for Jerry. Gonna be tougher than I thought.

He headed south on the A 5 towards Strabane. It was early enough, he would make it home at a decent hour, but he would have to eat supper on the road somewhere. On the highway, he relaxed and thought over his day. Interesting visit, from both a political standpoint and a personal one as well. It's going to be very interesting to hear what the Unionists have to say. O'Coyle makes them sound like a bunch of Fascists. I wonder if I can get sufficiently absorbed in this thing to keep Meagan out of my mind? Not likely. I wonder what she'd make out of what O'Coyle had to say? What would she make out of my asking her to discuss it? Better be careful what I do, sooner or later, she's going to tell me to fish or cut bait.

Tom reached over to turn on the radio; maybe he could catch the weather for the next day. He tuned into a news broadcast. There were the usual traffic accidents, a truck overturned, a three-car pile up at a roundabout, and a botched bank holdup in

Armagh. He remembered some of the news stories that he and Barbara had listened to on the car radio when they had been traveling in Ireland on vacations. One concerned an accident in which a car hit a sheep, which had wandered out onto the road. It happened during "rush hour" and caused a bit of a delay. At the end the announcer had said, "Oh well, there's nothing can be done about it." He and Barbara had adopted that statement as a kind of in-joke. How many things they had enjoyed together. Each able to anticipate what the other would find funny. Each saving little incidents from the day to tell each other that night. Would Meagan think they were funny? Might she be too sophisticated to find humor in some of the wacky, silly things that he found funny? Maybe humor between a man and a woman is a joint project that takes years to put in place. Maybe not. It shouldn't be a problem; in her own way, Meagan can be pretty funny.

Strange, thinking about Barbara and then Meagan. It was always the other way round. Think about Meagan and then feel some nagging sense of guilt, or sometimes, a sense of loss, which brought him back to grieving for Barbara. It was okay to think about Barbara and only her. Was it some kind of a test of the love that he'd had for her, and still had, that he could not think only of Meagan without coming back to Barbara? Maybe that's how I'll know when it's okay to go ahead — when I can think about Meagan and only Meagan.

The last words of a weather forecast caught Tom's ear. He had missed the entire program. Daydreaming, wool gathering, one of his teachers had called it. He reached over and turned off the radio. Try again later.

In Enniskillen, he stopped to stretch his legs and get a cup of coffee and a scone. He took O'Coyle's literature into the shop. Settled at a table, he began to scan through it. There were pictures, which he recognized as being the same as the posters on the Sinn Fein office walls. Pictures of British soldiers committing mayhem on demonstrators or standing over a child, semi-automatic rifle in hand. He began to read. There was strong emphasis on the reuniting of Ireland, one republic, thirty-two counties. The term Republican was used in connection with this. The British had to withdraw — "end their occupation of Ireland." But the Unionists had nothing to fear; their civil rights would be fully protected under the new Socialist Democratic Republic. Socialist? O'Coyle hadn't mentioned that. Later on, he read that the means of production had to be owned or controlled by the government. They can't be serious, even Castro is trying to find a face-saving way out of that quagmire. God, it sure would be great to talk to Meagan about this.

He got back to the farm a little after midnight, so the next morning got off to a slow start. He was sitting in his office going over the previous days' mail when there was a soft knock at the door. He turned in his chair expecting to find Brid standing in the doorway. Instead, there was Jimmy, holding a book in his hand.

"Brid said it was all right to come in," he said

"Of course it is. I'm delighted to see you, Jimmy. Come in."

Jimmy walked over to Tom and held out the book. "I came to return your book. It was very good." He was holding the copy of Treasure Island, which Tom had given him weeks earlier.

"Did you finish it?"

Jimmy nodded.

"Were you able to read it yourself, or did somebody help you?"

"I read some of it myself," Jimmy said, "but my Uncle Philip read most of it."

"I'm glad you enjoyed it. But I don't want it back; the book was a present. You can read it again when you're older. Or give it to a special friend."

Jimmy held the book to his chest. "Thank you very much," he said, and he turned to leave.

"Jimmy, before you go."

Jimmy stopped.

"Is your mother home?"

"No, she's out. Would you like to see her?"

"Uh — Actually, I was just wondering if she'd give her permission for you and me to go fishing. That's if you'd be interested?"

"Fishing! She would say yes, I'm sure. When?"

"We better ask her before we make plans, but we could go later this week."

"I'll ask her," Jimmy said, and he disappeared before Tom could say another word.

Well, there it is. I didn't say that I would avoid any contact with her. Besides, Jimmy's a sweet kid. I'll have fun with him. I'd have fun with him even if his mother was — was somebody else.

He turned back to his mail.

CHAPTER EIGHT

Meagan came in the back door with her packages and went straight into the kitchen where she put the fresh fruit in the refrigerator. She picked up the rest of her packages and went into the hallway. Kiki failed to materialize to greet her and get a pat on the head. Jimmy and the dog were either upstairs or out somewhere. She placed her other packages on the hallway table and removed from one of them the book that she had bought for Jimmy. It was about pirates; one he could read himself — He had certainly gotten excited over <u>Treasure Island</u>. Crossing the hall, she peeked into the library. There was Philip sitting in his usual chair, newspaper in hand.

"Where's Jimmy?" she asked.

Philip looked up from his paper. He stared at her as if he was wondering who she was, or was striving for an answer to her question.

"Out in the yard, I believe. Digging worms, or some such."

"Worms?"

"Yes, Tom's invited him to go fishing."

"Really?"

"He's quite keen to go. He'll tell you all about it."

Meagan was standing next to the table in the center of the room. She placed the pirate book down and stood there pursing her lips. Philip started back to his paper but noticed that she had not moved. "Is there a problem?" he asked.

Meagan crossed her arms and walked slowly toward the fireplace. "No — No, I guess not," she said, as she sat down on the couch.

Philip waited a moment and then said, "You did say that Tom was a good influence on him."

Meagan had leaned back and had one arm out along the back of the couch. "*You* could take him fishing," she said.

"You know that I've been fishing once in my life. And I didn't like it."

Meagan sighed and looked off into the distance.

"What's wrong with Tom taking him?"

"Nothing. It's just that we had agreed that we wouldn't see each other for a while."

"Maybe he's changed his mind."

"He can't do it this way."

"Why not?"

Meagan got up and started to pace about the room. "We stopped seeing each other because he's still grieving for his wife, and he felt guilty about seeing me."

"Does it have to be total, one way or the other?"

Meagan stopped and looked at her brother. "Yes, it does," she said. "It can't be an occasional, sometime thing. He's either feeling guilty, or he's not. I don't want to be going up and down."

"He means a lot to you then?"

Meagan clenched her jaw and sat in the closest chair.

Philip said, "I think that you should let him do it his way."

"It's not you that will be losing the sleep."

"Are you going to let Jimmy go fishing with him, or not?"

Meagan sighed and got up. "Yes, of course." She scooped the pirate book off the table on her way out of the room.

Tom shuffled around the kitchen making breakfast. He had insisted that Brid not get up just because he was going fishing. He looked out the window. Damn, it sure looks like rain. It's early; maybe it'll burn off. With my luck, I'll probably bring the kid back soaking wet and without a fish. What the hell, we'll have fun — one way or the other.

He sat down to eat some cereal and drink his coffee. Why am I so excited over this stupid fishing trip? I feel like I'm going out on a date or something. Christ, it's just a kid. He's only seven. What are we going to talk about all day?

There was a gentle tap at the door. There was Jimmy, fully outfitted with raingear, fishing pole and a lunch bag.

"Come in, I'll just be a minute," Tom said.

He went about the kitchen, putting things away and gathering up the lunch that Brid had prepared. He put on his jacket. "I've got my gear in the car," he said. "Did you bring the beer?"

Jimmy looked at him, his expression indicating that he had forgotten something.

"Just kidding," Tom said. "Did your mother drive you over?"

Jimmy nodded. Tom patted him on the shoulder and guided him out.

"I rented a boat. We're going out on Lough Allen. I hope it doesn't rain."

"Uncle Philip says that the fish bite better when it's raining."

"I'd just as soon have sunshine."

"I want to catch a fish," Jimmy said.

When they arrived at the lough and were motoring away from the dock, Tom checked the weather. It did not look as if it would rain soon, but the top of nearby Iron Mountain was shrouded in a glowering, rolling mist. Not a great day to be outdoors, but Jimmy did not seem to mind in the least. They stopped at a spot not far from shore, and Tom got Jimmy's hook baited.

Jimmy operated on the theory that if the fish didn't bite in three minutes, or less, they should move to another spot. Tom figured that if they didn't catch any fish, it would be far better to have done it Jimmy's way. He loved the boy's energetic enthusiasm and he knew that with enough action, Jimmy would not be bored. The morning passed with Tom baiting Jimmy's hook, untangling his line and moving the boat.

At eleven o'clock they beached the boat and got out to eat lunch on some rocks.

"Maybe we should leave our lines in the water," Jimmy said. "In case some fish come by."

Tom put a bobber on Jimmy's line and cast it in. They sat down to eat. Tom looked up at the overcast sky and out across the lake. There were other boats moving slowly in various directions. It felt good to be doing nothing for a few minutes. "Well, at least, it's not raining," he said.

"Maybe the fish would bite, if it did," Jimmy said.

Tom smiled and continued to eat his lunch. "We should try trolling after lunch."

"What's that?" Jimmy asked.

"You motor along, slowly, with a lure on your line. Like those boats out there."

"Yes, let's try that."

The bobber on Jimmy's line began bouncing up and down, making strong ripples in the water. Jimmy slammed down his sandwich and ran to his rod. Frantically, he started reeling. "I got one!" he yelled.

"Don't fall in," Tom yelled back.

He raced to catch Jimmy, whose feet were already slipping down the rock and into the water. Jimmy continued to concentrate on catching his fish. Tom grabbed the scruff of his collar. Jimmy was sitting in the water. Tom was down on one knee, just behind him. "Don't lose him!"

It was too late. Jimmy reeled in his line. There was nothing on it; the line had broken. Tom helped him out of the water. Jimmy held up his rod, looking at the bare end of his line. He looked up at Tom, a mute question in his eyes.

"That was *some* fish, Jimmy. I'm glad the line broke. He might have pulled you across the lake."

Jimmy nodded with enthusiasm. "He was really big."

"We better get you home," Tom said.

"I'm not cold," Jimmy said.

He pulled Jimmy close, his arms seemed to slip around, and he held the boy in a strong hug. "I know, but we need to get you home."

"I caught a really big fish!" Jimmy said to his mother as he stepped in the door.

She helped him inside to remove his wet shoes. Tom stood on the porch, a few feet behind. Meagan looked down at Jimmy's wet pants.

"He got a little excited, and fell in," Tom said. "But only up to his waist."

Meagan looked up at Tom "Oh, is that all." she said and then turned back to Jimmy. "You go up, get out of those things and into a hot bath."

"It broke my line," Jimmy said. "It was really big."

"Yes, I'm sure it was," Meagan said. She pushed Jimmy toward the stairs. Kiki showed up and followed Jimmy up the stairs. Meagan turned to Tom, "You look as if you could stand a drink," she said.

He stood there, arms hanging down, his eyes reaching out to her.

"It's up to you," she said.

"I'd like to come in."

Meagan stepped back from the doorway. "You go in and say 'hi' to Philip. I'll be right along."

Tom stepped in to remove his boots while Meagan headed for the stairs. He put on some slippers and went to the living room.

"So that's fishing?" Philip said.

Meagan walked in just as Tom finished telling Philip about the grand adventure.

"I see that Philip's helped you to a drink," she said. "Thank you, Philip."

Philip raised his glass and offered to fix a drink for Meagan.

"Thanks, I'll wait till later," she said, and then turned to Tom. "Jimmy's really excited," she said. "He's ready to go again tomorrow."

Tom laughed. "I need a little more rest than that," he said. "But I did have fun, and I would like to take him again."

Meagan sat down, directly across from Tom "Have you been keeping busy?" she asked.

"Oh, yes. I've been working on the farm, and I've been to the North a few times." He looked at her wondering if he was staring too long and too hard and if that made her uncomfortable.

She put her hands together on her lap and looked at him. "You're working on that report?"

He nodded.

She said, "Going up there and looking into things must be something of a culture shock, for an American."

"True," he said. "It's difficult to read through all the emotions. It would be helpful to have someone to discuss it with."

"Yes, I can certainly understand that." She glanced at Philip who had been listening politely. He looked straight back at her with the blandest expression on his face. She turned back to Tom. "Well," she said, "if I can be of any help, I'd be glad...."

There was an awkward pause.

"Thank you. I'll call you — soon," Tom said. He tossed down the last of his drink. "I'd better be going."

ો ો ો

"Another trip to Derry, Mr. Brogan? You must like it there."

"Yes, Brid. I'll be gone overnight."

Tom had just sat down to lunch in the dining room. He had spent the morning supervising some carpentry work in the barn while most of his mental energy had been expended thinking about his brief visit with Meagan the previous day.

"Of course," he said, "I don't go there for the scenery."

"I've never been, myself," she said. "I understand it's quite lovely."

"It is. You and Sean should go up on holiday sometime. You can drive up through Donegal and approach from the west. The scenery's great."

"It's quite safe now. Is it?"

"Very peaceable. You'll feel perfectly safe."

Brid nodded and left him.

I better call Meagan before I go. What to say? He had been thinking about it all morning. Maybe I could just pop over? No, that might be pushing. What is she thinking? She didn't mind my taking Jimmy fishing. Seemed to think it was a good idea. She was perfectly polite yesterday. But she would be perfectly polite no matter what was going on inside. What can I expect? I'm the one that called it off. I can't expect her to welcome me with open arms. Open arms — God, what I wouldn't give...

Tom waited until late in the afternoon before he phoned. "I wanted to thank you for inviting me in yesterday."

"Not at all. Jimmy's still talking about his big fish."

"I'll take him again soon. We'll see if we can't bring one home."

"Don't feel obligated."

"I enjoyed myself. I really did."

Tom stood right next to the phone; his left hand down at his side, twirling the cord. He looked across the room at the window, which faced in the direction of Meagan's house.

"I'm taking another trip up to Derry tomorrow. I'll be talking to a Unionist this time. I was wondering if when I get back, we could get together?"

"A political discussion?"

Tom took a long breath. "No."

"No?"

Another deep breath, "I'd like to take a drive and have dinner someplace."

"That might be very nice. Why don't we talk about it when you get back?"

Tom didn't feel that he should hang up. He wanted to say more. But what? "I will. I'll call as soon as I get back. And — I miss you, Meagan." There, he'd said it.

"Have a nice trip, Tom." She hung up.

Have a nice trip? He put the phone down. Have a nice trip? Christ!

CHAPTER NINE

It was mid afternoon when Tom crossed the Craigavon Bridge and headed up Bond's Hill. He had an appointment with Ian McIntyre, Ulster Democratic Party leader for Derry. McIntyre's office was in the Waterside district, an area which Tom understood to be exclusively Protestant. At the top of the hill, overlooking the road, there was a large, dark green guard tower, heavily protected by fencing and concertina wire. The cloudy sky above it, a sky that Tom would normally have considered to be beautiful, added to its menacing appearance. As he passed the tower, he had the feeling that he was entering a fortified city, a compound, a foreign country. Continuing onto Limvady Road, he turned onto a side street and found a place to park. He walked back to Limvady Road. Almost directly in front of him, on the other side of the road, was a structure, which looked like a prison. High dark green walls with guard towers strategically located along the top. A small convoy of armored cars, carrying English soldiers, came down the road and went through the gate.

    Tom turned back to the row of small apartment houses on his side of the street. McIntyre's office was in one of them. They were built of red brick, had bay windows and some fancy parapets along the roofline, and turrets at the corners. The brick and stonework around the entrances matched the roofline. All of it done in a "castle" motif. Six or seven stone steps led up to the entrance doors, which were weather-beaten and had not been painted in years. Curtains in the windows were dirty, and some were torn. The little bits of shrubbery in front, along the sidewalk, were trimmed but tired and sparse. He guessed that the buildings were at least fifty years old, and had probably been luxury apartments when new. There were few pedestrians on the street.

He came to McIntyre's number, went up the steps and tried the door. It was locked. He looked for a bell, but someone inside was already undoing some locks. The door opened, and McIntyre introduced himself. He was much younger than Tom had expected; less than forty, slender, reddish hair, gray eyes and a tentative handshake. He led Tom down a dingy, poorly lit hallway and into a small office with a roll top desk, a small table, piles of dust covered papers, and lighting only slightly better than in the hallway. McIntyre sat behind the table, and Tom took the only chair on the other side. As he sat down, he looked around; the contrast to the Sinn Fein offices surprised him, no people, no phones ringing. The place looked as if it had not been used in years.

As McIntyre waited for Tom to initiate the discussion, he watched Tom examine his office. "Most of our work is out in the community," he said. "We rarely have need for this place."

"I can understand that." Tom turned and gave his full attention to McIntyre. "Well, as you know from our conversation on the telephone, I'm working on a report."

"Yes, there was a letter to our party headquarters from an American senator explaining your assignment."

Tom looked at McIntyre, wondering how best to begin. So far the guy had not exchanged any pleasantries, or even smiled. Tom had the feeling that he would have to work hard to establish some level of trust and openness. "I understand that it's Unionist policy to remain associated with England," he said. "Is that correct?"

"No, it is not. 'Associated' is not accurate. Northern Ireland is an intrinsic part of Britain."

Tom wanted to pursue this point, knowing that there were distinctions. He had heard from someone that the Unionists were embarrassed and angry over the fact that their currency was not accepted as legal tender in Britain. But to avoid antagonizing his host, he decided to change the subject. "As you know, it's my job to look at both sides of the problem here. The Catholics, or Nationalists — "

McIntyre interrupted. "Republicans."

"Okay, 'Republicans' feel massively discriminated against. How do the Unionists see that?"

"There was discrimination in the past, but now it's the Unionists that are getting the short end."

"They *are?*"

"Yes, I can show you the figures. Most of the jobs and the new housing are going to Catholics."

Tom was tempted to say "Republicans."

McIntyre continued. "Unemployment in the Protestant community is approaching twenty percent, and housing is deteriorating."

"So, the economy is pretty bad for both sides?"

"Yes, it is. Especially when you consider that over forty percent of all jobs are government funded."

"You would think," Tom said, "that both sides would have a strong common interest in attracting outside investment."

McIntyre moved forward in his chair. "There has been a strong industrial base, here in the North. If the Republicans would turn in their weapons and renounce violence, the outside investment would come, and there would be jobs for all."

"You make it sound as if it's the Unionists that need to be looked after?"

"That is absolutely correct. Our way of life is under siege. We have no self-government; Northern Ireland is being run from London. The Republicans are getting help and weapons from outside, especially from your own country. They want to unite with the South. They'll drive us out of *our* country."

"Interesting." Tom said, needing time to think about this new thought, an entirely different way of looking at the problem. He knew that the Protestants owned an overwhelming share of the wealth in Northern Ireland. They held a large percentage of the elected positions and of government and industrial jobs, including almost all of the police force jobs. And yet, they felt beleaguered.

The conversation went on for another hour. Tom felt more comfortable with McIntyre, he pressed him for details and elaboration, but tried hard not to cross-examine, or trap him.

"How is it," Tom asked, "that the police force is almost exclusively Protestant?"

"The RUC has been trying for years to recruit Catholics. The numbers are small, not because of the Unionists, but because the Catholics turn on any Catholic who joins. They murder their own."

"Why do they do that?"

"Ask them. That's the mentality that we're dealing with."

In the end, Tom felt that many of McIntyre's arguments were illogical and inconsistent. He was especially bothered by the absence of a means for the Catholics to get equality, without the Protestants giving up anything. Perhaps it would make more sense at another time. He put one last question to him. "If you were king for a day, how would you solve the problem?"

McIntyre looked at him; the question had clearly caught him off guard. Finally, he said very softly, "I don't know. I'm not sure it *can* be solved."

Tom heard the locks being reset in the door behind him as he went down the steps and turned toward his car. It was a little before five o'clock, and the green monster across the street was disgorging groups of armored cars. As they passed, he looked up at the faces of the young soldiers, barely visible between the top of the high armored sides and the helmets, which they all wore.

Glancing at his watch, he realized that he had over an hour to kill before his next appointment, an appointment set up by O'Coyle with a former member of the IRA.

Instead of going straight to his car, he turned up another street and soon found himself on a street filled with shops. Most of the shops looked just like those one would find elsewhere in Ireland. Ordinary store fronts, many with goods on display out on the sidewalk. People went about their business in a relaxed atmosphere. Corner stores were more security conscious, having walls where display windows should be and narrow entrances. In particular, Tom noticed, both on this street and on others, that any place of social gathering — pubs, betting parlors, social clubs — looked like a vault. The walls were thick, windows either small or non-existent, and the entrances were narrow and set back in from the street. Little fortresses every one, the very places that should look warm and inviting. You probably had to pass some kind of test to get in, like the old speakeasies.

As he turned down the street toward his car, he looked at the houses and apartments. None were new, but all were well maintained, if somewhat drab by American standards. They were built of yellow brick, or if of wood, were painted gray or a dull blue. Did they all have sturdy doors and locks? How did friendly callers identify themselves before the doors were opened? He returned to his car and headed back to the center of Derry, to Paedar's Pub where he was to meet Jack Galvin, recently released from Long Kesh Prison.

He walked straight up to the bar and ordered a pint. Following O'Coyle's instructions, he gave his name to the barman as he paid for his drink. The barman nodded; Tom picked up his pint and found an empty table near the back. The place was cheerful enough, mostly filled with young people engaged in quiet conversations, occasional laughter here and there. The ceilings were high; and large windows at the front allowed a generous amount of daylight to penetrate well inside. He had barely gotten past the foam on his Guinness, when he noticed a man come in and speak to the barman. The man turned and walked in his direction.

"Mr. Brogan?"

"Yes."

"I'm Jack Galvin."

They shook hands, and Jack sat down. He appeared to be in his thirties, a little less than medium height, thin build, dark curly hair and the complexion of someone used to working outdoors. He was wearing jeans and a navy blue pullover long sleeved shirt.

"Can I get you a pint, Jack?"

"Thanks, no. I'll get a Coke later."

Tom took a drink while he thought about how to begin. "I appreciate your coming," he said. "Did Daniel tell you what it's about?"

"He did. You're working on a report for your government, and you want to know about the IRA. Daniel said that I should extend my full cooperation."

"That's pretty much it," Tom said. "I'm not sure exactly where to start."

"There's no rush." Jack made an open gesture with his hands and sat back. "I understand that you got Brendan Greenan to the States?"

"Yes, that's right. It was a great relief to his parents."

"That's good, saves the lads the trouble of going after him."

"They won't look for him there?"

Jack leaned forward, as if to say something in confidence. "Not a chance. They know where their bread is buttered."

"You mean that they won't risk offending their American contributors?"

"Exactly." Jack reached into his pocket and withdrew a pack of cigarettes. He showed it to Tom. "Do you mind?"

"No. Go right ahead," Tom said.

Jack proceeded to take out a cigarette and light it. "Terrible habit," he said.

Tom made a simple gesture. "What can you do?"

"Getting back to the IRA," Jack said, "I sometimes wonder if it isn't all a show for American opinion. In the old days, they just wanted American money. Now, they're chasing after American politicians. Both sides are at it."

"Our politicians know that there are over forty thousand Irish-Americans," Tom said.

"That many?"

"Yeah. If it wasn't for them, I doubt that the U.S. would pay that much attention to Northern Ireland, with its population of one and a half million people."

"It all comes down to politics in the end doesn't it?" Jack said. "Were there some things in particular that you wanted to know about the IRA?"

"Yes. It's a question which I believe bothers a lot of Americans."

Jack snuffed out his cigarette. "Ask away, I'll not take offense."

Tom leaned forward and watched Jack's eyes. "Why, in spite of all the condemnations that come from everywhere, does the IRA resort to violence and terrorism?"

Without the slightest hesitation, Jack answered. "Because, it's the only language the English understand."

"But it seems only to harden their position?"

"That's what they say. Their propaganda is very good, but, if you want to understand the English, you must look carefully at how they act. Look at how they behaved during the cease-fire. What did they do but raise one false issue after another. They baited and taunted the IRA, and they rejected the good recommendations of your own Senator George Mitchell. They were never sincere about peace."

Tom was somewhat surprised at the sudden intensity with which Jack spoke. He paused before reacting. "I agree that the

English are not exactly the innocent victims that they pretend to be, but still, does the end ever justify the means?"

"When you put it that way, one has to say 'no'. But, when you look at the way the English are constantly pushing and degrading anyone who disagrees with their policies in Northern Ireland, you have to wonder who is actually causing the violence."

"You mean that the English cause the violence by frustrating any other form of dissent?"

"Exactly. Look at how this whole thing started. There was no IRA to speak of before the 'Troubles' began. In the beginning there was only a civil rights movement, a peaceful one. The people took your own Martin Luther King as their role model. There were peaceful civil rights marches, and then, right here in Derry, the English paratroopers opened fire on the marchers. There were women pushing baby carriages, for Christ sake! The English said it was an 'unfortunate' accident. Do you know that there were snipers up on the walls? It was premeditated murder! Now, there's your violence."

"I never heard about the snipers."

"The English have tried every way to cover it up, but it's coming out in spite of them."

"So that's when the IRA came back into business?"

"Yes, at first it was to protect the Catholics, but of course, later it changed. What can you expect when you take away people's basic dignity?"

"I don't know the answers, Jack, but there's got to be a better way than violence."

Jack nodded.

"I understand," Tom said. "Are you hungry?"

"Tom, I'd love to stay and keep talking, but my mother's not well, and I've got to get home and fix her a bit of supper."

They parted with Jack expressing an eagerness to talk some more. Tom could contact him through O'Coyle.

"I'll do that, Jack," Tom said. "I'm feeling a little overwhelmed, there's so much to learn."

Outside the pub, they went in opposite directions. Tom turned toward the Guild Hall. He was on a wide pedestrians-only street, crowded with people on their way home with little bags of groceries and produce for that evening's meal. The shops were closing, steel doors and grates made a banging and clanging sound as they dropped down in front of the shops, and then were locked. He came to the near corner of the walled city, the Center, the heart of Derry. Young people were already gathering in groups for a night of fun in the pubs and restaurants. At the Guild Hall which stood just across from the main gateway in the wall, between the wall and the old dock area, he turned and went in through the gate and then up the hill on Shipquay Street. There were young people everywhere. Many, no doubt, were students from elsewhere. In small groups, they drank, laughed, nuzzled, kissed and enjoyed themselves. Tom strolled along, up the hill, checking out restaurants as he went. He never liked eating alone away from home. His sense of loneliness was all the more acute in the face of his surroundings, all the laughter, the chatter, the open affection. He decided to call Meagan.

"I was thinking," he said when she came to the phone, "that maybe the next time I come up here on a trip, you might like to come along."

"That would be interesting," she said.

"It would be all very proper," he said. "We could bring Jimmy and have separate rooms, and all that."

"Ah," she said, "I'm certainly relieved to hear that."

Tom knew that she was pulling his leg; he struggled, but could not come up with a comeback. After another minute of awkward conversation, he said, "I miss you."

Silence.

And then, "I miss you too."

Tom got to the farm the next day, just after lunch. On the drive back, he had been thinking that this had been his third trip to Derry in the past few weeks and it had been the first trip on which he had thought more about Meagan than about Barbara. Spending time there, a place that he had visited with Barbara, a place where he felt close to her, had something to do with it. Then too, perhaps he had just run out of grieving energy.

He went into the barn and said "hi" to Sean and then into the house where he left his briefcase and notebook on the desk. From there he went to the kitchen and exchanged pleasantries with Brid. "I'll be up in my room for a while," he said and left her.

He closed the door to his room and put his overnight bag on the foot of the bed. He sat on the side of the bed, facing the window. He was not exactly sure why he was there. Just a feeling he had — something to do with Barbara. There was her picture on the nightstand. It was a studio portrait, the one he urged her to get on her forty-fifth birthday, a celebration of what he insisted was her growing beauty. He reached for it and then got up to go over and sit in the wingback chair in the corner. He sat there in silence, holding her picture in his lap and staring at it, as if he could transport himself through the glass. Then, in a soft whisper, as if he were praying, he began to speak.

"Barbara, I love you, I always have, and I always will. But I can't keep going like I have been. It feels wrong. I can't explain that, maybe I'm just weak. I feel that I should move on with my life. I'd like to think that you approve. I know that you do."

He gazed at the picture for several more minutes and then got up to place it back on the nightstand. At the window, he looked out over green that went for miles in every direction. It was a beautiful day. He went downstairs, put on his boots and walked up the hill towards Meagan's house. Reaching the top, he stood next to the tree, the one that stood by itself at the crest of the hill, keeping watch in all directions. He raised one arm overhead and grasped a branch. Leaning against the tree, he gazed down across the meadow to where Meagan's house sat on a knoll. Meagan, Meagan, I hope you're up for this.

He slid his hand down off the branch and then turned and headed back the way he had come. He bent to pluck a stalk of grass and put it in his mouth, twirling it with his tongue as, hands in pockets, he strolled down the hill. I'll call her later. Don't want to come on too strong.

Back at the house, he flipped through the mail and spotted a letter from Helene. She planned a week's vacation with her friend, Sheila. They would meet in London, but Helene planned to stop first for a few days with Tom. Great! Hope she likes Meagan.

He went out to a section where workers were still planting some seedlings. When he got back, he knew that Brid would be planning supper. He decided to call Meagan so that he would know if he was eating in or out. She was out but Philip came to the phone.

"Tom, we've had a bit of a surprise. Gregory, that's Meagan's ex husband, called to ask if he could get Jimmy early this summer. It seems he has to take a trip later. You know, it was arranged at the divorce that Gregory would get Jimmy for a few weeks every summer. Anyway, she's gone off to deliver Jimmy."

"When will she be back?"

"Not sure. I was out when she left. I'll tell her you called."

Tom hung up and went in to tell Brid that he would be eating in.

ૢ ૢ ૢ

"But I wanted to go fishing again with Tom," Jimmy said.

Meagan held the wheel firmly with both hands. She glanced aside to Jimmy sitting next to her. "Jimmy, I've explained this several times now. It's only fair that you spend this time with your father. He has to be away later. So, this is the only time when you can go."

"Tom will forget that he promised to take me."

"No he won't. He said that he enjoyed taking you. He won't forget."

Jimmy was momentarily distracted by a passing bus. He turned back to Meagan. "Tom's more fun, he really listens to me."

"It's nice that you and Tom get on so well, but we're going to your father's."

They were driving north toward Monaghan. From there, they would go to their destination in Portadown. It was a bright sunny day. "Isn't it a beautiful day for a drive, Jimmy? You can see the mountains so clearly."

Jimmy remained slumped down in his seat, his eyes barely level with the bottom of the window. She glanced over at him. "You'll have fun. You always think that you won't, but then you do."

"There are no horses there."

"After you get back, there'll be lots of time for riding before school starts."

He squirmed around a little in his seat, but did not sit up. She had the feeling that he was marshaling his next complaint.

She said, "I don't like it either. I miss you when you're gone. I'd much rather be making this trip in the other direction, bringing you home."

"Why doesn't Daddy come and visit us?"

"Well," she weighed her answer, "for one thing, your father is a very busy man, as I'm sure you've noticed when you've been there. And — I'm not sure that I would care for it."

He sat up and looked in her direction. "Why did you and Daddy get a divorce?"

She didn't answer; she was checking road signs.

"Why did you?"

She glanced over at him for a second. "It's hard to explain, especially to some one your age, but I'll try. Your father is a politician, and I was expected to be a politician's wife. That meant that I had no life of my own. I had to do what was expected of me and nothing else. Your father was out every night and often went on trips. I was left alone and had to do for myself. When he came home, he was too tired to do anything but eat and sleep. We had nothing to talk about."

"Are you going to marry Tom?"

Meagan laughed, and then smiled over at him. "Jimmy, you are a wonder. It's much too early for such talk," she said. "But, promise me; there will be no mention of Tom while you're with your father."

"I promise," Jimmy said, and he turned to take an interest in a Golden Retriever looking down at him from the window of a nearby lorry.

It was mid afternoon when Meagan found Gregory McDonald's new address in Portadown. She pulled off the street, through an open gate and onto a pebble driveway. The house was of recent construction set back about ten yards from the street behind a black, pointed-top iron fence of medium height and an attractive garden. Finished in white stucco, it was two stories, unattached on its own little plot.

A garage, painted white, sat back from the house at the end of the driveway, and behind that stood a high chain link fence with barbed wire along the top. McDonald came out the front door and walked down the short flagstone walk to greet them. He wore brown slacks, tan casual shoes and a tan shirt. He parted his brown hair almost in the middle and combed it almost straight back. Fringes of gray showed at his bushy temples. His hair lay close to his scalp causing his head to appear a bit wide and flat-topped. Heavy eyebrows accented his dark brown eyes. He was of medium height, barely as tall as Meagan.

Meagan got out of the car. "We've come up in the world," she said.

McDonald waggled his head as he opened the door to pull Jimmy out. "Party leader now," he said, "have to look the part." He gave Jimmy a kind of sideways hug, one hand on a shoulder, pulling him against his hip. "It's wonderful to see you, Jimmy. We'll have some good times."

Meagan opened the boot, and McDonald went around to get Jimmy's bags. As he came close to Meagan, he tried to give her a kiss on the cheek, but she stepped back and forced a smile.

"Stop in for a bit. I'll show you the house."

"It's a long drive back," she said.

"It won't take that long," he said. "Besides, there's plenty of room, you could stay the night."

"Thanks," she said, "but we wouldn't want to give your new neighbors the wrong impression."

Inside the house, Jimmy clung to his mother. McDonald put the bags down just as a woman appeared in the hallway.

"This is Claire," McDonald said. "She's my housekeeper."

Meagan decided that Claire was just old enough to be believable as housekeeper. They exchanged greetings.

"Claire, would you put these bags in Jimmy's room," McDonald said. "I want to show them the house."

He led Meagan and Jimmy down the hall. "Jimmy, wait till you see the basement," he said. "I've got a snooker table, darts and a television with computer games on it."

They went downstairs to a finished basement. The floor was carpeted in dark green, the walls paneled with a light wood veneer. Recessed fluorescent lights in the ceiling made everything look colorful and new. McDonald turned on the computer game and showed Jimmy how to work the controls. He led Meagan over to a small bar in one corner.

"What can I get for you?" he asked.

"Just water. Thank you."

"Two waters then. You'll love the rest of the house. Wait till you see the kitchen. All the latest."

"I'm sure it's lovely."

"And so are you," he said. "If you don't mind my saying so. More beautiful than ever."

"Thank you," she said. She looked over at Jimmy, who had gotten completely absorbed in the computer game. "He will get his proper exercise?"

"Yes, he will. I just wanted a chance to talk." He came around and sat on the stool close to Meagan. "Listen, things are different now," he said. "Why don't you stay the night; I saw your bag in the car. Give us a chance to talk. I can tell you about my new job. Party Leader is a very prestigious position, as you know."

"There would be no point to it, Gregory."

"Where's the harm?"

"We went over, and over, all of that years ago. We're not compatible. And there was the matter of those little 'birds' on the side."

"That was all in my youth. I'm different now."

"Leading a celibate life, no doubt."

McDonald grimaced and got off his stool. He went around behind the bar and leaned across, his face close to Meagan. "I made my mistakes, I'll admit, but that's all in the past. Things are better now. The hours are easier; there's more money. I should never have let you go. I want you back."

"That's neither realistic, nor possible."

"There's someone else?"

"No." She glared at him. "And that has nothing to do with it."

He came out from behind the bar. "Jimmy," he called, "leave that off now. We have to see the rest of the house." He turned to Meagan. "This was all for you, you know. I had you in mind when I bought it."

"It's all very nice," she said, her facial expression as bland as she could manage.

The rest of the tour was perfunctory. Meagan politely complimented what she saw. Jimmy's room was particularly well done. The wallpaper featured a series of horses and riders jumping fences, and a fully maned male lion stared into the room from a large colored poster. A small table lamp held a miniature ship's wheel. Gregory demonstrated how you turn the wheel to switch the light on and off.

Back in the driveway, Meagan bent over to give Jimmy a goodbye kiss. She whispered in his ear, "We'll have a party when you come home." She smiled and nodded at McDonald as she got into her car.

He came over to her window. "Think about it," he said.

She tried to be especially careful backing out of the driveway.

CHAPTER TEN

Tom was passing his office just as the phone rang. He went in and picked it up to hear Meagan's voice.

"You're back," he said.

"Yes, Philip said that you called while I was gone."

"I did. I was surprised to hear about Jimmy."

"It was rather sudden. Gregory couldn't take him later, as we'd planned, so..."

"So, now who's going to go fishing with me?"

Meagan laughed. "Perhaps someone from the pub?"

"Funny," he said. "Do you miss him?"

"I do."

"I was thinking about getting some better fishing stuff for when he gets back."

"I'm sure that will help the two of you to fill the boat with fish."

Tom walked over to a window, stretching the phone cord to its limit. He ran his finger through some light dust on the window frame.

"I was wondering if you'd help me pick it out?"

"Fishing gear?"

"You can't do any worse than I do."

Tom jiggled the keys in his pocket while he waited for an answer.

"Where would we go?"

"That depends. Do you need to shop for anything?"

"I promised Jimmy a party when he gets back."

"Great! We can get some games and some little gifts for the kids that will come. We'll go to Sligo. I'll pick you up in an hour."

❧ ❧ ❧

"Look at all this stuff," Tom said, picking up a toy car. "We should have the party here."

They were in a department store in Sligo. The toy section filled with toys and novelties of every description, a cacophony of garish colors, all competing for attention, and yet harmonizing to create a festive air. Tom held the little car between his fingers and drove it along the edge of the counter before placing it back where he'd found it.

She said, "I don't want to be too materialistic about this."

"No, but it's nice to have a little something for the kids to take home. How about these dinosaurs? God, they look scary, don't they?"

"What about the girls?"

Tom was busy picking out twelve of the fiercest looking, four-inch-high dinosaurs. "Tough age, isn't it?" he said.

"Yes, it is. Of course, it wouldn't have to be toys."

"Right," he said. "We could get them some writing paper — or something like that."

"I can see that you're going to be a big help on this part."

They wandered around to where they could pick out some party games. After they had picked several, Tom held one up which had a picture on the cover of a young couple playing the game and positioned in very sexy contact. "This one looks like fun."

"It does," she said. "I'm sure that some of the mothers would love to play it with you."

"There's only one that would interest me."

"Oh dear, I'd better not invite *her*. We have to think of the children."

They picked up their selections and headed for the cashier.

She said, "I'll think of something for the girls and pick it up in Dublin next week."

"You're going to Dublin?"

"Yes, I'll be gone for more than a week. I'm taking a course."

"Well, at least the timing overlaps with Jimmy's absence."

"True," she said. "Shall we go and look at fishing gear?"

They were at the cashier's counter. Tom insisted on paying for the dinosaurs. Out on the sidewalk, moving along with other shoppers, Tom listened to Irish voices blending like chimes in a garden to make a musical sound. It was a sound that he never failed to notice — soothing — a massage for his soul.

"You know," he said, "the fishing business was just an excuse to have some time with you."

"Was it now?"

Tom laughed. "I knew that you'd be missing Jimmy, and I was missing you. Why don't we just go and get some coffee, or tea, and scones?"

"I'm having a nice time," she said. "Let's do that."

They went up a staircase to a small restaurant on the second floor over the shop-lined street. It was busy, and they had to wait by the entrance for a table to be cleared. Tom noticed the many white porcelain teapots on the tables and on trays, waiting to be washed. When they were seated and settled, Meagan said, "I keep expecting you to bring up Northern Ireland."

"I'm not ready for that," he said. "It's a bit of a muddle. I want to go through my notes and at least get some of the questions straight in my head."

"It will probably get worse before you're through."

"I'm beginning to get that feeling."

The waitress came and took their orders. He chose tea over the powdered coffee offered.

"There's a chamber music concert in Boyle tonight," he said.
"Yes, Philip and I are planning to go."
"Oh."
"Philip would be delighted if you came with us."
"Are you sure?"
"Positive, and I will be too."
"You got a deal."
"Another Americanism?"
He shrugged.
"Philip and I will pick you up."

ša ša ša

"I really did enjoy that concert," Philip said.

He was driving; Meagan sat in the passenger's seat, and Tom sat in the back behind Philip. Meagan offered to sit in the back, giving the front seat to Tom, but he declined. There was no way to get it right with three people; he felt slightly separated from her, but at least he could see her, and she half turned in her seat to make conversation more natural.

"I didn't start enjoying chamber music until a few years ago," Tom said. "I only heard it on the radio when I was younger. To my ears, at the time, it didn't hold up very well against large orchestras."

"It's a different experience," Meagan said. "Somehow, with chamber music there's an intimacy, a communication with the players, that you don't get listening to an orchestra."

"That's true," Philip said. "But an orchestral concert can be very moving in a different way."

"Barbara and I used to go to a place called Tanglewood in Massachusetts," Tom said. "It's the summer home of the Boston Symphony Orchestra. They had chamber music on Friday night and a big orchestra concert on Saturday night and on Sunday afternoon. We got to the point where we preferred the chamber music. The big concerts had too many distractions."

Tom had no sooner closed his mouth when he realized that he had not spoken about Barbara in that manner before. It was a casual comment, not born of emotion — no grief involved. And — he had said it to Meagan.

"Let's look for the next concert, and go again," Philip said.

They pulled up to Tom's front door. He invited them in for a nightcap, but Meagan declined.

"Why don't you come over for supper on Thursday?" she asked.

"I'd love to." He got out of the car and stood next to Meagan's window. "I've got some Schubert chamber music on CDs. I'll bring them over."

Philip leaned across Meagan's lap to look up at Tom.

"Do you have 'Death and the Maiden'?"

"You bet I do."

Meagan waved and winked as she rolled up her window, and they drove off.

🙢 🙢 🙢

Thursday finally came, and he arrived bearing a bottle of wine. After a cocktail, they went into the dining room. "This looks good," Tom said, as he came to the table. "Where's Sarah?"

"I gave her the night off," Meagan said. "I like to cook, and the two of us in the kitchen doesn't work very well."

Meagan uncovered a dish of lamb stew, and handed Philip a serving spoon. Tom helped himself to some broccoli and cauliflower. She left them and went back to the kitchen for another dish.

"I actually prefer Meagan's cooking," Philip said, looking at Tom around the candles and flowers occupying the center of the table.

She came back in and sat down. "Philip, I think if the music was a little softer.."

"I'll get it," Tom said. He went first to the sideboard. "I almost forgot to pour the wine." He held up the bottle of red Bordeaux, which he had brought. He poured the wine and then went in to turn down the volume on the CD player. When he returned to his chair, they raised their glasses. "To Jimmy's return," Tom said.

Meagan smiled. "To Northern Ireland," she said.

"Up the IRA," Philip said.

"Philip! Please." Meagan said.

The dinner passed pleasantly, with conversation ranging from stories about Jimmy when he was a baby, to a discussion of the difficulties involved in bringing the European Community to a common currency. When they finished, everyone pitched in to carry plates into the kitchen and get things cleaned up. Then they went into the sitting room for coffee and dessert.

Meagan opened the conversation. "Is the work you're doing on that report getting any clearer, Tom?"

Tom looked down into his cup and gathered his thoughts. "You two are Protestants, living here in the Republic. Maybe your perspective is better than I'll find in the North. One thing that I see, without dragging up ancient history, is that the Catholics are getting a raw deal."

"A Unionist would say that they bring it on themselves," Meagan said.

"I agree with that as it applies to violence," Philip said. "Violence can't be allowed to be part of a process which is political in nature."

Tom said, "They tried peaceful means, and were the *victims* of violence."

Meagan placed a piece of cherry pie on a dish and set it down in front of Tom. Philip shook his head and mouthed, "No thank you."

"In recent years," Meagan said, "there's been plenty of blood spilled by both sides. I think that you need to look a little further back to understand the problem. The Unionists feel that what they built, they deserve to keep."

"And," Tom said, "the Catholics feel that what the Protestants have, they got, and kept, by force of British arms."

"Of course, Tom," Philip said, "if you go back far enough, your own country would have to give back land to the Indians and to Mexico."

"It's really not a land issue. Is it?" Tom said.

"There is the question of reunification," Meagan said.

"That's a false issue, in my opinion," Philip said. "There's no way that the Republic of Ireland wants those northern counties back. We couldn't afford it!"

"It's a wonder that the British taxpayers put up with it," Tom said.

"Well, I'm going to leave you two to solve this one," Philip said. "I'm going to go upstairs and read for a bit." He got up from his chair and went over to Tom. "We'll see you soon," he said. He gave Meagan a kiss on the top of her head and left them. Tom and Meagan waited for Philip to leave before resuming.

"More coffee, Tom?"

"No thanks," he said. "Do you really think that the Catholics are that much in the wrong?"

"I'm not saying that they are in the wrong. Although, it does appear that some of them think that they can obtain by violence that which they are unwilling to work for. I'm concerned that you haven't as yet understood the Unionist side of things."

"I'm sure that the Unionists are rational people, and have reasons for their positions, but so far I haven't heard anything that's defensible."

"Is it going to be possible for you, as a Catholic yourself, to see things from a Unionist perspective?"

"I think so. I believe I can see the issues more as an American, than as a Catholic. Besides, even the people up there don't see this as a religious issue."

"Don't be so sure. They're just very wary of whom they mention it to."

"That would be Unionists that you're talking about?"

"Not just Unionists, but religion *is* more of an issue for them."

Tom sat back on the couch. He put his hand up to his chin and gazed off at one of the paintings on the far wall, seeing it, but registering no awareness of it. He turned back to Meagan. "I could use another cup of coffee," he said.

"Stay right there." she said, picking up his cup. "Would you like more pie?"

"No thank you," he said. "It was delicious. Did you make it?"

She laughed and left the room. He got up and walked over to the piano. I wonder if I could listen to her play, without hearing Barbara? He wandered back over to the couch, as Meagan came in and put his cup back onto the low table.

"So, you think religion is a big part of it?" he said. "That's hard to believe when you look at the way the Church's influence has diminished here in the South."

She said, "The main reason why Ireland was partitioned in 1922 was that the Protestants in the North did not want to come under the dominance of the Catholic Church. They threatened civil war if they were not left out of the Republic. At that time, and since then, the Church has been a major political influence here in the Republic. Unionists believe that the Church still interferes as much as it can."

"That may be true of the Church," he said, "but I still don't see what it's got to do with Catholic citizens having equal rights."

"I'm not arguing against equal rights, Tom. I just feel that you should try to see the Unionist side. We would not want this report, which you're working on, to add to the problem. After all, the Unionists are citizens too."

Tom sat back and nodded. "Yeah, 'First, do no harm.' Right?"

"I'll drink to that," she said, holding up her cup.

Tom took a drink from his cup. As he set it down, he said, "I've had enough politics and confusion for one night. Let's talk about something else."

"It's getting a bit late," she said.

He looked at his watch. "You're right. The time flew by." He got up. "The dinner was wonderful. I do appreciate the invitation."

Meagan got up slowly and led him to the front door. When they got there, she stood with her arms hanging down, hands clasped lightly. He stood directly in front of her. Neither reached for the door.

"Will I see you again, before you go?" he asked.

"That might be nice," she said. "Do you ride?"

"Horses?"

"Yes, horses."

"If that's what it takes to see you, I'll give it a try."

"You might find that you enjoy it."

"I might."

Meagan placed her left hand on Tom's right forearm. She opened the door with her right hand, and he moved out onto the porch, turning to face her.

"Saturday morning," she said. "And don't get anything. We have everything you need."

"Saturday morning," he said.

She reached out and took one of his wrists in each hand. She pulled him down and kissed his cheek.

"You are a nice man," she said.

"Nice?"

"Yes, *nice*. Good night, Tom."

She closed the door.

ès ès ès

Tom dismounted with an audible "Whew," grateful for having survived over two hours of horseback riding without falling off or hitting his head on a tree branch.

"It couldn't have been that bad," Meagan said.

"It wasn't. I enjoyed it," he said.

He meant it. He had been riding Philip's horse, Alfie, a very well behaved and tolerant animal. Meagan gave him a few simple pointers to start and added helpful comments every so often. She left him to sit on a rock for a brief time while she exercised her own horse, Bernadette, with a good gallop. He had been grateful, both for the respite and for not having to attempt a gallop.

She led Bernadette into the barn, and Tom followed with Alfie. It was cool inside, dark, and except for the horses, quiet. The smell, which he noticed immediately, was not unpleasant, pungent, almost sweet. Horse people seemed not to notice it at all. She left her own horse and came over to show Tom what to do. He learned to remove the saddle, and then she demonstrated how he should rub and brush Alfie.

"Always maintain control of the horse," she said. "And mind where you put your head."

She left him, with towel and brushes in his hands, and went off to attend to Bernadette. At first, he stood there, looking at Alfie with a renewed appreciation for the massive size of the animal he had been riding. Once he started, it was a pleasant experience, which Alfie seemed to share in his own mute way. He kept working until Meagan had put Bernadette into her stall and came over. She ran her hand over Alfie's flank and took his bridle.

"Alfie says 'thank you' and that you can ride him again." She led Alfie into his stall.

"I appreciate Philip's letting me ride him."

"Philip's back is bothering him," she said, "he's glad to see Alfie get some exercise."

As she closed the stall, Tom stood behind her, waiting for her to turn around. She turned and seemed not at all surprised to find him standing so close.

"I think I'll be able to sit down again by dinner time," he said.

She leaned back against the stall. "I have to leave for Dublin this afternoon. There's an orientation session tomorrow morning." She didn't move.

"So soon?"

"We could have lunch," she said.

He nodded and reached for her left hand. He held it, looking down and massaging it gently with his thumb. He moved it to his other hand and began to slip his right arm around her waist. She didn't resist. She moved to him, but turned sideways, so that her left shoulder rested against his chest. She took his left arm and held it to her waist. He moved his right hand up around her right shoulder.

"I won't pretend that I'm not enjoying this," she said. "But we're not kids."

"I know," he said. He began to nuzzle the side of her head.

"I mean, I don't think we should let things go without talking it through."

"You want a commitment?"

She turned to face him, keeping her forearms against his upper chest. "No. There doesn't need to be any commitment, just a clear understanding. I don't want to be hurt."

"I'll never hurt you, Meagan, not for anything."

She pulled her arms down and encircled his chest, pressing against him with her face against his shoulder. He felt a rush, all over, and all at once. The shape and feel of her body amazed him; for an instant, her breasts were all he knew. He kissed her head and inhaled, deeply, through her hair. They held each other for only a moment, and then Meagan slowly pulled away. She kissed him lightly on the lips. Just a touch, before taking his hand, and leading him out of the barn.

CHAPTER ELEVEN

With Meagan and Jimmy both gone, it seemed a good time to make a trip to Belfast. Tom had never been there. He knew it to be Northern Ireland's capital and largest city, and in recent times a hotbed of confrontation between Republicans and Unionists. He made arrangements to interview David Taylor, the leader of the Ulster Unionist Party, and he arranged to stay at a B&B outside the city. The B&B was expensive and sounded somewhat luxurious. For that reason, he was fairly sure it would be run by Protestants, and he hoped to get their opinions on the conflict.

He arrived at Paley House, the B&B, late in the afternoon and was greeted by Dennis and Karen Holmes. The house was a large Georgian style structure with a stable just to the rear and cobblestone paving between the house and stable. Dennis explained that they had bought the place only two years earlier when he had sold his insurance business, and they had been refurbishing ever since. Everything was being done first class. Tom's room was large, elegant, and furnished with everything that he could imagine wanting, including a terrycloth bathrobe and slippers. There were numerous pieces of bric-a-brac, small statuettes in the French style, dainty flowers in small vases, and scented rose petals on tiny trays. The chairs were too small, and he felt slightly out of place in what he considered to be feminine surroundings. It might be a great place to bring Meagan. Karen brought him some tea and cookies to enjoy while he settled in and took a shower before going out to dinner.

The next morning, he had breakfast with two other guests, a father-daughter couple, on holiday from France. Only the daughter spoke English, but they were very congenial, and Dennis made an effort to encourage conversation. The breakfast room was in an extension of the kitchen itself. Both Dennis and Karen took an obvious pleasure in showing off all their modern appliances. Tom told them where he was going that day. Dennis and Karen were clearly interested but were too polite to press him for details.

Belfast proved to be a substantial and modern European city, much like London, albeit not as large. Driving around the city center looking for a place to park was difficult. Streets were closed off, and concrete barriers were erected in locations so as to slow traffic, and to require many turns and stops. All this was to prevent a fast getaway by terrorists fleeing from a shooting or bombing. When he finally got to a suitably located parking garage, he had to open the boot of his car for inspection before he could park.

Several blocks from the garage, he found the UUP headquarters. Simple utilitarian offices in an old building. At least, it was bright and airy inside, and in contrast to Sinn Fein offices, there were no posters depicting scenes of violence. David Taylor greeted him and, after they were seated in Taylor's office, offered him tea or coffee. Tom declined and Taylor got right down to business. He was about forty-five, medium height, dark hair and brown eyes. He wore a business suit, dark blue, double breasted, a white shirt and tie. Neither the suit, nor tie, was of recent vintage.

Taylor's office was much larger than those at Sein Fein. There were two windows about ten feet apart in one wall, and Taylor's large desk was located between them, facing the interior of the room. A portrait of Queen Elizabeth hung on the wall behind Taylor's high-back chair. Tom sat in one of two cane-back chairs facing the desk, and there was a table with six chairs behind him. The walls were painted an off-white.

Instead of starting by talking about his party and its policies, Taylor put a series of questions to Tom. How long had he known the senator? What would be the form and nature of his report? How would it be used? Tom couldn't tell whether Taylor was trying to find out if this interview was a waste of time, or if he wanted to know how to put the Unionists in the best light possible. Tom decided to take the initiative.

"This report will be used by Republican Party members in the United States Senate, to cross check what they're being told by the Democratic administration regarding the situation here in Northern Ireland."

"Thank you," Taylor said. "I want to give you my complete cooperation. But I must tell you that there is a deep mistrust of the American government and its ability to be an honest broker in our country. American politics seem to favor the other side."

"This could be your chance to balance things up."

"I'll do what I can."

"Could you start with a brief overview of where you stand on the issues which most strongly divide Nationalists and Unionists?"

"Well, one fundamental issue is that of reunification with the Republic of Ireland. I should say, at the outset, that I recognize that many Nationalists don't want reunification either. We Unionists will never accept it because there are deep seated cultural differences between the North and the South, not the least of which is the role of the Catholic Church in their government. In addition, we see the Dublin government as less than fully competent."

"I understand that reunification is not a defining issue at this time. What else keeps the two communities apart?"

"I believe that it's the lack of accountability."

"Accountability?" Tom, who had been sitting back up to this point, leaned forward. "I've not heard that mentioned before."

"Yes, the country is being governed from Whitehall in London: there is no representative government here. That allows every group to hold out for their own narrow interests. There is no need to compromise. No one has to get results."

"And meanwhile, there's stagnation and rising unemployment," Tom said.

"Precisely. And look around you," Taylor gestured as if Tom had a view of the city. "There's an industrial base here, a well educated work force, reasonable wage costs. With an end to the violence, prosperity would come."

"So why don't you just let Sinn Fein be a full fledged partner and get on with it?"

"The IRA has already been rewarded for their violent behavior, and more violence was the result. We cannot give in to violence."

"Isn't it a 'chicken or the egg' kind of situation?"

"No it is not!" Taylor used his index finger to tap forcefully on his desk. "Look at what's happening within the Catholic community. The IRA has become a Mafia type organization. They mete out punishments, beatings and knee cappings, to their own neighbors. Somebody turns someone in. And that's it. There is no due process of law; there is no review. Just blind violence. Catholics are afraid to speak up — afraid to talk to the police. It's how the IRA keeps control. How will encouraging Sinn Fein put a stop to that?"

"It might show Catholics that there's another path to equal rights."

"And it might demonstrate that violence pays."

Tom nodded and sat back. "That's a point to consider," he said. "What about the other side of that coin, the violence by Loyalist paramilitary groups? There have been more Catholics killed than Protestants in the last few years."

"That's true, and it's regrettable. But you'll notice that the Loyalist groups have been very peaceful lately, compared to the IRA."

"And what about British justice? Like the suspension of civil rights, the beatings and forced confessions, and the falsified evidence used to convict the Birmingham Six and Guilford Four?"

Tom was uncomfortable with the way he was questioning Taylor. He did not want to come across like a prosecuting attorney, but he did want to get at the basis for, what to him, looked like unreasonable foot dragging by the English and Unionists.

Taylor swung slightly from side to side in his swivel chair. He leaned forward and put his elbows on his desk to answer Tom's question. "It's a dirty business. I think you Americans have an expression 'Good guys finish last.'"

"The English seem to encourage more violence, by the IRA, with their own outrages."

"I doubt that very much."

"All right, one more IRA question. Why is the IRA expected to give up their weapons while the Loyalists keep theirs?"

"It's a question of who has to prove a genuine desire for peace. It's the IRA that has resorted to the gun whenever political negotiations don't go their way."

Tom was itching to debate some of Taylor's points. Some things just did not make sense in light of other things that he knew. He wanted to ask about Unionist gerrymandering. Confrontation might get more out of Taylor, but it also might make it difficult to get information out of any other Unionist later.

"What *would* be a way to bring about peace?" he asked.

"I don't know all the answers," Taylor said. "But it would have to start with the IRA giving up their weapons and renouncing violence. Because of their past record, it will take a long period of non-violence before people will have enough faith to begin meaningful talks."

"That makes some sense," Tom said. "Is there anything else that you feel I should know?"

"Yes." Taylor stood up. "We don't want English soldiers here, and we don't like being governed by Whitehall. However, the

Nationalists have got to understand that they cannot get everything they want by taking it away from Unionists. They have got to work for what they want. They'll not get it by violence, or by getting your government to interfere."

Tom felt that this last statement was one of the most revealing things that Taylor had said. He said nothing, but stood up and shook hands with Taylor. A few minutes later, he was sightseeing in Belfast. Overhead, the sky was clear blue, and the temperature just right for a midsummer's day.

❧ ❧ ❧

He walked to Donegall Square and through the park, which surrounded the civic office buildings in the center of the square, to Donegall Place, Belfast's most famous shopping street. If nothing else, he wanted to be able to tell Karen Holmes that he had seen it. At the head of the street was a security barrier. Only pedestrians and busses were allowed to pass. The busses were emptied and searched before being allowed to proceed. Each of the major stores had its own security as well; bags were searched before a shopper could enter. For all of that, the stores seemed lively enough once inside. Tom walked down the aisles, checking a few items of men's clothing and their prices; he had no idea of whether the prices were good, or not.

He had been into two stores. As he left the second, he couldn't suppress a laugh. What the hell am I doing here? I'm not going to buy anything. Although — a little present for Meagan might not be a bad idea. He found a place to have lunch and thought about what he had seen in the department stores. He decided that he would rather get her something at a craft shop. Something that shows a little thought.

After lunch, he walked up to Queen's University. Dennis had told him that there was an excellent art museum there. As soon as he walked onto the campus, he sensed a different atmosphere: relaxed, friendly, people going about talking, laughing. This could be Any College, U.S.A.. He went into the museum, located in a tall gothic building near the edge of the campus. There was a desk in the middle of the high-ceilinged lobby, presumably for security. There was no one at it. He waited, thinking that there might also be an admission fee. Finally, he wandered off and toured the museum. There were no security cameras, no guards. No nothing.

Outside, on the front steps he passed a group of students, enjoying the sunshine and each other. One said "Hello." Tom stopped.

"Great day, isn't it?" he said.

"Are you an American?" a girl asked from her perch on the low wall.

"How did you guess?"

They all laughed. He joined their group.

"Things seem very peaceful, here on campus?" he said.

They looked at each other. "Peaceful enough," another girl said. "Were you looking for a fight?"

They all laughed, including Tom. He told them briefly why he had come to Belfast. They were all interested. "What do you think, so far?" one asked.

Tom explained that he was still confused and needed to learn a lot more. Then he asked, "What happens to you people, if there's no real peace by the time you graduate?"

"We leave," the first girl said.

"That's it?"

They all nodded. A young man spoke up. "If there's peace, and there are jobs, we'll stay. But there are plenty of opportunities elsewhere."

"Does that apply to both Catholics and Protestants?" Tom asked.

Again, the students looked at each other. "We don't care about that here," the second girl said.

Tom thanked them and began to walk away.

"We *all* love Americans," the first girl called after him.

When Tom arrived back at Paley House late that afternoon, Dennis greeted him and offered lemonade and some cookies. He seemed to be angling for a chat. Tom knew that he would be curious about his visit with Taylor so he summarized Taylor's comment's without adding any of his own feelings about them.

"More, or less, what one would expect of him," Dennis said. "My own view is a bit different."

"I'd love to hear about that."

"To begin with, this dispute, this fight, is essentially a blue collar issue. We in the upper middle class are not that concerned with how it turns out. We don't stand to gain or lose that much, either way."

"Really? I would have thought that the upper classes would want to maintain the old system. That's how they got rich in the first place, isn't it?"

"I wouldn't want to argue that."

They were seated on a brick paved patio on the shady side of the house. The table and chairs were of white wrought iron. The table was round with a frosted glass top. Trellises covered with a flowering vine, blue blossoms that resembled morning glories closed in two sides of the patio. The rear facing third side consisted of a low railing over which Tom looked out across a large meadow where horses grazed near the far side. "Your horses?"

"Oh yes, but they're available to guests."

Tom turned back to his host.

"Not many of my peers would agree with this," Dennis said. "But I think it was a mistake to partition Ireland in the first place. There might have been a fuss at the time, but it would all be behind us. In fact, I wouldn't mind seeing reunification now."

"Interesting. Most non-Catholics seem deathly afraid of it."

"I would not have said that a few years ago. Karen and I used to go down there on holiday. It was like visiting a banana republic. The roads were terrible, infrastructure third rate. And the people are a bit lazy. Much more industrious here in the North. The government was thoroughly incompetent. Do you know that, at one time, they passed a law requiring that all automobiles coming into the country had to be assembled in the Republic? My God! They needed a Margaret Thatcher more than the English."

Tom smiled and took a drink of his lemonade. "As we would say in the States, Margaret Thatcher couldn't get elected to dog catcher in the Republic of Ireland."

Dennis laughed. "Be burned at the stake, more likely."

He pushed the plate of cookies closer to Tom, who picked one up, and munched on it idly while he looked out across the meadow.

"So, why do you feel it's different now?"

"I see three things," Dennis said. "First, they *did* make a major commitment to education in the South. Second, the influence of the Catholic Church has greatly declined. Whenever you see a priest mentioned in the news these days, you can bet that it will be for some type of perversion. And then, there has been a massive infusion of funds from the EU. Funds dedicated to building up the Republic's infrastructure. All in all, they're doing pretty well down there."

"What do you think will happen when the EU funding stops?"

"I'm optimistic. They're doing a lot of trade with the rest of Europe."

Tom nodded and took a long drink of his lemonade. Dennis picked up the pitcher and offered to pour some more. Tom declined. "I'm going to shower and have an early supper," he said. "Long drive tomorrow. Thanks for the conversation, even if it does add to my confusion."

"That's Ireland, Tom. Every man is his own philosopher."

🙢 🙢 🙢

For the trip home, Tom selected a route that took him through Portadown. He thought of Jimmy. Wouldn't it be fun to spot him on the street and stop for a talk? What a great story to tell Meagan. One in a million chance, but how would I introduce myself to his old man? What would Jimmy tell him? Passing through the city, he drove slower and looked at any kids he passed. It was only a game.

Just outside of Armagh, he was stopped at a checkpoint. A young English soldier came up to his window. Tom reached for his passport and opened his window.

"Where are you going, sir?" The soldier could not have been more than nineteen, freckled face and a cockney accent, which made it difficult for Tom to understand him.

"To County Leitrim." Tom held his passport in obvious view but did not offer it.

"And, where are you coming from?"

"Belfast"

"And your business?"

"I had a meeting with David Taylor, the leader of the Ulster Unionist Party."

The soldier stepped back to consult with his sergeant, who was standing several yards to his rear. He came back to Tom. "Thank you, sir. Have a good trip."

Tom put his passport away and drove off, wondering what would have happened if he'd told them that he'd been to see Gerry Adams, the leader of Sinn Fein.

Back at the farm, he found a letter from Helene with her itinerary and flight number. She would be there in a week. He taped the letter to the post of the lamp on his desk. Wow, that's only three days after Meagan comes home from that course in Dublin. Three days. He called Philip and got a number where he could leave a message for Meagan at Trinity College. She returned his call that evening.

"I went through Portadown today," he said. "I thought I might spot Jimmy."

"It's just as well you didn't," she said. "I wouldn't want him to feel that he's caught in the middle of anything."

Tom sat at his desk, rocking back and forth, doodling on his desk pad. "You're right," he said. "I got a letter from my daughter, Helene, she's coming next Thursday."

"How wonderful."

"Anyway, I was thinking — "

"Dangerous thing that."

"I was thinking that you'll be home Sunday, and I would cook dinner for you and me on Monday night."

"Hamburgers?"

"No, I'll fix steaks. We'll have some kind of fancy dessert. One that you light up."

"With a match?"

"Yeah, I'll show you how to work the fire extinguisher."

"I'll bring some hors d'oeuvres."

For the next few days, Tom busied himself with farm work and drawing up an outline for his report on Northern Ireland. He needed to get a fix on what additional information and interviews were required before he could finish it. He also made a couple of short visits to Frank's pub. Frank listened with great interest when Tom told him of his trips to the North. Occasionally, he would ask a question which gave Tom some pause to think. On Saturday, he checked with Brid to see what he would need to buy for his dinner with Meagan. On Sunday, Meagan called to let him know that she was back.

He started his preparations at three in the afternoon on Monday. First a tossed greens and tomato salad, then the dressing. The recipe was one he had been using for years, lots of garlic. Then the potato salad, lots of onions. He went upstairs to his dresser and found a roll of breath mints. He put them in his pocket. Downstairs he checked the refrigerator and discovered some chocolate mints, way in the back. He thought about barbecuing the steaks. No, too disruptive. I'll grill them in the oven. The dessert would be peaches flambé with a scoop of ice cream added.

In the dining room, water glasses, wine glasses, napkins and candles. So what if it's still daylight. Too warm for a fire though. He went upstairs to shower and change, rehearsing the evening in his head. Back downstairs, he sat in the sitting room in his favorite chair. Just look laid back. Ice. He got up, grabbed the ice bucket, a quick trip to the freezer, and he was back in his chair when Meagan arrived at six.

She handed him a tray. "Anything I can help with?" she asked.

"Nope"

"I'm impressed already."

They went into the sitting room; Tom put the hors d'oeuvres on the coffee table and made drinks. Irish with ice and lots of water. They brought each other up to date. Meagan was very interested in Tom's trip to Belfast.

"I still think that you're being unfair to the Unionists," she said.

He deflected her attempt to discuss it seriously. This was an evening for lightness, for talking about themselves. He gave her the present he had bought in Belfast, a hand carved wooden barrette, painted on the outer surface with a delicate bright floral design. "It should contrast nicely with your hair," he said.

She thanked him, got up and walked to a mirror near the door to hold the barrette up against her hair. "You have good taste. I love it."

They moved easily from subject to subject. He told her stories of his early life, even some that included Barbara. "I met her at a tea dance. She attended an academy for Catholic girls, and I was at a prep school with a partial scholarship and a waiter's job. I remember being a little uncomfortable; most of the girls came from wealthy families. Somehow, I got up the nerve to ask Barbara to dance. Afterwards, I started writing to her. I was blown away when she took me seriously. I just knew that some handsome guy with money and a car was going to take her away from me, but it never happened."

She told him how, as a student activist, she had gotten involved with Gregory. "He was very colorful. Thought nothing of getting up in front of large groups and making fiery speeches. I thought that I could help him to save the world. I was enamored of the academic environment and had a rather inflated view of myself. My real education came later."

They moved into the kitchen to broil the steaks.

"Where is Brid?" she asked.

"She's gone with Sean for an overnight to visit her sister in Galway. I loaned them the car."

"You mean that we're all alone?"

Tom laughed, and held up his glass to her.

"Here's looking at you, kid," he said, "Humphrey Bogart — Casablanca."

She clinked her glass against his. "Here's looking at you too, kid. I've seen it — three times."

The steaks were ready. Meagan helped carry serving dishes into the dining room. He lit the candles and poured the wine.

"This is very nice," she said. "We're having such a delightful time."

"I certainly am," he said.

She drank some wine. "This wine is special," she said. "California, no less."

He drank and then held the wineglass down near the table. He turned it gently, examining the ruby liquid. "And so are you. I guess you know that I'm falling in love with you."

"I think that it's a little premature to be saying that — but I'm glad you did."

They raised their glasses to each other and drank.

The dinner went smoothly. Tom had forgotten the water, but that was quickly remedied. Even the flambé worked well. Meagan, by then a little giddy, stood there holding the fire extinguisher until Tom took it and put it away. Afterwards, they leisurely cleaned up and then went back into the sitting room. Neither one made a move to sit down. Conversation slowed to a stop.

Meagan went over to the window. "You really do have a nice view from here."

He came over and stood right behind her. Slowly, but firmly, she leaned back against him. She reached back, took his arms and held them around herself. She pushed her head against the side of his neck. A delicate fragrance wafted into his nostrils. He breathed deeply, pulling in more.

He kissed her temple. "You are so beautiful."

She turned her head to look into his eyes.

"Are you sure that you want to do this?" she asked.

"I'm sure."

She reached up behind her neck and undid the first button of her blouse, and then the second.

He took over and unbuttoned the rest. "I feel so klutzy," he said.

"Clutchy?"

"That too."

She slipped off her blouse and laid it across the arm of a nearby chair. She undid her skirt and stepped out of it; turning to him to begin unbuttoning his shirt, starting at the top. He unbuttoned the cuffs, slipped off his shirt, laid it on top of her blouse, and then reached for the bottom of her slip. He raised it up, and she helped him take it off over her head. She undid his belt buckle, and then held the two ends.

"Should we go upstairs?" she asked.

"It's now, or never."

They went up to Tom's room, holding each other and leaning together. His legs felt watery, and his breathing was audible. At his bed, they separated. She to one side, pulled down the covers; she stood there and without a trace of shyness removed her bra. He sat on the other side of the bed and scrambled to remove his shoes, pants and underwear. She got into the bed, pulled up the sheet, and underneath, removed her panty hose. He rolled over to her and grasped the top of the sheet.

"The socks, too," she said.

He looked at her, his eyes wild. Her face, so demure, such eyes, so much hair spread out on the pillow. He rolled back to his side and tore off his socks, scratching one calf. Back again to Meagan. She had already removed the sheet.

"My God!" he said.

He moved over her, she encircled him in her arms and moved her hips and thighs to help him get it right. She pulled him in, surrounding him with arms, legs, warmth, wetness, and the sound of her breathing. Her breath came strong and over his face like a warm breeze. There was a sweetness to it along with a hint of onions and garlic, which added to the intimacy, making her feel so much more real.

It felt like seconds. It was probably minutes.

"I'm out of practice," he said.

She caressed the sides of his head with the inside of her forearms. "Let's not ruin things with expectations," she said.

"I can do much better," he said.

"I'm sure," she said, "but you were wonderful tonight. Don't move. Just stay."

Later, as they lay side-by-side in the dark, he spoke of Barbara, and she stroked him gently on his chest.

"I'll never be able to forget her, you know."

"I wouldn't want you to. It wouldn't be right, or natural."

"You're okay with that?"

"Yes. I just hope that you are."

He did not answer immediately. "I am," he said. "I've given it a great deal of thought, and I want to be with you. I want you, and I'm sure that I have Barbara's blessing."

She raised herself up to kiss him and then snuggled back down.

"She died a gruesome death," he said.

"Do you want to tell me about it?"

"I think I have to," he said. He told her of the bicycle ride and how Barbara had died. "Time stood still. I wanted to die. I've been over it a thousand times. I should never have left her behind."

Meagan turned slowly and took a corner of the sheet to pat his eyes. She kissed him gently. "Everything I know about Barbara tells me that she would never want you to blame yourself for an accident like that. She would want to be remembered by having you celebrate the fact that you had those years together. Remember, she loved you too."

❧ ❧ ❧

Meagan left early in the morning, after Tom fixed her breakfast, which included some of his world famous coffee. After she left, there were heavy showers. Tom used the opportunity to go around checking on the drainage ditches, which had been put in along with the trees. He found a number of places where the ditches were spilling over with water. Back at the house, he noted the locations on his plot plan.

After lunch, the sky cleared, and later in the afternoon, he walked up the hill and over to see Meagan. Philip was sitting on the porch. Not reading, for a change; just enjoying the sunshine. He waved when he saw Tom approach. Kiki strolled out to greet him.

"How was your trip to Belfast?"

Tom sat on the steps and turned his face upward to feel the warmth of the sun. He turned back to Philip and told him briefly about his trip, including his experience at the checkpoint.

"I was stopped there once," Philip said. "The soldier asked for my name, and I refused to give it to him. When I refused the second time, he went back to get his sergeant. The sergeant came up and asked me, 'Why won't you give him your name?'

I said, 'It wouldn't be fair.' 'Why?' he asked. I said, 'Because, then he'll have two, and I won't have any.'"

Tom laughed. Somehow, coming from Philip, the joke was all the funnier. Meagan had come out onto the porch, just at the end of Philip's joke. "Don't encourage him," she said.

Tom stood up, still chuckling. "Nice day to grab a few rays," he said to her. "California expression."

"I'll get a hat," she said.

Tom waited and exchanged pleasantries with Philip until Meagan reappeared. They strolled off toward the hill.

"Are you excited about Helene's coming?" she asked.

"Yes. I wish she was staying longer, but she just started a new job."

"Does she know anything about me?"

"No."

"Well, you do whatever you think is best."

He held her hand, and they swung along. He reached down, snatched up a flower and presented it to Meagan. "I love her dearly," he said. "But she's a puzzle sometimes. The totally modern woman. And then at times, so old fashioned. Good values though. She's a brick."

At the top of the hill, they turned around and returned to the house. Philip was still on the porch.

"I got a letter from Jimmy," Meagan said. "Wait here, I'll let you read it." She did not tell him about the letter from Gregory that came with it.

Tom read the letter, smiling the whole time.

"The boy's funny," Philip said.

"And he's not even trying," Tom said.

Philip got up and went inside. Tom gave the letter back to Meagan.

"I won't be here tomorrow," she said. "Taking Philip to Galway for a checkup."

"All right. I'll see you soon, depending on how things go with Helene." He kissed her.

"The horses are watching," she said.

He glanced over toward the horses. "You know what the horses can do," he said.

"That sounds like an American expression, which I would probably not care for, if I understood it."

"Right, on both counts," he said.

He kissed her again and then walked back over the hill.

CHAPTER TWELVE

Tom waited outside of Customs at Shannon Airport and greeted his daughter with a big hug and a bouquet of flowers. After a light breakfast, they drove north. It was an all-day trip. By the time they arrived at the farm, Helene was ready for a quick bite, a shower, and bed. Brid had gone out leaving Sean in charge. He made a sandwich for Helene. She ate it, drank a glass of milk, and then Tom showed her upstairs.

When she was asleep, he called the Clarks' and told Philip that he would walk over. Meagan and Kiki were waiting for him on the front steps. "How's Helene? She must be exhausted with the time change and all that driving."

"Yeah, she went right to bed, but she's young, she'll be up tomorrow full of piss and vinegar."

"That sounds like another vulgar American expression."

"You're right. I'll try to be more careful. It's just that some of those things get used so often, they flow into everyday speech."

"I *do* want to believe you."

"Okay, enough already. Want to go for a walk?"

"Yes, I'd love to."

They started walking across the yard. Tom took her hand, and she put her other hand on his upper arm and leaned softly against him. Kiki went along, meandering about.

"How did it go?" she asked.

"Great. She's pretty tired though."

"So, you haven't told her yet?"

"No."

"That's probably best."

Tom let her hand go and slipped his arm around her waist. They walked slowly.

"She'll like you. How could she not?"

"What's that expression of yours? 'Don't count your chickens'? It could come as a bit of a surprise to her."

"Maybe. She's pretty mature. She's going to love you — not as much as I do, of course."

They reached the fence for the horse paddock — what Tom called the corral. He leaned his elbows on the rail and looked off at the setting sun. "You know," he said, "I think we get better sunsets in the States. It's the pollution. Ireland doesn't have enough pollution in the air. What can be done about that?"

She had her arms around his waist, resting her head on the back of his shoulder. "Maybe, you should have started a steel mill instead of a tree farm."

He took his arms off the fence and encircled her. He gently kissed her forehead. "It wouldn't work. Too much rain. It keeps cleaning things up." He bent to find her mouth and kissed her hard. He held her tighter and began to nuzzle her neck.

She laughed and pulled her head back. "Do you have any idea of what you're doing?"

He laughed and let her go. They started walking again along the fence. "It looks like it will be a nice day again tomorrow," he said.

"Yes," she said. "Do you think you'll be bringing Helene over?"

"I'd like to; we'll see how it goes. Like you said, 'Don't count your chickens.'"

ờ ờ ờ

Helene opened her eyes and blinked a few times while she waited for her brain to tell her where she was. Ireland, of course. She relaxed stretched under the covers and admired the stenciled pattern along the bottom edge of the smooth curve which blended the walls into the ceiling. Getting up, she went to the tall window nearest her bed and opened the drapes. The sunlight flooded over her, forcing her to step back and hold her forearm up to protect her eyes from the glare. She had been in Ireland for over twenty-four hours, and no rain yet. She stepped back closer to the window, bent down to open it and then leaned on the windowsill breathing the fresh air and wondering at the beauty of the fields and meadows. She could see the rows where seedling trees had been planted, a garden plot near the house, and some old farm equipment stored under an overhang along a back wall of the barn. Why do farmers keep that junk lying around? They know they'll never use it again.

She was enthusiastic, wanting to get dressed and get the day moving. What to wear? It seems to be warm enough, but jeans would be best. Not the real tight ones, just good walking-around pants.

Downstairs, things were so quiet that she had a sensation of having been abandoned. Before moving around the house she stood at the bottom of the stairs and listened. A faint sound came from the back of the house. She walked toward it and pushed through a swinging door.

"Did you have a good rest, dear?" Brid asked

Helene had to look around to see who was speaking.

"It's Brid, dear, I'm the housekeeper. I've been waiting to fix you a fine Irish breakfast."

"It's Helene, Brid, and I'm starving. What comes with an Irish breakfast?'

"Well, dear, you can have oatmeal, eggs, and bacon, and sausage. There's toast, jam, and some fruit, if you'd like."

Helene decided not to make an issue out of 'Dear' versus 'Helene'. "Oh well, maybe just a soft boiled egg and some bacon. Do you have any coffee."

"Yes, dear, it's all ready. You just sit yourself in the dining room, and I'll bring it right in."

"Is my father around?"

"He's just gone out for a bit to check on some work that's being done. He'll not be long."

Helene thought to argue that she should sit in the kitchen, but she simply did as she was bid and went into the dining room. How strange it all was to be a guest in her father's house, a strange house in a foreign land. Even the furnishings looked different. Apparently, the Irish valued furniture by the pound. Everything looked thicker and heavier than she was accustomed to. What would it be like, being with her father in this place? What did he really think of all this? Would he tell her? Or, was he too invested in what he was doing?

She moved about, looking at the pictures on the wall. A curious blend of watercolors that she remembered from the house in Woodcliff Lake and some oil paintings of Irish scenes. Who picked those out? She heard a soft rustling behind her and turned to see Brid with a tray. She sat down in the nearest chair.

Brid smiled, "Your father likes to start with his coffee," she said. She poured some for Helene and left the pot along with a silver sugar bowl and creamer.

Helene tasted her coffee, and Brid reappeared with her tray. There was an egg in an eggcup; some toast in a silver rack, a plate with what Helene assumed must be the bacon, and some marmalade.

"We've some lovely oranges. I'll bring one?"

Helene nodded, and Brid disappeared again leaving Helene to wonder if her stomach was up to the slab of fried ham, which passes for bacon in Ireland. She regretted having said that she was starving. Where was her father when she needed him? She did not want to do the wrong thing on her first day. She did not want to eat the bacon either. Brid returned with an orange, neatly sliced on a small dish. Helene would have preferred to peal it herself or have it quartered, but she appreciated Brid's effort at tasteful presentation.

"Is the coffee hot enough?" Brid asked.

"Oh, yes. It's fine."

"It's very expensive here in Ireland, you know."

"Really, why is that?"

"I don't know, dear, but your father tells me it's much cheaper in America. Is there anything else you'd like?"

"No, everything looks very nice."

"I'll leave you to enjoy your breakfast." Brid started toward the door.

"Brid?"

"Yes, dear?"

"Has my father made any friends here?"

"Oh my, yes. Every one who meets him thinks that he's grand, a real gentleman."

"I mean, is there anyone that he spends time with?"

"Ah now, I wouldn't want to spoil the telling for your father. I can see how proud he'll be to take you around and show you off."

Brid continued out the door. Helene cracked the shell of her egg, and scooped it into the cup. She picked out a piece of toast, noting its rough texture and decided that, with marmalade, it would be delicious. There was a noise, a door, and then feet, stomping on a mat. Good, he's back. Tom came in, immediately going to her and giving her a warm hug around the shoulders and a kiss on her forehead.

"Off to a substantial start, are we?" he said, gesturing at her breakfast.

"Dad, what am I going to do with this?" She pointed at the bacon

"Yeah, I know. Just leave it. I'll explain to Brid."

Tom sat in another chair and watched Helene work on her breakfast. Brid came in with a coffee cup for him. She poured some coffee for Tom and refilled Helene's cup; they both thanked her. When she left, Tom turned to Helene. "Well, what do you think, so far?"

She looked at him. "Dad, you've got to be kidding. I just got here."

"Right. Nice house though?"

"It's beautiful."

"I'll show you around as soon as you finish."

A little later, when Helene had finished her breakfast, they went to the back door.

Tom said, "Here, I got these for you to wear around outside." He handed her a pair of bright yellow slip-on boots. He sat on a stool and exchanged his shoes for a similar pair of black boots. Helene waited to use the stool.

She held up the boots for inspection. "Wow, are these a fashion statement, or what?"

"They'll see you coming," he said.

They went outside. Tom gestured at the house. "You remember the pictures I sent you of this place when I bought it. It's shaping up very nicely."

"It's very impressive," Helene said. "I've always liked stone houses."

He showed her the rest of the farmyard and barn. Then they went out into the field. Tom bent down here and there to examine one of the seedlings.

"How are they doing?" she asked.

"I'm not sure," he said. "They seem okay, a few didn't make it, but that's to be expected."

"They're so small!"

"Yeah, it will be a year, or two, before we really know if all this is going to work."

He continued to lead her through the field and up a hill where he pointed out the view of Iron Mountain and Lough Allen. They sat on a large stone enjoying the sun and gazing out into the distance. Sheep were visible on the near hillsides, little spots of light gray, in small clusters, or singles, widely spread to the very tops of the hills. A small white panel truck wended its way up Iron Mountain, looking like a toy in this vast diorama; the road beneath its wheels barely defined by widely spaced utility poles. Its destination? Not a structure was in sight.

"It's beautiful," she said. "Mom would have loved it here."

"Yes."

"You must miss her terribly."

Their eyes met. Tom looked back into the distance, and nodded.

"I do, but I try not to dwell on it," he said. "Life goes on."

"Of course, that's very healthy," she said.

Tom got up and held his hand out for her to grasp. They started back down.

"Am I going to meet any of the locals?"

"Yes, I thought we'd drive into town after lunch."

"How about the neighbors?"

"Sure. I've gotten pretty friendly with a couple that live over that hill." He gestured casually at the hill, which separated his farm from the Clarks'.

"That's nice. Do they have any children?"

"Uh — yeah. They're not married. They're brother and sister. She's divorced, has a seven-year-old boy. Nice kid."

Helene said nothing. They walked. A minute or more passed.

"Do you see them often?"

"Yes, actually. I've done a little skeet shooting with the brother. His name is Philip."

"And the divorcee?"

"Her name is Meagan. She's a history teacher. She's shown me a few of Ireland's significant historical sites. Not the usual tourist thing."

Again, they walked in silence.

"I like the boy," he said. "His name is Jimmy. We've been fishing together. Haven't caught anything yet."

He looked at Helene who ambled along, seemingly studying the placement of each footfall. "Ready made family," she said.

Tom looked up at a hawk circling high overhead. A few steps later he bent to examine a seedling. He straightened up and

153

stood in front of her. "I think maybe I haven't explained the situation very well. These are nice people. It's all very proper. And, I have to tell you; I *am* fond of Meagan. Maybe someday — Well, we'll see."

He hesitated, waiting to see if she would react. She said nothing. He turned away, they continued to walk. And then, "You're taking on an awful lot, Dad. All these changes. Mom died less than a year ago. You've left John, his family, and me to fend for ourselves while you go off to a foreign country and — and go fishing with this kid, Jimmy — or whatever his name is."

He waited to be sure she was finished before he answered. "No man ever loved a woman more than I loved your mother. I still do. I miss her terribly. Not a day goes by that I don't come close to tears for the hurt I feel. I miss you and John too, but you have your own lives. I can't just wallow in it; I've got to move ahead. I'm only fifty-two, for Christ's sake."

"It feels like you're moving ahead a lot faster than I am," she said. After a pause, she continued, "It was bad enough when you left John and me to go off to another country. We lost somebody too. She was my best friend."

They stopped and faced each other. Helene pulled out a tissue and blew her nose, obviously fighting to hold back the tears. "We're still your kids, you know. I'm not ready to lose my father, too."

"You're not losing me, Helene. I just can't live the rest of my life through my kids. I need to do some things that are challenging — take some chances. That way, there's no dependence; we have interesting things to share — You, John, and me. Make sense?"

She nodded. "That part does."

Little more was said for the rest of their walk back to the house. A few neutral comments about the weather and Ireland. On the back porch Tom hesitated and then said, "I've really been looking forward to your visit. It's only a couple of days."

She sat on the stool to remove her boots. She made no attempt to hide her tears.

❧ ❧ ❧

Meagan came into the dining room and sat in her chair at one end of the table, the sun still bright on the window at her back. She sat upright with her hands folded on her lap, a stern look on her face. Philip sat at the other end making little finger sandwiches out of his cold plate supper while reading the Irish Times, which was folded on the table to his right. He took notice of Meagan and placed a finger on the paper to hold his place. He peered at her over his reading glasses.

"Have you had your supper?" he asked.

"I'll eat later. Anything exciting in the paper?"

Philip shook his head. He pushed his paper aside and put his glasses down on top of it. He took a drink of his tea. "Wasn't Tom supposed to come over?"

"He called. It seems we won't be seeing him until after his daughter leaves for London."

"Oh. That's too bad, I was looking forward to meeting her."

"It might have been nice," she said. "At least her visit will be short."

Sarah brought in a cold plate and a pot of tea for Meagan. She set them on the table and then stepped back. Meagan thanked her, and Sarah went out through the swinging door.

"Is that important?" Philip asked.

"She seems to be a strong influence on him."

"You're upset," Philip said.

"Tom won't cross her," she said. "He has very strong loyalties, even to people back at his old company in America."

"Then he'll be loyal to you," he said. "He'll just have to take some time to work things out."

"I don't think you understand how I feel."

"Maybe not, but if you love him, you'll give him whatever time he needs."

"Philip, sometimes your logic can be very exasperating."

"I'm trying to represent Tom. You don't expect him to tell his daughter to go to hell. Do you?"

Meagan began to eat her supper, and Philip went back to his. Meagan chewed slowly, and, when her mouth was empty, she said, "Of course not. She's still grieving for her mother, and so is Tom. I'm sure that she's a lovely girl. She's just not ready for this kind of a surprise. It hasn't been that long since her mother died, and Tom says that they were very close."

They went back to eating their suppers. Philip began to take a renewed interest in his paper.

Meagan interrupted him. "I'll call Tom and tell him that everything will be all right, that he should be gentle with her. I just hope that she doesn't answer the phone."

Philip smiled at her as he picked up his reading glasses and put them on. "You know what they say 'If a woman answers.....ring off.'"

Meagan made no move to get up. Philip went back to find the point were he had stopped reading.

Meagan persisted, "Sometimes I wonder if Tom is as ready for a new relationship as he thinks he is. I just hope that she doesn't play on his feelings of guilt and sense of loyalty."

Philip folded his paper and put it aside. He took off his glasses and gave Meagan his full attention.

"I had hoped that Helene and I would become friends," she said. "Of course, it could never be as it was with her mother."

"That would be largely up to her. Would it not?"

"Yes. Now, I just hope that we're not to be rivals."

"Rivals?"

She got up and went to his end of the table. "Philip, sometimes you can be as naive as you are logical." She kissed him on the top of his head before leaving the room.

"I'm sorry if I wasn't as much fun as you thought I would be," Helene said. "But I'm glad I came and had a chance to see what you've been doing."

They were standing in the lounge at Galway Airport awaiting the boarding announcement for the plane that would take Helene to Dublin and her flight to London. The other passengers were a mixture of businessmen and people dressed as though they were off to visit relatives, or to do a little shopping. Tom noticed several young men take a particular interest in Helene. He concluded that she had just the right mixture of Irish-American beauty and the sophistication of a New York woman to intrigue a young Irishman.

"We decided that we wouldn't discuss it any more, remember?" he said.

"I didn't mean to bring up that. I was referring to the farm."

"Oh."

"I did have a good time, meeting your friends, and seeing Ireland through your eyes. The work you're doing for Jerry on Northern Ireland is fascinating, and I think, very important."

"Sure," he nodded, "I feel as if I've only scratched the surface so far. I only hope that I can make some kind of coherent sense out of it. It's so hard to not get sucked into taking sides." He went over and looked out the window at the planes on the tarmac. "Why don't we sit down?" he said. "It doesn't look like anything is about to leave." He picked up her bag and led her to the side where they could sit by themselves.

"I can't wait to tell Sheila about my proposal of marriage," she said.

"That was pretty funny; I wonder if old Andy really thinks he can get a wife that way, or if he's having us all on."

"Is he in Frank's pub all the time?"

"No, I only see him every other week, or so."

There was an announcement saying that the Dublin flight would start boarding in twenty minutes.

"The folks in the pub seem to treat Andy pretty nicely," she said, "considering his obvious mental deficiency."

"The Irish are fairly laid back about that sort of thing," he said.

They fell into silence. He looked around the lounge area, casually wondering if the plane would be full, or not. They looked at each other. He lightly clamped his hands together. Helene's were folded on her lap. They each started to speak at the same moment and then stopped to let the other go ahead. Helene began, "Dad, I can't go off without saying something about you-know-what."

He nodded. "So?"

"I won't say anything to John about it." She paused, watching his face.

He sat and continued to listen for what she had to say.

"I hope that you can hold off," she said, "step back and see if you really want to be doing what you're doing."

"Helene, if you're trying to tell me something, why don't you come right out with it?"

"It's not that easy. I just think that you never really gave a fair chance to building a new life back in the States, near your real family. I think this Meagan woman may be taking advantage of your vulnerability, even unintentionally. There, I've said it."

Tom sighed, and looked aside to consider his response. "I'm sorry," he said, "I'm sorry that I sprung this thing on you, and I'm especially sorry that I didn't more fully appreciate the effect on you of my leaving so soon after your mother died. I was selfish, I thought that I was the one with the biggest problem."

"Will you leave all this and come home?"

"I love you, Helene. Right now, I don't know what I'll do. I really wish you had met her. I think it would have made a big difference in how you feel."

"I'm not ready for that. Mother was — so much to me. I just can't see anyone taking her place."

"No one's going to take her place," he said.

They sat side by side, Helene blinking, Tom biting his lower lip and looking down at his folded hands. A minute passed before he spoke. "I didn't think about my importance to you and John. He has a family and a career. You were getting ready to graduate and start your career. I didn't want to be dependent on you guys for my social life, for my sense of who I am. Maybe even, become a drag on you. I thought that what I was doing was best all round."

She looked at him and nodded. They spent their last few minutes talking about Helene and Sheila's plans for their London vacation.

He watched her go through the gate. She blew him a kiss. He stood at the window, watching the plane taxi and then leave the ground, and finally become a speck, disappearing into the clouds. Why does there always have to be a parting? What do I have to do to get the people I love together?

❧ ❧ ❧

"Am I too late for a bite of lunch?" Tom asked, having just arrived at Meagan's front door.

She stood in the open door with her head cocked to one side. "Well," she said, "seeing as how you're in no position to complain, I suppose we can come up with something." She stepped aside to invite him in.

He followed her down the hall watching the toss of her hair and the sway of her skirt. Her bearing bespoke an elegance, almost regal. How independent and self-assured she could be at times. At others, so warm and tender. Was the outward Meagan a schooled mannerism with the real Meagan just inside? At times, in conversations with her, he had to work hard to tell if she was serious or having him on, and he knew that she enjoyed his efforts.

"Sarah's not here," she said, as they entered the kitchen. "I'll fix you something."

Tom sat at the table, and Meagan began to take some things out of the refrigerator. He had been in this kitchen before. It was different, as all Irish kitchens are from those in the States. *Why?* Why did it have such a special feeling about it? The appliances were similar enough, the refrigerator, stove, coffee maker. They just looked as if they all came from far away places at different times. That's it. Everything came in at a different time. The whole room is a distillation of as much as a hundred years of adding and throwing away. Some of the pots, hanging over the stove, looked as if they had come in over many generations.

Meagan finished making a salmon salad sandwich. She put it on a plate adding a sliced tomato and a stalk of celery. She put the plate in front of Tom along with a glass of water.

"I'm making some tea," she said. She sat down, put her elbow on the table and rested her head on her fist.

It was up to him to start the conversation. "She's pretty upset," he said, "misses me more than I thought she would."

Meagan put her hand down. "Yes, I can understand that."

"Makes me wonder about my son, John, and what his feelings are."

"Of course."

Tom chewed on his sandwich and took a long drink. Just as he put the glass down Meagan got up, holding up a finger to indicate that she would be right back. She poured the water for tea, put the pot on the table and got the cups and saucers out. She sat back down. "What are you going to do?" she asked.

"I don't know," he said. "I sure don't want to lose her."

"Of course not."

"I've got to think about how to bring her around."

"Maybe you can't."

Tom looked at her, not quite sure of her meaning. He finished his sandwich.

She poured the tea. She watched him, waiting on his thoughts. He put some sugar in his tea and stirred it, staring at the cup as if waiting for some genie to rise up and tell him what to do. "I've got to think it out."

"Take your time," she said. "I'll be here."

They passed the next minutes in silence. Tom finished his tea, declined a refill. Meagan got up to remove his cup. She bent and lightly kissed his ear before moving to the sink.

"I'll call you," he said, getting up to leave.

CHAPTER THIRTEEN

Late that afternoon, Helene finally arrived by taxi at the Kensington Hilton in London. Sheila was waiting in the room that they would share for the next six days.

"Wow," Helene said, as she put her bags on one of the beds, "these rooms aren't very big. Are they?"

"What do you want for two hundred and fifty bucks a night," Sheila said. "At least it has a view." She went over and parted the translucent outer drapes and stood there looking down at the street.

Helene came over to see for herself. "Looks like a nice park," she said.

"It looks good from here," Sheila said. "Wait till you see all the dog shit."

"You've been *busy* on your one full day in London," Helene said.

She moved away from the window and sat on the bed next to her bags. The room felt oppressively small. The colors were too somber, mostly tans and browns, and the furnishings looked old and worn. She ran her hand over the bedspread. At least it looked clean. "I guess we won't be in here much," she said.

Sheila came over and sat on the other bed facing her. "Are you hungry? I found a great pub, right around the corner."

"Good, maybe I'll get another proposal," Helene said. "Let me just unpack a few things and use the facilities. Then we can go." She opened one of her bags and started to unpack

"Sounds like I've got a story coming," Sheila said.

"I'll tell you later," Helene said, disappearing into the bathroom.

Sheila came from Connecticut, but she looked like a farm girl from the Midwest, buxom with long blond hair in a braid down her back. Her smile revealed a gap in her teeth, the kind that young boys use to squirt water through when playing in the water. Helene could easily imagine Sheila doing the same.

They had roomed together in their freshman year and became close friends. In the following years, they drifted apart as Sheila became increasingly involved in radical student politics while Helene concentrated on her studies. But when Barbara died, Helene went instinctively to Sheila for the sympathy and support she needed. They had been seeing much more of each other ever since.

They were lucky and got a booth in the pub, now crowded with office workers having an after-work pint. As soon as Helene entered, she could see that this place was a far cry from the simple little Irish pub that she had been in with her father only two days earlier. The floor was white tile, the walls heavy wood paneling, and there were elaborate cut and etched glass partitions and mirrors everywhere she looked. From where they were seated, she could see a section of the bar. There must have been hundreds of glasses hanging from wooden racks over the heads of the bar men.

Their booth was at the far end of the pub, and their entrance had not gone without notice. They were barely seated when men began coming by, holding their pints and offering to buy drinks. When their intentions to be left alone were clear, the men stopped coming. One of the last to make overtures went back to his companions saying rather loudly, "Coupla dykes." His companions had a laugh, and so did Sheila and Helene.

"You know," Sheila said. "That first guy wasn't bad. What do you think, should we have given him a bit of encouragement?"

Helene shook her head and gazed around at the decor.

"This place is certainly more fancy than the pub my father goes to," she said.

"Your father hangs out in a pub?"

"Not really, it's just a little neighborhood place. I don't think he spends much time there."

"How did your visit go?" Sheila asked.

The waitress came by and Sheila ordered two shandys.

Helene looked surprised. "What in God's name is a shandy?"

"You've got to try one of these," Sheila said. "You won't believe what the English do with beer. Or maybe, it's *to* beer. Tell me about your dad."

"We had a good time. Well, except for one little surprise."

"Don't tell me. Let me guess what the surprise is," Sheila said. "She has red hair and the most fantastic blue eyes?"

"Sheila, you're sick — Besides, I have no idea what she looks like."

The waitress came and left their drinks. Sheila asked for menus. When the waitress left she turned to Helene, waiting for her to continue.

"He's been seeing someone," Helene said, "She's a divorcee."

Sheila took a sip of her drink, continuing to look at Helene over the top of her glass.

"She has a boy. My father's been taking him fishing."

"Sounds serious," Sheila said.

"*And* it's been going on for a while," Helene said.

"You didn't get to meet her?"

"I refused."

"Why?"

"Are you kidding? My mother's been dead for less than a year."

"Ten months," Sheila said

Helene sat back in her chair and then leaned forward to pick up her drink. They sat sipping their drinks, saying nothing for the moment.

"It's not as if he didn't have a family at home," Helene said.

"I don't want to be crass about it," Sheila said, "but there are some things a son and daughter can't do for a man."

"I know. But a divorcee?"

"You're making it sound worse than it probably is. What do you actually know about her?"

"She lives on the next farm with her brother and her seven year old son. She teaches history, and she rides horses — Oh — and her name is Meagan."

"Great name! And is that all you found out about her?"

"I'm afraid I'll be finding out more later."

Sheila picked up the menus, which had been dropped off by the waitress. "We should order something," she said.

When they had made up their minds and were waiting for the waitress to return, Helene asked Sheila, "Did you find a job?"

"Yes, I start right after we get back. And I have an apartment with a roommate from Massachusetts. She's a writer. I think her parents are paying her share of the rent."

"Is she nice?"

"Yeah, pretty naive too."

"Tell me about the job."

"It's with Citicorp. Systems work, credit cards and that kind of stuff. Don't know much at this point."

"You should be good at that."

"The only problem is that I have to commute over to Long Island City every day. It's not exactly the glamorous Manhattan life that I'd envisioned."

"How are the men?"

"Not bad, but I expect to be making the literary scene now that I've got a writer for a roommate."

The waitress interrupted to take their orders. They both opted for the roast beef special.

"You made the literary scene at Princeton," Helene said. "They were a bunch of creeps."

"Yeah, well, this is New York."

The waitress returned and arranged the dishes to fit on the small table in their booth. They began to eat. Helene commented on the food. Sheila apologized for wolfing her meal down. The noise from the bar grew louder as more patrons joined their friends and each group had to talk over the rising tide of greetings and laughter. Sheila leaned forward, swallowing a last morsel as she did so. "This fellow you met at work sounds interesting."

"Bob?" Helene said. "Yes, he's nice, but it's not serious."

"That's too bad."

"What do you mean?"

"Oh, I don't know. I just think it would be good if you had somebody that you were serious about."

Helene toyed with her fork before using it to place a small piece of beef in her mouth. She chewed three or four times before responding. "Because of what I told you about my father?"

Sheila shrugged. Helene continued, "I'm too tired to get into it any more tonight."

"Okay," Sheila said, "we can just go back, read our tour guide books and get to bed early."

"It's okay?"

"Sure."

ᔑ ᔑ ᔑ

Tom spent much of the day thinking of Helene and how to bring her around to accepting Meagan. After supper, he drove into town and took a walk before heading for Donohue's pub. The day was fading; the high clouds taking on a pinkish hue on the sides still seen by the sun and light gray shadows on the sides from which the night would come. He paused on the bridge to watch and listen to the stream endlessly passing under. People strolled by; "good evenings" were exchanged, along with a nod of the head or a hand to the cap. He listened to the sounds of children laughing and running, playing at games which became more fun as bedtime approached.

There were a couple of regulars in the pub, but Frank was not busy when Tom entered and took his usual stool. There were polite greetings, a wave of the hand, a nod and a smile. Frank left off from a conversation and came over. "Has she gone?" he asked.

"She left this morning."

"Fine young woman. It was a pleasure to meet her. Will she be back soon?"

Donohue put a glass under the tap, and waited for Tom's nod before starting.

"It may take a bit of persuading to get her back here."

"Ah, now. Was there something she didn't like?"

"Someone."

"Did you introduce them?"

"No. I wanted to, but Helene was upset with the whole idea."

Donohue came over and placed the pint in front of Tom. "She never did like the business of you coming to Ireland? Did she?"

"No, but she was getting used to it."

"Well now, it will just take a bit longer for her to get used to the idea of you being with another woman."

"I don't know. She was pretty upset." Tom took a sip of his pint and reached out with the tip of his tongue to lick the creamy foam from his upper lip.

"She's young," Frank said, "it will take her a while to understand that you living like a monk isn't going to make the loss of her mother any easier."

"You're right, Frank, but I'm her father. I love her. I don't want to make her miserable. It's very painful for me to see her unhappy because of me."

Donohue moved away to take care of a new arrival. When he came back to Tom, he said, "In time, she'll realize that your happiness is important too. Make sure you take care of things with Meagan, in the meantime."

"Good point, Frank. I have a tendency to get too focused on one part of the problem. I better make sure that my intentions are clear."

ta ta ta

"Oh, God!" Helene said, as she flopped backwards, arms outstretched onto her bed. "I don't think I've seen as much history in one day in my whole life. I'm exhausted."

Sheila sat on her bed unlacing her shoes. She slipped them off and rubbed her feet, one at a time. "Tell me about it," she said.

"Let's just eat here in the hotel tonight," Helene said.

"Good idea. You want to shower first?"

"I was hoping you would."

"Yeah." Sheila lay back on her bed.

The two of them lay there, staring at the ceiling.

Helene said, "The English sure know how to make a buck on history."

"A pound."

"Whatever. I wonder what all those people would do for a living if the country was fairly young, and they didn't have all these historical sites to make money on?"

"Go to Australia for jobs?"

"Or Canada. My father says that the English are the most professional parasites the world has ever known."

"Sounds like he's been in Ireland too long already." Sheila got up and started preparations for her shower.

"I guess that's what I think too," Helene said.

"Poor baby," Sheila said, as she disappeared into the bathroom.

An hour later they were seated in the hotel restaurant. The place was nearly empty, the lighting was soft, and their waiter — they decided that he was an Indian — seemed relaxed. They ordered a bottle of red Bordeaux and were in no hurry to order their meals.

"Do you think I'm being selfish?" Helene asked.

"Didn't say that," Sheila said. "I don't know all the circumstances."

"But you think I should have met her?"

"It wouldn't have hurt."

"I might have gotten upset and said something awful."

"You? Miss Self Control?" Sheila held her glass up to the light and peered through the wine. "What do you think? Do the French send better stuff to the English or to the States?"

Helene left her glass on the table. She turned the stem slowly with her fingers, and looked absently at the red liquid. "Maybe, I overreacted."

"You know, I've told you before, your dad is an attractive guy. If you weren't my friend, I could go for him myself."

"Oh, Sheila."

"I'm just saying that he's an attractive and sensible guy. He's not going to go for some woman just because she wiggles her finger at him. Maybe this Meagan isn't so bad."

"But my mom?"

"Still hurts a lot, doesn't it?"

Helene nodded, sniffed, took out a tissue and blew her nose. She picked up her glass. "To Barbara," she said and took a healthy drink.

"To Barbara," Sheila said, as she reached over to touch her glass to Helene's.

After a pause, Sheila said, "If your mom is in heaven, or something, she's probably happy for your dad. Guys who weren't happily married don't generally do it again."

Their waiter stood patiently, not wanting to interrupt. Helene checked the contents of the wine bottle. "We better order," she said.

Later, when they had finished their meal and were waiting for the check, Helene came back to the earlier subject. "I should meet her."

"I think you owe it to your dad."

"If I'm going back to Ireland, I'll have to leave earlier than we'd planned."

"That's okay, maybe I'll have a better offer by then."

❧ ❧ ❧

"I'm so delighted that you could come, Helene," Meagan said. "Please come in."

Tom and Helene had just arrived and were standing on Meagan's front porch. She folded her umbrella, and he shook some of the rain off his coat. Helene hesitated; Tom took her elbow and ushered her inside. He removed his coat and hung it up. Helene stood looking down at the pool of water gathering at her feet.

"Sorry about the water," she said.

Meagan gave a small wave of her hands. "Irish floors were meant to be wet," she said. "That's what the tiles are for."

Tom helped Helene remove her coat. He took off his shoes and put on his usual pair of slippers. He offered another pair to Helene.

Meagan intervened. "Don't bother with those," she said, taking Helene's hand to guide her down the hall. Tom followed. When they reached the parlor, and Helene was seated, Meagan said, "I'll ask Sarah to make some tea."

"I'll go," Tom said, and he left the room.

Meagan sat in a chair just across the coffee table from Helene. Helene had been looking about. This place was different from her father's house. It didn't feel as much like a farmhouse, more like a mansion, although it was not that big or ostentatious. The pictures on the walls — all oil paintings in ornate frames impressed her. Some were portraits. Family members? Others were simple country scenes, similar to some of those that she had seen in her father's house. When her eyes had completed their tour, she saw Meagan smiling at her. She smiled back. "I'm sorry that I didn't come before," she said.

"You had so little time with your father," Meagan said. "I don't blame you for not wanting to dilute it."

"You're kind."

"Not at all."

"An ancestor?" Helene asked, gesturing at the painting over the mantel.

Meagan looked at the portrait. "My grandfather. He was responsible for the family owning this property."

"I understand that you teach history," Helene said. "Do you specialize in any particular era?"

"Not in my teaching; it's really quite general. I do have a personal interest in Irish history."

"I don't know much about that," Helene said, "I've got my hands full with our own. And that's relatively short."

"America has done so much and means so much to the rest of the world. There's a lot to know."

Helene took note of Meagan's posture, not stiff, just poised and erect. She found herself straightening up and moving further back in her chair. Meagan's physical attributes had been obvious to her from the moment she had arrived. This woman had presence and beauty combined. "Class" was the word that came to mind.

Tom reentered. "You haven't been talking about me, have you?"

Meagan looked at Helene. "Do all American men have big egos?"

"We were talking about history," Helene said.

"In that case, I'll go back and help Sarah," he said and left.

"Well," Meagan said, throwing up her hands and laughing, "Back to history."

"You have a particular interest in Irish history?" Helene said.

"Yes. You might be interested as well. America has taken the lead in empowering women in modern times, but Ireland has some great, and indeed some lusty, women in its history."

"That is interesting. I suppose Saint Patrick put a damper on that."

"No. The damper came much later, from the Church in Rome. Women were in positions of real power in the early Irish Christian Church. Saint Patrick worked with the Irish as he found them. He taught them to love each other. He melded Christianity into the culture."

"I've got a lot to learn," Helene said.

"Not at all, but it is fun when you get into it. Tell me about the new job you're going back to."

"Actually, I was about to ask about your son, Jimmy. Can I meet him?"

"Unfortunately, he's just gone to spend a couple of weeks with his father."

"Does he enjoy that?"

"No he does not, and it takes me a week to straighten him out when he comes home. But it's only fair that he spends some time with his father."

"He must be a nice boy, my father speaks fondly of him."

"I'm glad to hear that. Your father's a good influence on Jimmy."

Tom came back in followed by Sarah. They were both carrying trays. One with sandwiches and the other with the tea set. Sarah left, and for a while they ate sandwiches, drank tea and made polite small talk.

"Meagan, I've been admiring your sweater," Helene said. "Did you make it yourself?"

"Thank you. No, I'm afraid that my domestic skills start and end with cooking. This was made by the wife of the groundskeeper at Jimmy's school."

"I've been looking to buy one, but the shops have nothing like yours," Helene said.

"Perhaps you'd like to go and visit Mrs. Clancy tomorrow morning. We could have lunch and be back by two?"

Helene glanced at Tom.

"I've got plenty to keep me busy," he said. "You two go right ahead."

Helene turned back to Meagan. "I'd love to go."

≥∎ ≥∎ ≥∎

Tom took Helene to Shannon for her flight to New York. It was almost ten in the evening when he returned, drove up to his porch and got out of the car. God, Shannon Airport, and back, in one day. Too much. He stretched his arms and then bent over to relieve his back. He straightened and looked at the moon, just rising over Lough Allen. It was partly hidden behind a passing slip of cloud, but the light still shimmered on the water and traced the black shapes of mountains against the sky. He went up the steps and glanced at his watch. It's late, but I'll chance it. He went into the office and picked up the phone. Brid came down the hall and peeked in, just to be sure it was he.

"I'm back," he said. And dialed Meagan's number. She answered. "You have another fan," he said.

"That goes two ways," she said. "I think we're going to be good friends."

"She never stopped talking about you the whole way. She said that it's clear to her why I fell for you."

"She's a delightful young woman, Tom. It took real courage to come back the way she did."

"I guess that's right. I am proud of her."

"You have every right to be."

"What have you got on for tomorrow?" he asked.

"I'm going north."

"To get Jimmy?"

"No, unfortunately. Gregory's insisting that I meet him to discuss Jimmy's future."

"Hmmm." Tom sat down. "That sounds like fun," he said.

"I'm not looking forward to it."

"Would you like me to drive you?"

"I don't think that would be a good idea."

Tom swiveled around in his chair. "When will you be back?"

"Oh, I don't know. Probably the day after tomorrow."

"I'll see you then?"

"Maybe. It might be late."

"Oh"

"I'm worried about Jimmy. I won't be myself, or very good company until I get him back."

"I understand; I'll stay cool. I kind of miss him, myself, you know."

"I know. I'll call you."

CHAPTER FOURTEEN

Meagan drove into the heart of Armagh, one of her least favorite cities. Flat, drab, no color, no signs of prosperity. It was six o'clock, drizzling, and the traffic was heavy and confusing. It took twenty minutes to locate the Bellcastle Hotel a six-story, red brick, Victorian structure, which appeared to have fallen on hard times. The bricks were coated with dark gray soot, as if it had stood for a hundred years next to a railroad yard instead of near the city center. She parked and went inside. The entrance to the restaurant was just off the lobby; she stood in the entry doorway; the restaurant was virtually empty. She cast her eyes over the room at the small faux-crystal chandeliers, the faded striped wallpaper, the white tablecloths, and the unlit candle on each table. A man approached, "Miss Clark?" She followed him to a secluded booth in the rear. Gregory got up to greet her. The table was moved out for her; she sat down against the wall, and Gregory moved in beside her. The table was moved to close them in, and the man left.

"I hope you don't mind meeting here," Gregory said. "I thought it best not to meet in Portadown. And this is closer for you."

"This is fine," she said.

"Well, as long as you're here, we might as well make a pleasant evening out of it." He made a signal with his hand. A waiter appeared with a bottle of wine and proceeded to open it.

"Gregory, I don't think that this is what I want to be doing."

"Relax, Meagan, there's no harm. I just want to talk. That's all."

The waiter poured a sip of wine into Gregory's glass. He tasted it and nodded his approval. She thought of Tom. What would he think of the wine? The waiter poured a glass for her. She forced a small smile. Gregory took a good drink, and smacked his lips.

"Better than we could afford in the old days," he said.

She took a sip and nodded. "You wanted to talk about Jimmy?".

"Yes," he said. "Well, as you know, I'm now Deputy Leader. I've a bit more money and a lot more influence."

"What has that got to do with Jimmy?"

"I want to play a stronger role in his upbringing."

"That was all settled five years ago, at the divorce."

"I don't think the court anticipated that he'd be going to a Catholic school."

"It's the best school in the area. And he's not being made into a Catholic."

Gregory raised his eyebrows and then his hand to signal the waiter. "Maybe you'll be a little less feisty if you've got something in your stomach." He asked the waiter to bring menus.

Meagan scanned her menu, looking for something light, easy to digest. "Why this sudden concern for Jimmy?"

"A lot of things have come together. Come to a head, so to speak."

Meagan said nothing, waiting for him to continue. She selected Dover Sole and a garden salad.

He ordered a steak. "Jimmy's reaching an age where he needs a father," he said. "We went fishing the other day; he caught a big one. He's really into it now."

"He can go fishing in Lough Allen."

"Who's going to take him? Your brother?"

"It would be best to leave Philip out of this."

"Right. The lad needs a real man."

Meagan sat with her hands on her lap, looking straight ahead. He looked at her and wrung his hands together. "I'm sorry," he said, "I shouldn't have said that. Besides, it's not just Jimmy."

Her eyes shot sideways at him. He leaned across to pour a little more wine into her glass, although she had barely touched it. He put the bottle down and looked out across the room as he spoke. "Things are different with me: I'm a little older, I have more time now, I've changed."

The waiter brought their salads and refilled Meagan's water glass.

"I'm glad for you, Gregory. On all counts."

"I've been thinking," he said, "I've been thinking a lot — about us."

Meagan stared down at her salad and continued to eat, slowly.

He took a few mouthfuls of salad. He looked at her and then reached out to break off a piece of bread. "I don't want to upset you. Why don't we just have a nice dinner, and talk after."

"Fine," she said.

"Do you get to the movies at all?"

Meagan put her fork down and cleared her throat. "Not that often," she said, "I'm trying to remember what I saw last."

The meal went on with Gregory raising one subject after another, and Meagan responding politely, but without enthusiasm. She took a sip of wine whenever he insisted, managing to down almost half a glass by the time the meal was over. Finally, when the dishes were cleared, and they were waiting for coffee, he came back to his agenda. "I said earlier that there were a number of things coming together. There's Jimmy. He's growing up without me. There's the new job. And then, there's the house. I was thinking of you when I got it."

He looked over at her. She continued to stare at the table.

"There's places to keep horses, just outside of town."

The waiter brought their coffees. Meagan turned to Gregory, but he spoke before she did. "I wouldn't expect anything in the beginning. There'd be no rush. Just the three of us together."

She continued to look at him and slowly shook her head. "Gregory, you're not the only one who's changed. I'm a different woman now. I have a completely different life. I have no interest in the old life — even with improvements."

"I thought for Jimmy's sake, you'd be willing to give it a try."

She shook her head.

"Well, I've got to think of the lad then. Don't I?"

She watched him, her eyes wide. "What does that mean?"

He hesitated. He scratched his chin and turned to face her. "I want you back, Meagan. I still love you." He waited for a reaction. Again, she sat, staring at the table.

"I've talked to a solicitor," he said. "I'm going to keep Jimmy."

Meagan did not move, not a twitch. She slowly turned her head and spoke in a hoarse whisper. "You'd use Jimmy to get to me?"

"I'm not using him, I want my son back. But I want you too. Maybe even more."

Meagan concentrated on taking a few deep breaths. Then, without looking up, she said very quietly, "There's nothing more to say."

"Please, just think about it," he said. "Look why don't you stay here for the night. No strings. I'm going back to Portadown. Maybe you'll feel different in the morning." He produced a room key and dangled it in front of her.

She got up from the table; she turned to look at him as if she were going to scream at him. And then, she turned and walked across the dining room. Everything was a blur; things seemed to be moving in crazy directions. She bumped into someone in a chair. She said nothing and kept moving as if in a trance. Everything seemed to depend on just getting out of there. Once on the street, she almost ran to her car. She had difficulty getting the key into the ignition. Oh my God, don't let me have an accident.

When she was on the highway out of town, the tears came.

~ ~ ~

It was three in the morning when Meagan arrived home. She left the car in front of the porch and went inside. Kiki padded out to greet her as she sat on the bench and removed her shoes. "Oh, Kiki, don't look at me like that. You're right, I should not have let Jimmy go."

Kiki nuzzled against her. When she had her slippers on, she went down the hall to the living room, Kiki in tow. She went to the sideboard, poured herself a drink and then slumped down in a wing-backed chair, holding the drink in one hand and absently patting Kiki with the other. "What am I going to do, Kiki?"

There was a sound behind her. She turned to see Sarah, in bathrobe and slippers, standing in the doorway. "Are you all right, Miss Clark?"

"I'm fine, Sarah. I'm sorry if I disturbed you."

"Not at all. Can I fix you something to eat?"

"I'm not hungry. You get your sleep. I'll be fine."

"Good night, then."

"Good night, Sarah."

Meagan took a drink. Why doesn't Philip wake up? What will he say if I wake him? She took another drink. Maybe he'll be upset if I *don't* wake him. She put down her glass and, followed by Kiki, went to wake Philip. He put on his bathrobe and followed her back downstairs. She poured herself another drink; he refused one. He sat in the middle of the couch and watched her. She put the drink down and walked about the room. "He's going to keep Jimmy," she said.

Philip said nothing.

"Did you hear me?"

Philip nodded.

"He said that he has seen a solicitor. It's all legal."

Philip shook his head. "That can't be," he said, "you're his mother. That was all settled years ago."

Meagan sat down, slumped over with her elbows on her thighs.

"Why is he doing this?" Philip asked.

Meagan sat back, still slumping. "He wants me back. Isn't that ridiculous?"

"No."

"What do you mean? *No?*"

"You're a very desirable woman, Meagan. Even you know that."

Meagan sighed and looked up at her grandfather's portrait over the mantel.

Philip said, "Who knows what his solicitor actually said. We'll talk to our solicitor, McBride, in the morning. We'll get Jimmy back."

Meagan got up and went over to pick up her drink. "This could take forever," she said.

"Maybe not. Tom might be able to help."

Meagan sat back down, facing Philip "How?"

"He's been spending a lot of time up there. He might know some people."

"Oh no. We can't do anything risky."

"Of course not. You are going to tell Tom about this?"

"About Jimmy — yes. But not about what Gregory wants."

"Why not?"

"I just don't think it's a good idea. Besides, I might have to do it."

"Go back to Gregory?"

"I'm *not* giving up Jimmy."

"Tom would just have to understand what you were doing."

"Oh sure," she said. "In any event, there's no cause to telling him now."

Philip got up, went over to Meagan and gently rubbed her back.

"You get some rest," he said. "I'll call McBride in the morning."

❧ ❧ ❧

The drainage ditches on Tom's farm had been put in before the trees were planted. Some were not functioning as intended. A project to fix the problems started during Meagan's absence. Workers were hired, and with Sean's help, Tom began to repair the system; he drove the tractor, and Sean handled the backhoe. When not needed in the fields, Tom spent time on his report. He concluded that in order to finish it properly he needed to interview John Hume, the leader of the Social and Democratic Labor Party, the SDLP. Their headquarters were in Derry, and Hume was the MP, the Member of Parliament in London, from that district. Going to Derry would also give him a chance to follow up with O'Coyle, and maybe Galvin, the IRA guy. The two of them had made the IRA sound almost reasonable the first time he had talked to them, but now, he knew more about IRA methods. How would they defend these — the knee-cappings, the beatings, and the absence of any form of due process in their ranks?

On the afternoon following Meagan's return, he sat at his desk looking over material for his report and making a list of questions as yet unanswered. Through an open window, he could hear the faint sound of workers' voices and the gentle scraping of shovels. The phone rang startling him; it sounded like a cymbal crashing against wall of his thoughts. It was Philip. "Tom, Meagan didn't get home until three o'clock this morning, and then, early this afternoon, we went to see our solicitor. She's resting now, but maybe you'd like to come over."

"Sounds like trouble. What happened?"

"Meagan wants to deal with this in her own way, and I don't want to make any problems. I think she'd like to see you."

"I'm on my way."

Philip opened the door and showed Tom to the living room. Kiki greeted him as a now familiar friend.

"I'm sure that she's not sleeping," Philip said. "I'll tell her that you're here."

Tom did not sit down. He moved about, looking blankly at pictures and bric-a-brac. On every previous visit to this room, he had found some little item that he had not noticed before. Today, nothing registered. It's something to do with Jimmy. The son of a bitch is giving her some grief about the kid. Meagan entered followed by Philip. She was still dressed in a linen suit, now slightly wrinkled. She extended her hand. "Thank you for coming over." He held her hand and kissed her cheek. She sat at one end of the couch, Philip at the other. Tom sat down facing them, directly across the low table.

"Sounds like it wasn't a very good trip?" Tom said.

She shook her head. "Gregory is going to keep Jimmy."

Tom sat up in his chair. "Jesus! Just like that?"

"He feels that Jimmy is not getting a proper education here, and that he needs his father."

"And what? He doesn't need his mother?"

"I don't know what he's thinking about that," she said.

"What did your solicitor say?"

"Not much," Philip said. "Except that the matter will have to be decided in Northern courts."

Tom got up and began to pace about with one hand up to the back of his neck. "This is crazy," he said, "the guy ought to be put away."

"The worst of it is," Philip said, "that no matter how it comes out, it will take a long time."

Tom looked at Meagan, and she at him. He said, "I don't know what to say. I'm going back up to Derry in two days. I'd been hoping to take you along and to pick up Jimmy on the way back."

"That would have been nice," she said.

Each of them looked down, and no one spoke for a moment. Tom went over to Meagan. She got up, and he took her hand. He caressed the top of her forehead. "You look tired," he said.

"Exhausted."

"I won't stay," he said. "I'm sure that you two have already considered anything I might come up with, but I want to help."

She nodded, and Philip did as well.

"Let me know if I can do anything," Tom said. "Even if it sounds crazy." He let go of Meagan's hand and walked to the door. "I'll see myself out."

Tom got in his car and drove slowly back to his house. I wonder if I could hire somebody to snatch the kid back? Better leave it for now. If anything went wrong... Good God! Maybe later, if things get desperate, it might be worth taking a risk.

He went back to the Clarks' late the next afternoon. He brought some flowers for Meagan and a book on the Lewis and Clark expedition, which he thought might interest Philip. Meagan was sleeping so he only stayed a few minutes, long enough to learn that she would go, the next day, to see a solicitor in Belfast. It comforted him to know that he would not be leaving her at home when he made his trip to Derry.

὜ ὜ ὜

Shortly after one o'clock, Tom found SDLP headquarters, located in an attractive, mostly residential section of Derry, not far from the River Foyle. The weather and parking both worked against him and he had to walk some distance in the rain. He arrived and was told, with great apologies, that John Hume had gone to London. Eugene Hagerty, his deputy, would talk with Tom. He went in to meet Hagerty with a feeling of resignation. It had been a lousy drive, his shoes were wet, and now he would have to talk with a flunky. What could he learn that he could not have gotten from the newspapers?

Hagerty got up to shake his hand. A big man, tall, well over two hundred pounds, blond, mustache, blue eyes. He looked to be a little older than Tom. His voice was strong and masculine. "John wants me to extend his personal apologies to you for not being here. I'll do every thing I can to see that you get all the information you need."

Tom sat down in front of Hagerty's desk.

"I can see that you've been treated to a bit of Irish dew," Hagerty said. "Let me get you some hot tea."

Tom nodded; things were looking a little better. In spite of the rain outside, the office was bright and cheery, high-ceilinged and not crowded with furniture and papers. No posters, either.

Hagerty came back with the tea. "Where would you like to start?" he asked, easing himself down behind his desk.

Tom said, "I already know that the SDLP is the most politically successful party for the Nationalist community. Can you tell me why that is?"

"Because we represent the mainstream of public opinion. In particular, we denounce violence as a means to gain political ends."

"So, you've gotten more MPs elected than Sinn Fein has, because they're seen as advocating violence?"

"That's part of it."

"The Unionists still have over seventy percent of the MPs."

"We've been making inroads. Things would go much faster without the IRA keeping tensions high."

"Do you think that the British and the Unionists would give up power faster without IRA pressure?"

"Yes, I do. The IRA gives them both an excuse to maintain power and control."

Tom took a swig of his tea and opened his notebook. This was getting interesting. "How would you gain power if the IRA didn't exist?"

"To begin with, you can look at the demographic trends here in Northern Ireland. The Nationalist community is gaining at the expense of the Unionists, particularly in the number of college graduates. The Protestant graduates tend to leave, and the Catholics to stay."

"Why is that?"

"The Catholics see growing opportunities, and the Protestants see them shrinking," Hagerty said. "Another point is that the Nationalist community, particularly SDLP, is better organized than the Unionists. Take out the violence and a lot of Protestants would come over to our side."

"Why would they want to do that? Don't they all want to remain tied to England?"

"Not all. Many would vote for an independent Northern Ireland, as long as their rights were assured."

There was a phone call for Hagerty. He motioned Tom to stay seated while he spoke to the caller. Tom took the opportunity to check back on the notes he had prepared for this interview. When Hagerty hung up, he asked, "Realistically, Mister Hagerty, what makes you think that the Unionists will voluntarily cede power over to the Nationalists?"

"It's Gene, and may I call you Tom?"

Tom nodded.

"I don't think that they will," Hagerty said. "I think it will have to be wrested from them by a combination of political power and world opinion."

"Okay," Tom said, "assume it happens. Would reunification with the Republic then be the next step?"

"It would not. As long as reunification is even an open question, there can be no real democratic government here in Northern Ireland. That's what Sinn Fein cannot seem to understand. Northern Ireland must be an independent country with both the Unionists and Nationalists fairly represented."

"If that depends on changes in demographics and public opinion, it could take years and years."

"Not necessarily. It's already started. The quick fix with Sinn Fein hasn't worked. People are more realistic now. It's time to put away the guns and work for peace."

Tom stayed for almost another hour. He listened politely as Hagerty went over various SDLP successes and programs. He half expected Hagerty to hit him up for a contribution, but he didn't. Tom left with a stack of position papers and brochures. The rain had slowed to a light sprinkle. He checked his watch. Over an hour to kill before his appointment with O'Coyle. He sought out a coffee shop and sat down to complete his notes and collect his thoughts.

ea ea ea

Meagan got to Belfast just in time for her four o'clock appointment with Steven Mulligan, the Northern Irish solicitor selected by McBride. She had no difficulty finding her way; things had not changed that much since her days at Queen's College. The city was cleaner, at least in the center, and the access roads were new, but all familiar nonetheless. She parked and barely took notice of the threatening clouds as she made her way to Mulligan's office on Victoria Street. She walked up the stone steps, banistered on each side with white marble. The building, four stories high, was itself faced with white marble. It had, undoubtedly, been built as a town house for some wealthy Belfast merchant or shipbuilder. She entered and went into the reception room on her right. The floor design was a pattern made of different colored marbles, largely covered with Persian rugs. The walls were paneled and held a combination of paintings and decorative mirrors. There were several dark oak benches set near the walls, and near one end a large wooden desk. The young man seated behind it addressed her. "Miss Clark?"

She was ushered into a side room, which looked like either a large study or small library. Everywhere she looked there were bookshelves, lots of leather bound books. A lush Persian rug covered the floor. A large window in the far wall was covered with white transparent drapes, and, standing in front of it in a large terra cotta pot, was a ficus tree. A small slender man, bald, about sixty, stepped out from behind the desk and extended his hand, not to take hers, but to show her which chair to take. He sat across from her, behind a low circular table.

"Well, you must be tired from your trip, Miss Clark. So we'll get right down to business."

She nodded

"I'd like to confirm the facts of the case." He went on to explain his understanding of the situation as he had received it from McBride. "Is that an accurate assessment?" he asked.

"Yes," she said. "I can't think of anything that you've left out."

The young man appeared with a silver tray on which there was a tea service, a selection of biscuits, and jam. He set it down, glanced at Mulligan, and then disappeared.

"I hope you haven't just come from tea," Mulligan said. He reached for the pot and poured two cups. "Sugar?"

"One, please."

He put in one lump, handed her the cup and saucer and moved the tray closer to her. "I'll leave you to help yourself to the rest," he said. He put sugar and milk into his own tea and then sat back, stirring. "We've had very little time since Mr. McBride called, but we did manage to obtain a copy of your divorce decree."

"Is it adequate to support my case?"

"Oh, indeed," he said. "It's quite straightforward; the child belongs with you."

"How long will it take?"

"Ah, now that may not be up to us."

"Why not?"

"He'll undoubtedly get a solicitor."

"He has one now."

"He does?"

"Yes."

"Has he said anything about what this solicitor may have told him?"

"I'm not sure, but he did say that he objects to Jimmy attending a Catholic school."

"Are you of the impression," he asked, "that he's keeping the child with the advice of his solicitor?"

"Yes, I am."

Mulligan put down his teacup. He sat back and put his hand up to rub his chin. "Hmm, this is interesting," he said, "I wonder what this solicitor can be thinking?"

"Could it be the Catholic school? Could he use that?"

"With some judges, that could be a factor, but, by itself, it's probably not adequate."

Meagan was famished. She picked up a biscuit and quickly ate it. Mulligan talked to her about what he saw as the legal precedents for her case. He was generally optimistic. Meagan was mostly interested in what could be done to speed things up. He consistently hedged on that question.

"We need to make some discreet inquiries," he said. "And I would like to talk with McBride again. It is important that we don't run into surprises later on. Could you possibly stay over, and come again tomorrow afternoon?"

"Yes," she said, "I'll do whatever is needed."

"I'll arrange rooms for you at the Victoria."

Meagan was vaguely aware of the expensive legal fees implied by all that surrounded her. She had in mind to stay someplace less expensive than the Victoria, but under the circumstances, it just did not seem to matter that much.

ta ta ta

Tom stood in the, now familiar offices of Sinn Fein.

"Ah, it's good to see you," O'Coyle said, as he came out to the reception area to greet Tom. He extended his hand and then helped Tom with his raincoat. "Come on in." he said, leading Tom toward his office. "It's a dismal day. Here put this on," he said. "You'll be warm and dry in no time."

He handed Tom a cardigan Irish sweater. Tom dutifully put it on, and they sat down. Instead of getting down to business, O'Coyle wanted to know all about the farm and Helene's visit. Tom told him but left out the details involving Meagan.

Tom asked, "And how are your mother and Grace, your lady friend?"

"They're grand. Grand. My mother never leaves off trying to get us married. I think that she and Grace are scheming. They'll have me going to church next."

When O'Coyle was ready, Tom introduced his subject. He summarized what he had been told in other interviews, and then he said, "I do understand the hatred for the British. And I see the injustice and inequities, but there are two things that I can't understand."

"I'll do my best," O'Coyle said.

"The first issue is the IRA. Their violence, against their own people, against innocent victims, is political suicide. I have great sympathy for Catholic victims of British and Unionist violence. But now, the IRA is turning support against you, here in Northern Ireland, and in the States."

O'Coyle sighed and took a moment before responding. "Tom, we've not known each other very long, but I like to think of you as a friend."

"I feel the same way," Tom said.

"Can I tell you something then, that you're not to repeat, or put in your record?"

Tom answered. "What do the Irish say — you have my bond?"

O'Coyle said, "Speaking, strictly for myself, the IRA is an embarrassment at times. Unfortunately, the ties to Sinn Fein, and the hatreds and mistrusts of the English, all run very deep. However, before you dismiss them completely, ask yourself: Would the Palestinians have gotten anywhere against Israel without violence? Would Israel be an independent nation today without Zionist violence? Would South Africa have gotten rid of apartheid? I could go on. It's all well and good for politicians to get up and denounce violence, but they only make changes when they're forced into it. Many times violence is the only voice available to the afflicted."

"Your points well taken, Dan, but I still believe that, in today's political climate, the IRA is counterproductive."

"I won't argue with you. By the way, speaking of the IRA, Jack Galvin wanted a word with you. He's out on a job somewhere, moving furniture. Can you stay over?"

"What does he want?"

"He said it was personal. I didn't want him to tell me."

"Yeah, I can stay over."

"You said there were two things that concerned you?"

"Yes, I wanted to ask about reunification," Tom said. "Not many people support the idea. The people in the Republic don't want it. And it's such a divisive issue. Why push it?"

"I'm going to argue this one with you, Tom." O'Coyle leaned forward and put his forearms on his desk. "To begin with, more people would be for it, if they saw it as a possibility. The reason is that, no matter what form an independent Northern Ireland takes, the English will still have their dirty fingers in it. And they can't be trusted. Also, we are not looking to do it right away. It could take years. I would agree with our friend, John Hume, at SDLP, the Unionists would have to be treated fairly. Look at the Protestants in the South. They still have their lands, their wealth. Nobody's talking about confiscating their property, or taking away their rights."

"Why does Sinn Fein sound so unreasonable on the issue?"

"We don't. It's the English who use it as a scare tactic to keep their people in line."

Tom smiled at his friend and waved a hand, as if to say "Fair enough." "Okay, Dan. I will do my best to represent Sinn Fein fairly. But just between us, I think that you guys should concentrate more on results, and less on dramatics."

"Oh, Tom. I'll pray for your enlightenment."

Tom laughed. "If I get any more *enlightened,* I'll need a shrink."

They talked on about other things, coming back and forth to the peace process, and politics. It was getting to be time for Tom to leave when O'Coyle said, "You know, Tom, there are a lot of special interests in Northern Ireland, and elsewhere, that depend on a continuation of the conflict. A lot of jobs and a good part of the economy are tied to it. You need to interpret what you're told in accordance with the narrow interests of who's telling you."

"How does that apply to you?"

O'Coyle sat back. He smiled and nodded. "Now, Tom. You show me the man that can see himself that well."

Tom got up to leave. "What are you doing for supper?" he asked.

"I'm expected to attend two wakes tonight. Believe me, I would rather be having dinner with you. It goes with the job."

They walked out to the reception area. O'Coyle told him that Galvin would meet him for breakfast in the city center.

"Next time, it will be strictly social," Tom said.

"I'll look forward to it, Tom. All the best."

CHAPTER FIFTEEN

The next morning the weather turned. The sun was shining, and it felt as if it was going to be warm. Tom looked forward to having his meeting with Galvin behind him so that he could head home and see Meagan. He found the restaurant, small, clean, white walls. Galvin sat in a corner with a cup of coffee. Tom joined him and picked up a menu. "How about some eggs?" he asked.

"That sounds good," Galvin said. "I don't usually eat much breakfast."

"It's the foundation of a good day," Tom said.

A waitress took their orders. Tom had thought earlier that he would question Galvin about the IRA. But he had changed his mind. There seemed little point to adding details and rationalizations to what he already knew about their practices and policies.

"O'Coyle said that you had something that you wanted to tell me?"

"Yes, but I want to say something first. I no longer have anything to do with the IRA. I couldn't even if I wanted to — which I don't; English spies watch me like a hawk. Understand?"

"Yes, I understand."

"Now and then, I'm given some information, or a message, to pass on. And this is it."

"You're going to give me a message from the IRA?"

The waitress arrived with coffee for Tom, and a plate of toast.

"It's *information*," Galvin said. "I'm told that you keep company with a woman in County Leitrim, and that she was married to Gregory McDonald. He's now a Unionist leader in Portadown. She was known then as a strong supporter of Unionist causes. Some believe that she still supports them."

Galvin paused and waited to see if Tom wanted to say anything. Tom felt his stomach starting to tense. "Go on," he said.

"The information is this. She still sees her husband. Last week they were at the Bellcastle Hotel in Armagh." He waited for this to sink in. "There was a room taken. The register was signed 'Mr. and Mrs. McDonald.'"

Tom did not know how to react. He was at a loss for words. He was tempted to laugh. "That's it?"

"That's all I was told."

The waitress came and served their eggs. Tom ate quickly, thinking furiously about how to react. He wanted to send a message back to the IRA like "Go fuck yourselves." He decided to let it pass. He looked at Galvin.

"I'm just the messenger, Tom. Please don't look at me like that."

Tom nodded. "I know. I know. What can I say?"

"Don't say anything. That's my advice. There's probably nothing to it."

"Yeah. Good advice," Tom said.

"I would say one last thing," Galvin said. "Here in Ireland, people can work in strange ways. I wouldn't totally ignore anything."

Tom drained his coffee and put some money down for the bill. He looked at Galvin. "Don't feel bad about this," he said. "I won't thank you for the message. But thanks for your advice. I've got to go."

Galvin stayed at the table. As Tom left, he turned back and waved.

🙢 🙢 🙢

Meagan spent her morning on a nostalgic walk around the campus at Queen's College. The day was beautiful and she comforted herself with the idea that, although it could take some time, she would have Jimmy back. After lunch, she stopped into a department store. There was a young man, probably a college student, demonstrating gyroscopic tops in the toy department. She bought one for Jimmy and hoped that the box included detailed instructions on how to do some of the tricks that the young man had so easily performed.

At three o'clock, she was back in Mulligan's office. The routine was the same, including tea and biscuits. She had neither. She just wanted to hear about getting Jimmy back. Mulligan put his elbows on the arms of his chair and placed the fingers of each hand against each other, steepling.

"We've made a few preliminary inquiries, and I had an interesting conversation with Mr. McBride. We still see the case as being straightforward. Unless, of course, they were able to show you to be an unfit mother."

"That would be ridiculous."

"I'm sure. But we must remember that this case will be decided by a judge in Northern Ireland, and some are not without their own prejudices."

"What does that mean?"

"Let me ask you a few questions. We talked yesterday about the Catholic school. That can only hurt. Is there anything else in your life that could, out of context, be made to look bad?"

"Not that I'm aware of."

"Tell me about your brother."

"Oh no! Oh, my God!"

Mulligan leaned over and poured two cups of tea. He put one lump in each cup and then turned the tray and pushed it over to Meagan. She reached down for the tea, being extra careful not to spill. Mulligan got up and reached over for the other cup. He poured some milk and sat back down.

"I personally have no qualms about your brother's sexual preferences," he said. "I've no doubt that he's a good brother and an uncle to your son. But you know how these things can be twisted in ways we never imagined."

Meagan shook her head. "This is insane."

"Perhaps. You are, if I may say so, a very attractive woman. Are there any men in your life?"

Meagan sat back; she did not answer at first. She sat there feeling her world closing in — closing down. "Yes. There's one. He's marvelous with Jimmy. He would make a far better father than Gregory ever could."

Mulligan waited, watching Meagan's reactions. "He's the only one?"

"Yes, I've not gone out with anyone else in years."

"He's a fine man, I'm sure. What we have to worry about is whether a confidential investigator could come up with anything that your ex-husband's solicitor could use. Could, for example, anyone have seen him leaving your house in the early morning?"

"No, but I did leave his house early one morning."

"While your brother was home with your son?"

"No, Jimmy was away. This is sick!"

"You are absolutely right. It's sick, and it's unfair. But we have to be prepared. Please remember that I'm on your side."

Meagan nodded and looked down. "What can we do?" she asked.

"It will take a little time to figure that out," he said. "I don't suppose you'd even consider going back to him?"

Meagan looked at him, her mouth slightly open.

"One day, you might take your son — give your ex the slip — Be back over the border.."

"I'm too upset to think about anything like that right now," she said. "I should just go."

"Of course," he said and walked her to the front door.

Meagan walked out onto the sidewalk and headed in the direction of her car. Bright sunshine warmed every surface, and people were all about enjoying the day. She walked, alone, no thoughts, just a numb feeling. In City Hall Park, she sat on a bench, oblivious to the flowers, sunshine and cheerful conversations going on about her. She remembered what Philip had said. "Tom would have to understand." She could not imagine it. She would lose Tom if she went back to Gregory. Jimmy, Jimmy. Get Jimmy back. Everything else comes after that. She found a phone and called Gregory. He would meet her. Same place, the Bellcastle at seven. She called Philip.

"Why don't you take a few days and think about it, before you leap?"

"Because, Gregory will be thinking about it too. I won't stay; I'll tell him I have to go home and get my things."

*。 *。 *。

After leaving Galvin at breakfast, Tom drove straight for home. He did not stop seething until he was almost in Strabane and he glanced at the speedometer, which read 125 km per hour. He slowed to 80 and then to 50 through town. I can't let those fuckers get to me like that.

He called as soon as he got home; neither Meagan nor Philip was in. It was still early, only three in the afternoon. He went out to see how the drainage work was going. Good progress had been made, but he noticed an unusual number of trees, which looked as if they were not going to make it. He made a note to be sure that Kevin was keeping accurate records of where they had used different fertilizers. He got back to the house after six, and immediately called the Clarks.

Philip came to the phone. "Things sounded good yesterday, Tom. But she had to go back to the solicitor today, and things sound complicated."

"What did he say?"

"I don't think I could keep it straight, Tom. And I know Meagan will want to tell you all about it, herself."

"When will she be home?"

"I'm not sure, exactly. Maybe not until tomorrow."

"Call me. If I'm out, have somebody come find me,."

"I will, Tom. I know that Meagan appreciates your support."

Tom hung up and looked down at the notebook on his desk. The one with most of his notes on Northern Ireland. *This is going to be* some *report. How the hell am I supposed to concentrate when Meagan has problems?*

ta ta ta

Meagan arrived at the Bellcastle shortly after seven. She did not go straight into the dining room, but instead, to the ladies room. She checked her makeup and her hair. She straightened out her suit jacket and skirt. Then she looked into the mirror, staring into her own eyes. *Don't you dare cry.* She took a deep breath, exhaled and went to the dining room. There were more patrons than last time, mostly men. She felt their eyes on her as she followed the same man to the same booth in the rear. Gregory was not there. The waiter offered to get her a drink. She asked for a glass of white wine. When it came she took a drink, and then looked down at the glass. "Dutch courage" is what Tom would call it. *Where is he now? What's he doing?* She could see him, the glint of his eyes looking into her, the feel of his hands, his arms guiding her to him, strong, gentle. She could almost smell him, steely, clean, musky. *Is it all gone?*

Gregory entered the dining room. He stopped at two tables to exchange a few words and to shake hands. He slid in next to Meagan. "You've been celebrating already," he said.

She forced a smile.

"I was delighted to get your call," he said. "It's going to be good news, I hope."

Again, she smiled and quickly took a drink.

"I'm ever the optimist," he said. He reached into his pocket and took out a room key, which he showed to her and then put back in his pocket. "What do you think?" he asked.

"I couldn't possibly. You said there would be time."

"Ah, yes," he said. "But how much time? That's the question."

"I don't know. Does there have to be an answer right now?"

He turned so that he could look straight at her. "No, I wouldn't believe you anyway. Are you really prepared to leave him?"

Meagan struggled to give away nothing and to come up with an answer. "Yes."

"Not sure I believe that either."

Meagan's stomach twisted inside. Under the table, she clenched and unclenched her fists, fighting to keep her face calm. The waiter came over. Gregory ordered a bottle of wine and menus. He said nothing more until the wine had been served. He held his glass up to Meagan. "I've got a proposition for you." He drank. "This guy, Brogan. He has got friends in high places. He's been all over the North here, talking with people for this report he's doing for his friend, the Senator. But, of course, you know all about that."

"Yes, I do."

"I notice that he didn't interview *me*."

The waiter came for their orders. Meagan did not even look at the menu; she simply ordered what she had had last time, Dover Sole.

"We want that report to balance out some of the political pressure we Unionists have been getting from Washington. We want it to solidly support the Unionist side of the argument. Are you following me?"

Meagan began to wonder if she might be getting sick to her stomach.

"You get this Brogan to turn in a report favoring the Unionists. And, when we've verified that, we can go ahead and get together. Just the three of us, you, me and Jimmy.

"What makes you think that he won't do that on his own?"

"Well, for starters, he's a Catholic, himself. We also know that he's been on very friendly terms with the Sinn Fein leader in West Derry."

The waiter returned with two salads. Gregory started right in on his. Meagan looked at the food but made no motion to pick up a fork. She continued to look at her salad. "What makes you think that I could get him to change it?"

Gregory continued to eat his salad. Then he paused, without looking at her. "I have information that tells me that he'd do a lot for you." He turned to watch her react. She turned and looked him in the eye. "And you'd hold Jimmy hostage to get this done."

"I'm *not* holding him hostage. He's my *son*." He went back to eating his salad. Meagan just sat there.

He said, "This is a way to set things right. We gain a little ground in Washington, I get you, and you get Jimmy. And me too, of course." He held up his wineglass to her, and took a drink.

Meagan took a small bite of salad. She picked up her wineglass and pretended to drink. She continued to look down. "How would it work?"

"You mean after we verify?"

"Yes."

"Simple. You just pack your bags and come on up."

"All right," she said. "I want to leave now."

"No, it wouldn't look good. Stay a while; eat something."

When Meagan got to her car, her head was splitting, but she was otherwise calm and in control. She promised herself that she would stop a little later, when her stomach settled a bit, to get something to eat. An hour later, when she reached the outskirts of Monaghan, the car began to buck. She checked the gas; there was plenty. The lights on the dash seemed to be going out. The engine quit, and she had to coast off to the side of the road. After a minute, she tried to restart the car — nothing happened. It was close to eleven o'clock. She looked out the front and back to see if there might be someplace open. She was in a commercial area; the buildings all contained light industrial businesses. Just to her right, there was a tall chain-link fence, behind that, a flat-roofed building with a faded sign on top, MacNair Scrap Metals. Other than streetlights, there were no lights anywhere. *How far will I have to walk?*

A car came by. It slowed, and its brake lights came on. It pulled to the side and looked as if it was starting to back up. She locked the doors. Another car pulled up behind her; a garda got out, and the first car drove off. She rolled her window open about three inches and told him what had happened. He went back to his car and after a few minutes returned to her window.

"We called a man named Garetty at his house. He has a garage in town; he's coming out with a tow truck. We'll wait until he gets here."

A half-hour later, she was seated in the small office of Garetty's garage, waiting to hear the results of his check on her car. She looked at the stacks of parts books, all well thumbed and stained with black grease. The same black grease coated the phone, and the pens and pencils which protruded from the holes in a round plastic car part sitting on the desk. On the wall, near the door to the garage, a calendar featured a pretty girl, lots of cleavage, but she was fully clothed.

It didn't matter what Garetty found. It just didn't matter. She felt that she was in some kind of chute, hurtling down away from Tom, and toward Gregory. It was going to be very difficult to fool Gregory, to pretend that she wanted to be with him. *How long will it take before he lets his guard down? And Tom, my one real chance?*

Garetty came in. "Alternator. I can pick one up in the morning. You'll be going before noon."

Meagan nodded.

"I can bring you down to the hotel," he said.

The Regal was a small hotel, just off the main street. There was a tour bus parked alongside; it couldn't be too bad. Garetty waited to be sure that a room was available and then, with a tip of his cap, he left. The night clerk made a fuss over her, offering to carry her bag up to the room. She let him take it up while she stayed in the lobby to use the phone. She called and woke Philip.

"I'll call Tom in the morning," he said. "And tell him that you're all right."

"Yes," she said. "You do that."

Upstairs, she undressed and sat on the edge of the bed, barely aware of her surroundings. How quickly things were slipping away, her house, her room, her job, Philip, and Tom. Tom, who had brought back feelings long forgotten: fragrances in every breath of air, colors, long faded, now clear and bright again, walking that felt like dancing, laughter at things which had earlier gone unnoticed. How can he understand? How can he possibly understand?

❧ ❧ ❧

Tom said, "I appreciate your call, Philip. It's good to know that Meagan is okay. I know she'll be tired, but ask her to call me when she gets in."

He finished his breakfast and then had a short meeting with Kevin to make sure that the record of where they had been using different fertilizers was accurate. Satisfied with the records, he tried to work on his report on Northern Ireland. He could not concentrate. He needed to see Meagan.

He went out into the fields, nominally checking on tree condition and drainage but, all the while, thinking of Meagan and Jimmy. He envisioned a protracted legal battle with Meagan totally caught up in it, and Jimmy trapped in Northern Ireland. This thing could take a year — maybe more. What will the stress do to her? To our relationship? Is everything on standby? How long can that last? Will it be possible to pick up again with Jimmy?

In his office, late in the day, he was still thinking about it. We have to talk about it. It's too important to just play it by ear. We'll discuss it. We'll come up with something that works — something supportive — not an added burden to her. He took out his notes on Northern Ireland and the outline he had started. He completed the outline and started to compose a summary.

The phone rang. "It's Jack Galvin, Tom. I've some more information to pass on."

"If it's anything like the last *information* I got, I could do without it."

"I know how you feel, Tom. I'm just trying to stay out of trouble. Just doing what I've been told to do. Okay?"

"Yeah, okay. But you should try to stay away from those people."

"I'll try. I will. Here's the information. Last night, the Bellcastle Hotel. Your friend and her ex husband. There was a room taken under 'Mr. and Mrs. McDonald.'"

"Great. Take care of yourself, Jack."

"I will, Tom. And, God bless."

Tom hung up, and leaned back in his chair. He stretched his arms behind his head and then leaned forward. He closed his notebook and put it away. He sat back again and looked off into space. What a fucking mess. Later, he got up and went into the living room.

"Cum sanctis tuis," music filled the room. Why had he chosen *that* CD, the Mozart Requiem? Majestic, deep tonal messages, which never failed to evoke somber thoughts, deep philosophical thoughts. He had not played it since Barbara's death, knowing that when he did, it would bring forth his sense of loss. He sat in his large easy chair, looking out the window across the fields toward the road. The music flowed over and around him working with and then against the effect of the early evening sunshine, now glowing and shining off the greens and the splashes of wildflower colors just outside. Yes, Barbara, you're gone. I was never meant to live without you. I'm only trying to get my life back; to have someone who makes me feel complete.

His thoughts shifted to Meagan. He loved her. That was certain. It had never occurred to him that he needed to be cautious, to look out for the intrigues of the Irish. He had been so preoccupied with his own guilt over not waiting long enough after Barbara's death; he hadn't seen that Meagan falling in love with him was too good to be true. And, what had he drilled into his subordinates at work over the years? "If it's too good to be true...etc."

There was a sound competing for his attention. Slowly, his mind left its meditation. He turned to see Brid standing in the doorway.

"It's Missus Clark to see you," she said. Brid always ignored the fact that Clark was Meagan's maiden name. If you had a kid, it had to be 'Missus'.

Tom got up, telling Brid to show "Missus" Clark in. He turned off the music. Meagan appeared in the doorway. She smiled at Brid and continued toward Tom. He moved to embrace her and kiss her cheek. "This is a surprise," he said. "I would have come over if you'd called." He gestured toward the couch and then walked over to the sideboard. "Would you like anything?"

"No," she said. "Maybe later." She sat down but did not lean back. She almost perched on the forward edge of the couch, legs together, ankles off to one side and hands folded on her lap. She wore a suit, dull gray in color, very practical looking. Tom was reminded of a school teacher come to speak to a parent about some unpleasantness in a child's behavior.

"I've not been home yet," she said. "I came straight here, on the chance you would be home."

"You were in the North?"

Tom sat in a chair directly in front of her. They were separated by a low coffee table.

"Yes," she said. "Life can take some odd turns in Ireland."

"That's for sure," he said, as he leaned back and studied her face. "Anything new on Jimmy?"

She raised her chin up and shook her head no.

"Your ex has got to be one mean son of a bitch."

Meagan lowered her head. She appeared to be biting her lip. There was a pause, and then she said, "I need to ask you for something."

Tom leaned forward, opening his palms to her. "Ask away."

She looked directly at him, the sharp clear blue of her eyes holding him, almost physically. She took an audible breath. "This is difficult."

Tom sensed that he was about to be hurt; briefly, he was tempted to respond with just a tinge of sarcasm, to strike out in a defensive reaction to what he thought was coming next. Don't be stupid, he told himself. Hold your fire. You don't really know a damn thing. He waited for her to go on.

"Your report. The one to your friend in the Senate."

Tom sat up with his hands folded. "Yeah," he said, "what about it?"

"I went north to see the lawyer in Belfast. He didn't hold out much hope. I went to see Gregory."

Tom sat back now. Meagan rattled on, as if trying to get through some memorized pitch. She told him the story of her visit with her ex, and the new deal he wanted to make for Jimmy's release. She left out the part that had her going back to Gregory.

"He says he'll free Jimmy if you turn in a report that's really favorable to the Unionists." She raised and lowered her shoulders in a soft sigh indicating that she had gotten through it.

Tom lowered his hands. The point of her story surprised him. He needed time to react, to get his mind around the implications. He continued to stare at her. Not because he expected her to say more, or because he was about to say something to her, but only because he had no reason to look elsewhere while his mind scrambled for something to latch onto.

Meagan broke the silence. "I know it's asking a lot."

He nodded. "I need a minute to think."

Was this what it had all been about? A neighborly meeting, a casual friendship turned into a love affair; all for the sake of his lousy report? Could he have been that blind? That much in need? Got to think about Jimmy, though. Christ, I miss the kid. And maybe — *Maybe* it's all on the level!

Meagan bit her lip. "I'm not asking," she said, her hands visibly trembling. "In truth, I'm begging."

"Oh, no," he said, "Don't do that. I'm just thinking. We have to think of Jimmy. Jimmy comes first."

She was nodded yes, her eyes watery.

Tom stood up; hands jammed into his pockets, and started pacing around. "I'll do it," he said. "I'll do it, I just have to rethink some things. It can be done."

What else could he say? He needed time to regroup, to sort things out. She stood up. Why didn't she come to him? Why didn't she push herself against him; let him enfold her in his arms; kiss the tears away? Good God! He needed her to say something — to do *something* to reassure him; to let him know that he wasn't being tossed aside.

"I'm tired," she said. "Just exhausted. On that drink — I think I'll take — What do you call it? A rain check?"

He walked her to the door. He kissed her lightly on the cheek, and she walked out. He said he would call her. She took a last look into his eyes and then walked down the steps. Clouds were lowering, rolling in; hilltops had disappeared, and he felt the chill of cold mist.

ða ða ða

Meagan let herself in the front door. She put her umbrella down to dry off and then she sat on the bench next to the umbrella stand and boot rack. She heard a soft, half-hearted bark, and Kiki came padding in to nuzzle up to her.

"Always glad to see me. Aren't you, Kiki? Sorry I didn't bring Jimmy."

The Lab pushed her nose into Meagan's hand as if to reassure her and express faith in her ability to produce Jimmy next time. Meagan settled for a moment and then reached down to remove her shoes. She was just putting on a pair of slippers when Sarah came into the foyer.

"It's good to see you're back, Miss Clark. Didn't the rain come on very sudden?"

Meagan gestured at her umbrella, still open and dripping near the door. "Yes, as you can see, I didn't quite beat it home."

"You must be tired," Sarah said. "Can I fix something for you?"

"That would be very nice, Sarah. If you would just make a sandwich and put it in the refrigerator, I'll help myself later. Is my brother home?"

"He's in the library."

Sarah hesitated a moment to be sure that Meagan did not want anything more and then left. Meagan gave Kiki a pat on the head and then stood up. The dog followed her down the hall.

Philip had several books spread out on the heavy round oak table that occupied the center of the library. He was deeply engrossed in looking something up in one of them when Meagan entered. He glanced up over his reading glasses. "Ah, you're back," he said, proceeding to mark his page with a slip of paper before closing the book and removing his glasses.

He came over and took Meagan's right hand in both of his. He gently led her into the room, bending his head to look into her face as he did so. He brought her to one of the large wingback leather chairs and then quickly bent to scoop up a newspaper from the seat so that she could sit down. "It's not been a grand day?" he said.

Meagan had almost sprawled into the chair. She leaned her head against the protruding wing on one side, stared off at the fireplace and raised her hand to her mouth. She shook her head, no. There were decanters of whiskies and of sherry next to the fireplace. Philip went over and poured two drinks. He added a generous splash of water to Meagan's and a little to his own drink. "Here," he said, handing her a glass, "I hope I got it right."

Meagan took a sip and smiled her approval. She looked around the room. It should be bigger. We do so many things in here. Shelves covered every wall, lined with a mongrel collection of books, an occasional, matched leather-bound set, here and there to hint at what a proper library looked like. The lighting pleased her, bright where needed, but the use of green lampshades made the general effect soft and calm. Kiki settled at her feet, snuggling against an ankle.

"It's nice and cool in here," she said

"Must be the books. They make good insulation."

"I hardly know where to begin," she said.

"What happened with the lawyer?"

Meagan shook her head. "At best it will be a long drawn out process. He said that in the end it would probably be more a political decision than a legal one. I went to see Gregory."

Philip took a swig of his drink. "And, what did Mr. Pompous Ass have to say this time?"

"I was hoping that Jimmy might be getting under his skin by now," she said.

She went on and related the whole story of her meeting with Gregory and the new bargain he wanted to make. Philip listened, nodding his head in sympathy and making an occasional soft sound for emphasis. "And, you've been to see Tom?"

She nodded and moved forward in her chair. "I left out the business of my going back to Gregory."

"We mustn't let it come to that."

"I think I'd better eat something," she said, starting to get up. "Sarah made me a sandwich."

"I'll get it," Philip said. "You rest yourself."

He went out the door. Kiki got up looking to see what she should be doing next. Meagan put her hand on the dog's head and Kiki rested her head on Meagan's lap. She stroked the dog. "Sometimes I envy you, Kiki."

Philip reappeared with the sandwich, a glass of milk, and a napkin. He set the sandwich and milk on a small side table next to Meagan and sat down again facing her. Kiki lay back down at her feet.

"What was Tom's reaction?"

Meagan waited to get down a bite of the sandwich and a drink of milk. She cleared her mouth before answering. "He agreed to do it."

"Just like that?"

"For Jimmy's sake, he said."

Philip got up and walked over to the fireplace. He put his elbow on the mantel and turned to Meagan. "I would think that report would mean a lot to him; he obviously has a great deal of affection and respect for his friend."

"I think you're right," she said.

"I haven't known Tom that long, but he strikes me as a man of real integrity."

Meagan chewed on her sandwich and nodded her agreement.

"I wonder what he's thinking?" Philip said.

"If he said he'll do it, he'll do it," she said.

"How did *you* feel about it?"

"Oh, I don't know, Philip. I can't think straight. I want Jimmy back."

"We all want Jimmy back. I'm sure Tom is sincere about that."

Meagan swallowed and wiped her mouth with her napkin. "I felt so guilty having to ask him. I wonder if it can ever be the same with us."

"Did you tell him how you feel?"

She shook her head. "I just wanted to get it over with. I don't want to hurt Tom any more than I have to"

"How could he agree so quickly?" Philip said. "He's going to lie to his friend in the United States Senate and then tell him later that he did it for his lady friend's child?"

"What are you thinking?"

Philip went back and sat in his chair. Meagan moved forward in hers, and Kiki got up, trying to get Meagan to pet her. She ignored the dog.

"I'm just exploring here," Philip said

Meagan paid close attention. Her brother was a bit inept at times, impractical, forgetful. But when he set his mind to reasoning something through, he could be positively brilliant. She wanted every bit of help she could get.

"You know," Philip said, "Tom hasn't been in Ireland all that long. And I think he really loves you, but he's known you for only a few months. He's a smart man — very smart." Philip paused to see how Meagan was taking it so far. She said nothing. She was sitting with her mouth slightly open waiting for him to go on. "Suppose he's thinking that holding Jimmy hostage might not be real? That it's just an elaborate scheme to pressure him on that report?"

"What! Oh, My God, Philip. He couldn't possibly think that!" Meagan was up now, pacing around nervously.

Philip waited for her to stand still before he continued. "You're probably right. We just need to consider the possibilities. After all, you did send Jimmy up there."

She stood by the table, glaring at her brother. She looked to be on the verge of shouting some obscenity at him. Suddenly, her expression changed. "Oh, My God! I better call him."

She ran out of the room. Philip got up, pausing to stuff the last bite of Meagan's sandwich into his mouth on his way over to freshen up his drink. Meagan came slowly back into the room; her arms folded in front of her. "He's gone out."

Philip left his glass on the drink table. He went over and put his arm around her. "You can talk to him tomorrow. I'll go with you — just for support."

She sat down on the edge of her chair. She leaned slightly forward, keeping her arms folded tightly across her stomach. "I'm losing everything, Philip. How can I expect to keep Tom after this, no matter what he's thinking? And Gregory — even if Tom does what he wants — Gregory can thumb his nose at me and keep Jimmy."

Philip picked up Meagan's glass. With a gesture, he offered a refill. She shook her head, no. "Things always look better in the morning," he said.

"Not *always*," she said.

CHAPTER SIXTEEN

After Tom watched Meagan's car disappear at the end of the driveway, he stood glaring at the darkening clouds. As he listened to the first drops of rain, he almost relished the cold clammy feeling now penetrating his clothes. "Shit!" He turned to go inside where he heard Brid noisily closing a window in the office to his right. He turned the other way and went back into the living room. The red power-on light on the CD player caught his eye. He crossed over and placed his hand on the smooth black top. What should he play? Could anything possibly cheer him up? He turned it off.

Brid came in and went immediately to the open window. She closed it and then turned to him. "It's surely going to rain."

"Yes." He wished that she would just leave; he did not want to be short with her; he just wanted to be alone.

"Will you be wanting supper, Mr. Brogan?"

"No, Brid, I'll be going out later. Thanks."

He said nothing more. She hesitated a moment and then left. He was relieved at not having to make small talk. He hoped he hadn't been short with her; the Irish are so sensitive to things like that, and Tom would never get used having servants, nor would he develop the detachment that normally went along with it. It was raining now. Some large drops hit the window with a sound more like soft pebbles than water. He walked over and gazed out in the direction of Meagan's house, hidden behind a hill now covered with dying trees, looking all the more pitiful as they got wet.

He went to the table along the sidewall, opened a drawer and removed a pad of paper. He set it down and pulled over a chair. Sometimes putting problems on paper freed his mind from just rehashing the problems over and over in his head and let him think first about how to define them clearly. Solutions came easier after that.

He wrote, "Trees." The trees had lost some importance in the last hour. He wrote, "BIG DEAL!" Who the fuck cares about a bunch of trees; they're dying anyway. He wrote, "Meagan." It was not working; his thoughts were just getting more jumbled. How could she just ask him like that, without even discussing other ways to get Jimmy back? She seemed cold. Was she prepping herself to kiss him off? Was his function over? His time in the sunlight ended? His time to look at the sky and see joy in the waltz of the clouds? He wrote, "Jimmy" and then, "Is he, or isn't he?" He drew some strong lines across the paper; he tore it off the pad, crumpled it and then threw it into the basket with a whump!

Twenty minutes later, Tom sat on his usual stool down at one end of Frank's bar. Frank greeted him when he came in and was engaged in slowly, ever so slowly, pulling a pint for him. Why he had come to the pub, he did not know. He was not up for conversation and he didn't feel like drinking. Maybe it was for perspective. Frank had a way of doing that, a quiet observation that helped Tom see things just a little differently. Maybe if he just talked around the problem, things would look a little better.

"You might have the place to yourself tonight, Tom." Frank wiped the bar and put a coaster down in front of Tom while he waited for the last injection into Tom's pint to settle, leaving a creamy foam at the top.

"Yeah, lousy night."

"Might help with the trees though?"

"I don't think so, Frank. We're doing something radically wrong there. I need a real expert to figure it out."

"The government man wasn't much help then?"

"No, he made a few suggestions, but we had already tried them."

Frank took Tom's pint from under the tap. He wiped the bottom and set it down in front of Tom as if it were a glass of vintage champagne.

"You know anything about lawsuits between the Republic and the North?" Tom asked.

"You mean like on a business contract?"

"I was thinking about a divorce agreement."

"Ah." Frank nodded his head and moved away as a regular entered the bar. "Freddy, isn't it a night for getting wet?"

Freddy took his hat off and shook it to remove some water. Tom raised his glass and nodded to acknowledge Freddy's arrival. He was glad to see that Frank was setting up a coaster for him at another spot along the bar. When Freddy settled with his pint and started to watch the television, Frank returned. "Divorce?"

"Yes, if someone was divorced in the North and then moved to the Republic, could the terms be enforced down here?"

"You're involved with her then?"

"You could say that."

"She's a fine looking woman."

"Yeah."

"I know very little about such things," Frank said. "But of course, you do know that divorce is still rare here in the Republic. We've had our referendum, but .."

"You think they wouldn't enforce something decided in the North?"

"That's what I would think, but you should talk to somebody like John Flaherty. I don't know the man, but I understand that he's a very good solicitor."

Tom took a healthy drink. "I think I better go get something to eat," he said.

"On a night like tonight, you'll do no such thing. I'll get Mary to fix you a bite."

Tom started to protest but changed his mind when another regular came in shaking off copious amounts of water.

❦ ❦ ❦

Meagan got out of bed. She could tell from the light on the window shade that the sun was just coming up, or would be very soon. She had been lying there, wide-awake, for some time. Probably she had gotten some sleep during the night, but not much. She went into the bathroom, flicked on the light and looked in the mirror. Oh God. Maybe I'll look better later when it's time to go over and see Tom.

When she finished in the bathroom, she put her toothbrush back in the rack, dried her hands, turned off the light and went back to her bedroom to raise the window shade. Yes, the sun was just coming up. It came glancing through the trees, softened by the mist rising from the ground. Tree trunks and branches glistened with a wetness that looked like a golden-silver paint. The valleys and low spots were still gray and filled with a thick fog. Every surface on every plant and structure was wet. The sky was yellow, going into blue, and high wispy clouds promised a beautiful dry day.

She put on field pants, a denim shirt, boots and a light canvas jacket. Back in the bathroom she added some lipstick, ran a brush through her hair and pinned it back with a barrette. She examined the result in the mirror. Good enough for a walk in the woods. Philip would not be up for hours, and she wanted him to go with her over to Tom's.

Downstairs she found Sarah padding around in slippers and bathrobe. Kiki was scratching to get back inside.

"She's never where she wants to be," Sarah said. "When she's in she wants out. When she's out she wants in."

"You can leave her out, I'll take her for a walk."
"Will you be wanting breakfast?"
"No, I'll wait and have some with my brother."
Meagan took an apple off the counter and headed out the door.

≈ ≈ ≈

Tom sat on the edge of his bed feeling old. He had gotten to bed early but never got his mind clear enough to sleep. When he finally convinced himself that thinking about his problems was a waste, visions of Meagan kept pushing into his imagination. Her neck, her breasts, the sweet, musky smell of her skin when he nuzzled and caressed her, the feel of her skin under his fingertips, radiating a heat that passed through his fingers into his entire body. He got up and walked to the window. The sun was just about to come up.

He had arranged to meet Kevin in the back field. They were to meet early so that Kevin could make his regular job on time. He dressed and went downstairs; Brid was not up yet. That was okay, he needed some quiet time; besides, she never really mastered the knack of making good coffee. Tom got a pot going — probably wouldn't be any better than Brid's. He went to the refrigerator and took out an apple and a piece of cheese. He sat down to peel the apple and wait for the coffee.

I have to get out of here — to get some perspective on all this. To talk to somebody. He started to inventory the people he knew in Ireland. Don't know anybody that well who could handle the whole thing. Nobody but Meagan.

"Meagan, Meagan, look, you've got me talking to myself."

Helene. She's the one. If I go over, I can see the tree professor while I'm there, and I can talk to Jerry. Maybe, he'll have an angle on this report problem that I haven't thought of.

The coffee was ready. He poured some into a large mug and carried it out the door.

He spotted Kevin out in the middle of the field and walked over to him. Kevin pulled a dead-looking seedling out by the roots and held it up for Tom's inspection. "These are the ones we gave extra fertilizer, last week."

Tom simply nodded and cupped his hands around his coffee cup for the warmth. Kevin continued, "It didn't make any difference. They're dying like the rest. The only ones not dying are up on the hill over there, and we did nothing with them at all."

"I know you've tried your best, Kevin. I think we should leave well enough alone, for now. We need some special help. Maybe I need to get somebody from the States."

"That professor you wrote to, he hasn't answered yet?"

"No, I'll contact him again. Perhaps he should come over and see the problem firsthand."

Kevin stood with his head down. He allowed the seedling to slip from his hand. "I'm sorry it's not working like we planned," he said.

Tom nodded and slowly walked away. Then he stopped and turned to Kevin. "Come back to the house for a few minutes. I may need a ride into town."

He called Aer Lingus. The New York flight was leaving two hours late. There was still space available if he could get there. Charter Air had a plane available in Galway; they would pick him up at the airstrip in Carrick-on-Shannon and get him to Shannon International on time.

❧ ❧ ❧

Meagan felt better as she arrived back at the house. The sun was full up, things were drying off, and Kiki's exuberance was infectious. Meagan had walked about three miles; she estimated that Kiki had run at least twelve. Kiki liked to run ahead where she flushed out lots of birds, but she constantly came back to check on Meagan, and of course, to get some approval for the fine job she was doing. Her last job was to run into the barn and check on the horses while Meagan waited for her at the back door. A little breakfast, a little makeup, and then, she could have a heart-to-heart talk with Tom. Just as I should have last night. Maybe he can think of some other way to get Jimmy back. Maybe he can get his friend, Jerry, to help. Philip was right. Things do look better in the morning.

Philip was in the dining room having some breakfast. His mouth was full, so he raised his teacup in greeting as she entered.

"You're up early," she said.

He waited to swallow. "I knew you'd be anxious."

"Right!" she said, sitting down. "I'll have a bit of breakfast, and then see what I can do about my face."

Sarah came in, set a pot of tea down in front of Meagan, and then left.

"He's not there," Philip said.

"Oh?"

"He called to say that he was leaving."

"When will he be back?"

"That wasn't clear. He's gone back to America."

Meagan slowly and deliberately poured some tea. "Was that *all* he said?"

"He said something about getting help for his trees and turning in his report."

"But nothing about when he would be back?"

"No."

❧ ❧ ❧

The cab turned off Woodcliff Avenue onto Corrine Lane. Tom leaned against the door so he could look upward at the tall oak trees lined up along the curb on each side of the street. The leaves were at their fullest and heaviest, clearly indicating that it was late summer.

"Nice neighborhood," the cabby said.

"Yes, I haven't seen it in a while, but nothing seems to have changed."

They were passing the spot where Barbara had been killed. What was a drunk driver doing speeding down a street like this? Where did he think he was going? The same questions. What difference did it make — no matter what the answers were? There was no one in sight. A lazy summer afternoon in New Jersey. No, it was later than that, almost six. The neighbors must be out in their back yards or on their back porches. Would Helene be home? He pointed out the house for the cabby.

"Wow! Some place. Must have cost a bundle."

"Thanks, we bought it some time ago."

"Lucky."

Tom counted out six twenties, and a seventh for the tip. It had been an expensive day. It did not look as if Helene was home; there were no signs of life in the house, and no car. Had Helene gotten his message? Shit, if she didn't get it, this could be embarrassing. Would he walk in and find the belongings of a live-in boyfriend all over the house? He left his bag on the driveway and walked around the side of the house. Grass is a little high, not bad overall, not seedy looking. Hope she's not doing it all herself.

He began to focus on specifics: the plants that Barbara had put in and nurtured, the rhododendron that she had wanted him to cut back, the curved flower bed along the fence. Whose house was this? It did not feel as much like his home as he had thought it would. Had Helene begun to put her own stamp on it? Inside, perhaps? Could it ever be anything but Barbara's? Barbara's in every nook and cranny? Encompassing and exuding the essence of Barbara?

He wandered back to pick up his bag. Had Helene changed the security code? He did not need a visit from the Woodcliff Lake police. The code was based on the date he had met Barbara, October 10, 1954. How many thieves would have access to that information? They can get your birthday, social security number, and just about any other number that you might find easy to remember. But, the day you met your wife? Not likely. He punched the code into the system. It worked. Inside, he set his suitcase down and went into the kitchen. Tidy Helene had left a cereal dish in the sink, but everything else was neat as a pin. The living room too. No sign of a boyfriend so far. He decided to sit down and not look anywhere else until Helene came home. At that moment, her car appeared in the driveway, and he went outside to greet her. She's alone. Thank God, I don't want to share tonight.

Helene jumped out of her car "Sorry I wasn't here when you got home."

They hugged each other. Tom squeezed her and kissed the top of her head and forehead. When they released each other, Helene stepped to the back of her car.

"I stopped to get some things for dinner," she said. "Help me carry them in."

"I had planned to take you out," he said, taking some bags out of the trunk.

"No," she said. "Not tonight."

Inside, they put the bags on the counter. Helene started to put things away.

"You can sleep wherever you like," she said, "I'm still in my old room."

"I'll figure it out later," he said. "I'll probably stick with the guest room."

"Why don't you pour yourself a drink?" she said. "You can keep me company while I fix dinner."

"You want one?"

"No," she said, "but we can have some wine with dinner."

Tom went into the dining room and opened the sideboard, which served as a liquor cabinet. It looked as if he had never been away. A bottle of Jameson's, almost full, a half bottle of Glenfidich, another of Black Bush, and a full bottle of sherry — Barbara's. No parties? No company, in all this time? He poured some Black Bush into a Waterford crystal tumbler — a gift from

Helene. Back in the kitchen he added some ice from the freezer and left his drink on the counter.

"What are we having?" he asked.

"Fish. I got some haddock."

"White wine then. Will I find some downstairs?"

Helene looked at him with an expression of mock exasperation. "I *think* so," she said.

He went down to the basement. The wine rack was, more or less, as he had left it. She hasn't been drinking any wine either. He picked out a bottle of Chalk Hill, Sauvignon Blanc. Pretty good, as I recall. Upstairs, he put the wine in the freezer to chill. He sat on a stool behind the counter, took a sip of his drink. Helene had the broiler going; the fish sat on a pan, waiting. She had her hands in a salad bowl, mixing some lettuce.

"I haven't done this since the time John was here playing chef," Tom said. "That was right after I was fired by Newcomer."

"And this time you've been deported from Ireland?" she asked.

"No, they're pretty tolerant. You've got to be a real weirdo to be deported from Ireland. No. It's the trees. A lot of them are dying. I need some help from Professor Gleason, the guy from Cornell."

"It must be a real emergency, for you to fly here on such short notice."

"Well, I've also got that report I'm doing for Jerry. I need to turn it in."

"It's a *verbal* report?"

"Not exactly."

Helene opened the oven door and slid the fish in. "Should be about fifteen minutes," she said. "I'm disappointed that you didn't bring Meagan."

Tom slid off his stool. "I better get that wine out," he said.

She watched him as he removed the wine from the freezer and put it into the refrigerator. He went back to his stool and took a sip of his drink.

"How is she?"
"Meagan?"
"*Yes*, Meagan."
"She's, uh, having a problem."
"Oh?"
"Yes. It has to do with Jimmy. Her son."
"Uh, huh?"
"It's a long story."
"I'm beginning to get that feeling. The fish won't wait. Why don't you open the wine, and we'll talk about it after supper. You do intend to tell it to me?"
"Yeah. Actually, that's another reason why I came home. I need to talk to somebody."
"I'm glad you're here," she said.
For the next ten minutes, little was said. Tom poured the wine; Helene set the table, lit some candles and served the meal with Tom's help. They sat down and raised their glasses.
"Here's to Barbara," he said.
"Yes," she said, "and I hope to Meagan as well."
The conversation switched to family matters, mostly an update on John, Anne and Catherine, the new grandchild. Tom kidded Helene about her tendency to use superlatives when describing Catherine's intelligence and beauty.
"And I suppose you just stick the pictures that Anne sends to you in a drawer someplace?" she said.
"You got me. She's pretty cute. The pictures are all mounted and on display."
They finished eating, and Tom got up to clear the dishes. Helene got up as well.
"We can finish our wine in the living room," she said. "Should I make a pot of decaf?"
"Good idea."
They finished cleaning up, loaded the dishwasher, and went into the living room. When they were seated, Tom waited another minute and then started.

"This is complicated. Why don't I just give you the bottom line and then tell you how I got there."

"Okay," she said, as she took a sip of her wine and watched him lean forward folding his hands and wringing his fingers together.

"I love her. You know that. I don't know when it happened, it just did. The problem is, I'm not sure that she loves me."

"Has she ever said that she did?"

"Yes, but there's this whole thing about Northern Ireland, Jimmy, Gregory, her ex-husband, this damned report I'm doing for Jerry. There may be some kind of game being played, and I'm feeling like I'm the only one that doesn't know what's really going on."

"Whoa, Dad. Slow down. Why don't you just tell me what happened."

Tom stopped and looked at her. She's doing it. She was doing exactly what he would do. All his life he had been dealing with emotional situations by getting people to concentrate on the facts. Slow down. Get the facts out. People can deal with facts, talk things through. It never worked with Barbara though. She claimed he was not really listening to her. Now he had a chance to see if he could take his own medicine. Carefully, and as objectively as he could, he reconstructed the situation. He told her of Meagan's defense of the Unionists whenever they discussed Northern Ireland, of her telling him that she had contacts in the North that might have been used to help Brendan. He told her of the IRA sending messages to him about her meeting with Gregory, her ex-husband, in a hotel, about her sending Jimmy to Northern Ireland in the first place.

He also repeated everything that Meagan had told him about her trips to the North and the rather cool way she had asked him to falsify his report. Helene interrupted only a few times for a brief clarification. When he had finally finished, Tom sat back and made a gesture with his hands to signal the end. He sat in silence, looking around the room, seeing and recognizing some items for the first time since he arrived: the pictures, including

Barbara's portrait; the carving of a hiker, a present from John when he was twelve; the Waterford Crystal vase from an early trip to Ireland.

Helene took her time before saying anything. "Dad, if the tree problem doesn't get solved for another six months, or a year, how big a deal is that?"

"As long as it gets solved," he said, "it's not that big."

"And the report? If Jerry cooperates, there might be ways to handle that in a way that satisfies the Unionists?"

"I suppose."

"Do you want some coffee?" she asked

"Not now."

"Okay then," she said, "here's my bottom line. I hope you'll be able to accept it."

He looked at her and waited.

She continued, "I think Meagan's the one that's getting the short end. I think that you left her just when she needs you, desperately."

"What?"

"Hear me out. You're expecting too much. Her son has been taken from her. You can't expect her to act in a totally rational way, to be considerate of *your* feelings. A mother will kill for her child; she will do anything, clutch at straws, anything that might seem to help in getting him back. She loves you, but she can't think about you, or anything else until she gets Jimmy back. Think of what Mom would have done, if one of her children was being held."

This last statement felt almost like a punch, or a red-hot knife, burning his heart.

"Yeah, you're right. Hard to imagine your mother hurting anyone. But for her kids — she would kill. But how do you explain Meagan's behavior?"

"There are all kinds of other things to look at, Dad. First of all, she's had a life in the Republic for years before you showed up. She has a job; she's been sending Jimmy to a Catholic school.

And this ex-husband — where's he been all this time? And lest we forget, you moved next to her — not the other way round. How could that have been set up?"

"So you think I'm all wet?"

"You've had a lot on your plate, Dad. A lot of stress. I think that you've over-reacted. I think that Meagan needs you. The woman is probably exhausted. How can she behave normally? Besides, suppose I'm wrong. Why should you be the one to end it? Let it play out. You don't want to lose her if she really does love you."

"That's for sure."

"Coffee?"

They both got up, picking up their empty wineglasses. He followed her into the kitchen, noticing on the way the bookshelves holding another picture of Barbara, a small trophy he had won playing racquetball, and the ornate clock he had given her for some wedding anniversary. There was the fancy crystal chandelier in the dining room, the one that he bought to replace the original when he made his first million. Barbara didn't want it; never liked it. What am I doing here? Discussing another woman — with my daughter, for Christ's sake. He half expected Barbara to step out and say, "What's this I hear about some woman named Meagan?" But inside, he knew it was okay, he knew that Barbara would approve.

In the kitchen, Helene reached up into a cabinet for some cups. Tom looked at her, thinking — not for the first time — that she had grown into a beautiful woman. Perhaps, more beautiful than her mother.

"You're beautiful," he said, in a simple statement of fact.

She turned to him, surprised at first, but then she smiled.

He said, "You can't tell me that there aren't a dozen guys chasing after you."

"There's only one that matters."

"Aah, when do I meet this guy and get him to state his intentions?"

"It's a little early for that, Dad. And — things are a little different these days."

"I can only imagine."

"Hmm, we were talking about Meagan, remember?" Helene had poured the coffee.

Tom picked up a cup and went to sit at the counter. "Yeah, I guess I should go right back, heh?"

Helene stood on the other side of the counter drinking her coffee. She took the cup down from her lips. "Yes, I think so."

"I better talk to Jerry," Tom said. He looked at his watch. "Maybe I can catch him now."

"I'm going upstairs to get ready for bed," she said. "I'll be back down."

❦ ❦ ❦

Helene went upstairs and down the hall to the room that had been hers since she was four years old. How many times had it been redecorated? The last time entirely to her own tastes. My God! Even in high school, how could I have done this? Look at those curtains. And Kevin, you've got to go. She went over and took out the pins holding a Kevin Costner publicity shot on the bulletin board over her bureau.

She would be moving out soon. No definite plans, but living, no — rattling around, in this large house in a neighborhood of families and older couples was not exactly what she had in mind for her post college, swinging single years. I'll talk to Dad as soon as this Meagan business settles.

Meagan. God, I hope I'm right about her. Suppose she is just playing a game? Dad sure would have been an easy mark. Recently widowed, alone in a foreign country, a beautiful woman.

She got into pajamas, a bathrobe and went back downstairs.

"It's all set," Tom said. "Jerry's going to play along, but I need your help."

"Great, Dad. *What's* all set?"

"Right — I told him about my problem, at least the nut of it, and here's what he suggested. He can wait a month for the real report. Meanwhile, we turn in a phony one, just a stack of blank paper, and he leaks that it favors the Unionist side."

"Sounds good," she said. "How does he do this leaking business?"

"I don't know. They do it all the time in Washington. I imagine that Jerry is pretty good at it by now. The idea is to let the information out to a few people, just enough so that the Unionists can find out that the report is what they wanted. Gregory should release Jimmy when he's informed."

She poured herself a cup of decaf and sat at the kitchen counter.

He said, "I need you to hand carry the dummy report, and to be seen turning it over. I can be back in Ireland tomorrow."

"Okay, I'll do it, if that's what you need. But what happens if Gregory doesn't give Jimmy back?"

"You mean, what do I do about the report?"

"No, I mean, what happens with Meagan?"

"That will depend on Meagan. I'm prepared to wait, or take some action, if she wants me to."

"You mean, like snatching Jimmy back?"

"No, that would be too dangerous. Maybe, Meagan can come up with some ideas."

Helene shook her head, slowly. "Okay, but that's not what I was asking. I mean, what if I'm wrong?"

"And she's playing a game?"

"Yes."

Tom rinsed his cup and put it in the sink. He turned to face her, leaning his butt against the counter. "I hear you. The way I see it, if she doesn't love me, I'm wiped. It doesn't matter what the rest of the story is. I'm not going back with any illusions. I just can't afford not to know."

CHAPTER SEVENTEEN

The clouds were high, higher than he had ever seen before; at least as far as he could remember. How nice to come back to the farm on a sunny day for a change. According to the weather forecast, it might not rain tomorrow either. Tom looked at his watch, which he had not bothered to reset for his trip to New Jersey. Wow, eight o'clock, not much daylight left.

He went in the front door and immediately heard Brid scurrying to see who was there. "Oh, Mr. Brogan!" she said, "you're back so soon." She came over to him and reached for his small carry-on bag. She studied his face. "Is everything all right?"

"I think so, Brid," he said, holding onto his bag. "I'll take this up. Am I too late for a sandwich?"

"Of course not," she said. "I made some fresh bread today."

"I'll have a beer with it," he said and then went up the stairs

He put the bag on his bed. I should call her right now. He sat on the bed, looking at the phone. I've been thinking about it for ten hours, and I still don't know what to say. The truth? Hell, if Helene is right, that would really blow it. The trees? I didn't even call Professor Gleason. I'll have to make up a complete story for why I left so suddenly. I'll just ask if I can come over. I'll tell her that I felt it was important to hand-carry the report and not to lose any time. I'll watch her reaction. If I'm careful, maybe she'll give me some clues, and I can take it from there. He picked up the phone.

Philip answered, "Tom, I never expected you'd be back so soon. Meagan's not here."

"Will you have her call me as soon as she gets back?"

"I will, Tom. I will, but it may be a while."

"Is that right?"

"We need to talk."

Tom took a deep breath; this was a new wrinkle. "I'll come over in about a half hour."

He washed his face and hands, put on a clean shirt and went downstairs to eat his sandwich. Brid wanted to chat; she asked him about his trip.

"I'm sorry, Brid. I'm that tired, and I need to think about something. I'll be better company tomorrow."

She gave him her best look of motherly sympathy and left him.

What the hell is Philip going to tell me? Is he the messenger? "Meagan asked me to tell you how sorry she is etc., etc." Christ! Wait till Helene hears this.

Philip met him at the door with a simple nod and led him down the hall. At least, Kiki was still there and happy to see him. They went into the living room, and Philip offered a drink. Tom declined, and Philip sat down across the coffee table, directly facing him.

There was an awkward pause; Philip cleared his throat, "Meagan's not been herself."

"Yes?"

"Tremendous stress, you know — this business with Jimmy."

Tom sighed. "We're all distressed, but certainly, Meagan's borne the brunt of it."

"She can't think straight, Tom. She can't make decisions."

Tom hesitated and studied Philip; he was taking an unexpected tack, "So what are you telling me?"

Philip leaned forward and locked his eyes on Tom. "I think it's time for others to act."

Tom was not at all sure that he was hearing the real message. He waved his hands at Philip for him to "come on."

Philip sat straight up. "I'm planning to abduct Jimmy."

When it sunk in, Tom started to shake his head, his hands flopping around in small random gestures. "You? You're going to snatch Jimmy?"

Philip smiled. "I know what you're thinking, but I've got it planned out, and I've got help."

Tom sat back in his chair and put his hand up to rub his chin, "Good god, Philip, this is crazy. You can't endanger Jimmy. And what if you get caught?"

Philip sat, nodding at Tom.

"And, why are you telling me this?" Tom asked.

"So that you can help."

Tom bent forward and laughed. "You've got to be kidding. If I'm not in jail, Meagan will want to kill me." He got up to walk around behind his chair, "Whatever gave you this idea, in the first place?"

Philip got up and moved toward the door. "I'll tell you, but first I need a glass of water. Would you like one?"

"Sure."

Philip disappeared, and Tom walked over to the mantel; he looked closely at Meagan's picture, the one that had caught his eye on his first visit, and in the glass covering a picture of Jimmy sporting a toothy smile, he saw his own reflection. There has got to be a way to bring some sanity into this.

Philip returned with two glasses of water, which he placed on the coffee table before sitting down. Tom returned to his seat, and they both drank some water; Philip downed some pills with his.

Philip put his glass down and began. "I know that you don't think of me as a man of action, or much of a risk taker, and normally, you would be right on both counts. The fact is that I don't expect to live very long, and that changes things." He stopped to take a sip of water and to affirm that Tom was listening. "You probably think that I'm a hypochondriac, but I honestly don't know how many years I've got left."

Tom nodded, "So what's the rush. Maybe, things will work out sooner than you think."

"Whatever it is, my time will be shorter without Meagan and Jimmy. And, Tom, I don't want to die alone. I'm dreadfully afraid of that happening."

Tom's left elbow was on the arm of his chair, and two fingers pressed against his cheek. He stared at Philip while gathering his thoughts. "I feel for you, Philip. I really do, but I'll probably stop you from doing this thing. You know that, don't you?"

Philip looked at him and nodded, as if he had said exactly what was expected.

"There's part of this that you don't know, a part that's important to both of us," Philip said. "And, if you do stop me, I'll find another way, without you."

Tom pressed his lips together, thinking that it would be best not to confront Philip or frustrate him. Best to hear him out and then try to reason with him. "Okay, I'm listening," he said.

Philip said, "Meagan didn't tell you everything. She couldn't bring herself to it; she loves you that much. That she loves you is as clear to me as your sitting there. What she didn't — what she couldn't tell you — is that Gregory wants her back. He's made it part of the bargain. She's there now."

Tom sat like a stone; he drew in a deep breath and pushed it out through his nostrils. He said nothing.

"She plans to escape, of course. But he knows that; he'll watch her like a hawk; never let her out alone with Jimmy. She'll have to build up his confidence, make him sure of her. It will take a long time. Time that I don't have — and you don't either." Philip raised his hands in a gesture indicating that he was finished.

Tom bent his head down, covered his eyes and rubbed his forehead. He sat back up, "I almost wish that you hadn't told me." He let out a long sigh. "Don't we still have to think of Jimmy's safety?"

Philip leaned well forward, "I'll die before I put Jimmy in danger. The plan is safe; I'm the only one at risk."

"Hmmn, I think I'll have that drink."

Tom got up and went to the sideboard. Philip sipped his water and waited. Tom came back, placed his drink on the table and sat down. "Okay," he said, "shoot."

"I've already arranged for a brief visit with Meagan and Jimmy. Meagan asked Gregory, and he gave his permission — probably to soften her up. Gregory has a very low opinion of me; thinks I can't tie my shoes. I should be able to get out of the house with Jimmy for a soda, or something. I have friends, some very dear friends from college days; they'll hide Jimmy and me. They're in the tourist business. They'll arrange for papers and transportation to London when it's safe."

Tom shook his head. "So you're going to be hiding out in Northern Ireland where secrets last about as long as an ice-cream cone on the fourth of July — until it's safe. And what's Meagan doing all this time?"

"That's where you come in. It will be up to you to get her across the border. She'll be upset."

Tom chuckled. "Yeah, right. She'll be upset all right."

Philip leaned forward again. "Do you love her?"

Tom just looked at him.

"How can you stand leaving her with that — that — that god damned son of a bitch?"

Tom took his time; Philip was getting upset, but at the same time, his own stomach was churning and binding. He leaned forward, forearms on thighs. He looked at his hands; they were trembling.

"I'll do it without you. I will," Philip said.

Tom sat up. "I believe you."

"Then?"

"Then, I've got to think." He took a healthy swig of his drink and sat back. "The longer you stay in Northern Ireland, the more surely something will go wrong. If you're going to do this thing, you've got to get everybody across the border before Gregory and his bunch can react."

"Tom, if you're in, I'll go whatever way you say."

"Yeah, well, I haven't got a way." Tom got up. "Let me sleep on it."

Philip got up to accompany him to the door. "It will be grand with your help, and safe for Jimmy. And Meagan will be pleased once it's over; the poor woman needs help."

Tom laughed on his way out. "We'll *all* need help before this is over."

ટ▲ ટ▲ ટ▲

Meagan held back the curtain and gazed out the window of Jimmy's room. Ostensibly, she had come upstairs to straighten things out, but she hadn't touched a thing, only wandered about between the guest room, which she occupied, and Jimmy's room. It was raining, a dull gray gloomy rain which added to her malaise. She was in prison. She could come and go at any time — without Jimmy — but it was a prison nonetheless. It even looked like a prison with its chainlink, barbed wired fence in the back and the wrought iron one in the front. There was a strange car in the driveway, and the gate, with its remote control, had closed behind it. She moved from the window and sat on the bed.

This was the start of her third day; she had come without any plan other than being with Jimmy and if possible, staying out of Gregory's bed until she could escape with Jimmy. It would be difficult; he was already putting on the pressure. When he agreed to let Philip visit, he rather cheerfully stated that he could sleep in the guestroom. There was no doubt about where he intended her to sleep. He would probably send the couch out for "repairs."

Jimmy waltzed in and plunked himself down next to her. This is what it was all about; he had been bubbling since she arrived.

He had also been asking some awkward questions about why they could not go anywhere without Daddy.

"Mr. Murray's here," he said. "We'll be going to Belfast tomorrow."

She gave him a little squeeze. "Have you brushed your teeth yet?"

He got up and flopped his feet toward the door.

"I haven't done mine either," she said, getting up to follow him, "We can brush together."

They went down the hall, passing the door to Claire, the housekeeper's room, or, as Meagan had begun to think of her, Claire, the assistant warden.

After they finished brushing, she led him into the guestroom. "I have a little present for you. This looks like just the day to give it to you." She handed him the small package — quite obviously a book. "Actually, it's from Tom, but don't breathe a word of that to your father."

Jimmy tore off the paper, Riders of the Purple Sage. He flipped to the frontispiece. "Wow!"

"I understand Zane Grey to be a famous American writer," she said.

Jimmy started to page through, looking for more pictures.

She sat on the bed and watched him, knowing that he would soon be lost in a corner somewhere. "Who is Mr. Murray?"

Jimmy closed his book and sat in the only chair. "He comes every week and gives Daddy money."

"Really. What's the money for? Does your father say?"

Jimmy shook his head. He was swinging his legs and looking toward the window, "It's in an envelope; Daddy counts it after he leaves." He looked back at her "He writes it in a book, and then he locks everything in his desk, and the next day, we go to Belfast."

Meagan got up to look and listen at the door. She turned back to Jimmy, "And you see all this?"

He shrugged. "I'm just around sometimes." He got up, leaving the book on the chair. He raised his arms. "Mom! Last time we went to the Heritage Park. You would really like it!"

"I'm sure. What else do you do in Belfast?"

"Oh, we just stop places." He retrieved his book. "I usually wait in the car."

She tousled his hair and kissed him on the forehead, "Let me know if I can help you with the book."

༄ ༄ ༄

Tom opened his eyes and, without moving his head, glanced at the windows; the sunlight on the curtains told him it was later than his usual seven o'clock wakening. He lazily raised his arm so that he could see his watch with a minimum of effort. Shit! Ten o'clock; what a night. He rolled over and sat up by swinging his legs over the bedside. He yawned, stretched his arms overhead, and rolled his head around to loosen the cricks. Then he reached for the phone.

"Philip, I've been up half the night thinking. I'm going to go north and see if we can get some help with this thing. Something that will get you and Jimmy back here, fast."

"What do you have in mind, Tom?"

"Nothing specific, and I don't want to discuss any details over the phone — with anybody. I'll see you in a couple of days. Sit tight."

"I'm scheduled to visit Meagan and Jimmy next week."

"I know. Wish me luck."

He called Daniel O'Coyle and left a message for him to return the call as soon as possible. Then he put on a bathrobe and went down to see Brid.

"Ah, Mr. Brogan, you're that tired from your trip. I'll put on the coffee right away."

"I'm going to take a quick shower. If a Daniel O'Coyle calls, tell him I'll get right back to him. By the way, I'm starved."

O'Coyle called just before he got in the shower. They arranged to meet the following morning. While eating his breakfast, he told Brid that he would be leaving again in a few hours.

"You've barely had time to shake off the dust. You'll need a good rest when you get back. Will you be seeing Missus Clark before you go?"

"She's gone up to see Jimmy for a bit. I hope to see them both soon."

"Well, she's certainly a good mother then, isn't she? Such a fine lad he is."

Tom made the now familiar trip to Derry. He stopped for a bite to eat in Strabane. It suited his mood to stop there instead of waiting to have dinner in Derry where every place he turned stirred feelings: memories of Barbara, thoughts of Meagan and how he had called her from there.

Strabane is a plain, matter-of fact, kind of place which reminded him of places like Youngstown, Ohio, or some of the old industrial towns in upstate New York. It was a place where he could eat and keep his mind on business, the business of snatching Jimmy.

O'Coyle greeted him in his usual cheery way, the welcome of a practiced politician, but one without the usual edge of saccharin which makes the greeted feel a bit silly. O'Coyle was either genuinely glad to see him, or one hell of an actor. His mouth opened slightly when, instead of following him, Tom grabbed his sleeve.

"I had in mind to take a drive — just the two of us."

O'Coyle turned and then bent to say a few quiet words to the receptionist before following Tom to his car. Tom drove out along Strand Road until they came to a spot with a view of Lough Foyle. Along the way, O'Coyle made casual conversation as if he and Tom did this sort of thing every day. When they parked, he said nothing and waited for Tom to begin.

Tom rolled down his window and gazed off into the distance before he turned back and said, "We haven't known each other for very long, but I believe that you're a man who can keep a secret."

O'Coyle smiled and nodded; he looked at Tom. "Whatever it is, you have my bond."

"I need a really big favor. I need to sneak somebody across the border."

O'Coyle pushed out his lower lip, "That shouldn't be too difficult; they hardly stop anybody these days."

"This is different."

"I'm beginning to see that."

Again, Tom looked off and then exhaled a deep breath before continuing, "You know that I've been seeing this woman. Her name is Meagan."

O'Coyle nodded.

"I'm very involved. She has a son, Jimmy. He went to visit his father, her ex-husband. The father's hanging on to him." He paused, "Meagan can't give up her son."

"I can guess the rest of it." O'Coyle said.

Tom waited.

O'Coyle let out a long sigh and sat still, watching a small boat wending its way up the Lough. Without moving, he said, "You realize what would happen to me if I were implicated in any way?"

"Yes."

O'Coyle turned back to him. "This is Gregory McDonald we're talking about? The Unionist leader in Portadown?"

Tom nodded.

"And, you think that I could find it in my heart to do that man a bit of dirt?"

Tom laughed.

O'Coyle put his hand up to his chin and paused a moment before asking, "What does Jimmy look like?"

"He's eight, a little tall for his age, blue eyes, reddish-brown hair — a good looking kid."

O'Coyle nodded. "How would he look as a girl?"

Tom grinned. "I'd have to sell him on the idea, but he'd make a cute girl."

O'Coyle gestured out his window. "Care for a stretch of the legs?"

They got out and strolled along the sidewalk at the edge of the hill, both taking in the sweep of the Lough down the hill and off in the distance.

"If those waters could speak, heh?" O'Coyle said.

"Yes, the waters of Ireland reek with history, don't they?"

"They certainly do," O'Coyle said. "I know this woman who lives across the border, in Monaghan. She's a good party member; done a few things for us in the past. She can keep a secret. She has a daughter, Irene, about ten years old — also a little tall for her age."

"With blue eyes?"

O'Coyle nodded. "A darling little thing, and you should see her step dancing. I'll get Mrs. Foley to come up with Irene's passport."

"Sounds great. We also need to talk about Philip, Meagan's brother. He's going to get Jimmy out and turn him over to me."

O'Coyle raised his hands, "Ah, no. This is my limit. Philip will have to fend for himself."

ฌ ฌ ฌ

She was expecting it, part of the almost constant pushing, the hints that she should begin to think of herself in the role of proper wife.

"We'll be going up to Belfast tomorrow," Gregory said, "Jimmy and me. I was thinking that you might want to join us. We'll have dinner at a fancy place — and maybe stay over?"

He had picked an odd time, probably calculated to exert maximum pressure on her. They were seated at the dinner table with Jimmy; Claire stood to one side, by the buffet, obviously waiting to hear her answer. Meagan wondered, What was her role in this? Was she in on the whole thing, or had Gregory made up some preposterous story to account for his ex-wife's presence?

Was she jealous, resentful of another woman's presence? Meagan glanced in her direction — a look to suggest that she leave the room, but Claire just stood there, her face set hard.

Meagan turned back to Gregory, "I think not," she said with no modifying explanation. She thought that she detected the merest flick of his eyes in Claire's direction.

"Well then, we'll definitely not stay over. Wouldn't want to be away any longer than necessary."

Meagan nodded. "That will eliminate at least one added expense." With this she turned and again looked directly at Claire, who averted her eyes and turned to leave. Meagan looked back to Gregory, "I wonder that you can afford all this," she gestured at the surroundings, "on a local leader's pay?"

He studied her, seemingly thinking about whether he should answer, or change the subject. "It is rather grand isn't it? But then, you needn't worry about the money. There are other sources." He stopped.

"Really?"

He waited. "Yes, I'm very much in demand for extra appearances. I get paid for that, you know."

"How nice."

Gregory left the next morning with Jimmy. Shortly after, Meagan announced to Claire that she was going out for a walk and might have lunch with some old friends. She then went to a small bakery on the corner and waited. Claire left the house and headed in the opposite direction — toward the shopping district. Meagan returned and reentered the house.

She went directly to the office. It was locked. Nothing fancy, just one of those old fashioned door locks, the keyhole just below the knob. Surely, Gregory wouldn't bother to carry such a large key around in his pocket. She knew him to be a creature of habit and was prepared for the desk to be locked. He liked to hide things in books.

She planned to look for the desk key in the books on his desk. Where would he hide the door key? Perhaps, she could pick the lock, as she had seen people do in movies. She decided to look in his bedroom.

A small desk key might go into a book, but a larger door key would go somewhere else. Where might a simpleton like Gregory hide a door key? She picked up each of his shoes and shook it; She looked in drawers and felt around, being careful to leave everything undisturbed. She checked her watch; was Claire just picking up a few items? She stood and turned slowly on her heel, scanning the room, questioning each item as it came into view. She went over to the nightstand and was about to open the drawer when she noticed that the lamp had one little foot off the doily, which protected the tabletop. Out of instinct, she grasped the lamp to reposition it, but then, she paused and raised it to discover the key.

Downstairs, she left the office door wide open and searched for the desk key. It did not take long; she soon had the book open and was scanning the names, dates, and amounts of money. She recognized several names. Names of men who had been active party members when she had been a member herself. There were about twelve names, which appeared on page after page; most of them were new to her.

She heard a sound and rushed to return the book, lock the desk and replace the desk key in its hiding place. She did not leave the office but simply turned her back to the door and pretended to be looking for something on one of the bookshelves.

When she sensed Claire at her back, she turned, "Do you know if Gregory has a good dictionary in the house?"

Claire stood at the doorway, looking alternatively at the doorlock and at Meagan.

"A dictionary?" Meagan said.

"Uh, yes, ma'am. There might be one in the bedroom."

Meagan lost no time in going upstairs to put the doorkey back in its place.

❧ ❧ ❧

Tom and Philip made their way to Northern Ireland separately, with Tom going first to see O'Coyle to make final arrangements before connecting again with Philip. He had arranged to meet Philip at a teashop just outside Portadown, which O'Coyle had suggested would be safe.

Tom arrived in a rented car, entered and found Philip sitting at a table in the corner. "It's all set," he said, sitting down.

"Is there a good place for me to bring Jimmy to meet you?"

"Yeah, there's a sweet shop right around the corner from Gregory's house. It's owned by Catholics; no self respecting Unionist would go near the place."

"Good. I phoned Meagan after you left; I'm to have the guest bedroom; it's at the front of the house — our signals should work"

The proprietress came over to take Tom's order. He ordered tea and a scone.

The woman left and he turned back to Philip. "Now all you have to do is get Jimmy out of the house."

Philip looked off and then back at Tom. "I'm counting on Gregory taking me for a helpless dolt."

Tom smiled. "Yeah, well, in-laws can do that."

❧ ❧ ❧

Philip arrived late, when he knew that Jimmy would be in bed. Gregory barely acknowledged his presence, and Meagan was very understanding of his fatigue.

"We'll talk in the morning," she said. "Jimmy will be delighted to see you."

She showed him to his room. "Gregory leaves early," she whispered. "We'll have a special breakfast, just the three of us."

After she left, he went to the window, raised, and lowered the shade three times.

※ ※ ※

Philip said, "I imagine that you're enjoying life a bit more now that your mother's here?"

Jimmy sat across the thick oaken table, which occupied the center of the dining room. Meagan was in the kitchen, having insisted on preparing the breakfast herself.

Jimmy shrugged his shoulders with a quizzical look. "We don't go anywhere."

Meagan came in with some eggs and toast.

Philip said, "Maybe things will improve when you get into your new school."

"I suppose," Jimmy said.

Meagan sat down and started to serve the eggs. "We certainly enjoy having Philip here, don't we, Jimmy?"

Jimmy smiled broadly and nodded.

"Has a school been selected?" Philip asked, looking at Meagan and Jimmy in turn.

"Oh, yes," Meagan said.

Jimmy nodded. "It's right nearby."

"Is that a fact?" Philip said, "Perhaps you can show it to me. I could use a stretch of the legs after yesterday."

Meagan sighed.

"We can have an ice cream while we're out," Philip said.

Jimmy smiled and looked to his mother.

"Well, I won't be able to go," she said.

"Ah, that's a pity," Philip said. "We won't be long."

For Claire's benefit, Meagan made a show of going upstairs as Jimmy and Philip got ready to go out. As soon as the door closed behind them, she heard Claire making a phone call. From a window in Jimmy's room, she watched him go out the gate with Philip; it was curious that they turned in the opposite direction from the school. She went back downstairs and feigned interest in a newspaper until she heard Gregory's car in the driveway.

"I thought that you wanted to see my school?" Jimmy said.
"I do, Jimmy, but I wanted to see if the sweet shop has a certain kind of candy. I have a friend whom I plan to visit, and I want to bring his favorite, if I can find it."
"Does your friend live in Portadown?"
"No, but not far."
Jimmy now satisfied; they strolled along, Philip with his hand resting lightly on Jimmy's shoulder.
"I saw Tom before I left," Philip said.
Jimmy looked up.
"He misses you, and so do I."
Philip bent to see if Jimmy was reacting. Jimmy nodded, but said nothing.
"We would be very happy if all of us could be back together: you, me, your mother, and Tom. What do you think?"
Jimmy shrugged and made a quick flap with his arms.
"I'm sure that your mother would rather be home."
Jimmy looked up. "I'd rather be home."
"That's good, Jimmy because Tom and I have an idea."
Jimmy waited for Philip to continue and then said, "What is it?"
"Well, it calls for a bit of bravery on your part, but Tom will explain it. We're meeting him at the sweet shop."
"Tom's *here?*"

Tom entered the small shop with large storefront windows and nodded to the woman behind the counter and glass display case. "I'm meeting someone," he said, and he sat at one of the few tables. There were no other customers until a woman came in, made a purchase and left. He ordered a pot of tea, and when he went up to the counter to get it he saw Jimmy and Philip crossing the street. He ordered another pot of tea, a glass of milk and a cookie. As soon as Jimmy entered, he went up to Tom for a strong hug.

When they sat down, Tom leaned close to Jimmy, "It's very important that we keep our voices down. Everything is a secret, okay?"

Jimmy nodded and held his milk with two hands.

"Jimmy, Philip and I are very sure that your mother does not like living here, but, of course, she won't leave without you, and your father won't let you go. Do you understand that?"

"Yes." Jimmy put down his milk and paid full attention to Tom.

"I want to take you back home so that your mother can leave and also come home."

Jimmy nodded.

"Unfortunately, we have to get you back home first."

Jimmy's mouth opened, "Mother's not coming?"

"Not with us, she's coming later."

Jimmy slumped down in his chair.

Philip said, "She won't leave until she knows that you're safely back home."

Jimmy remained in his slump, shifting his eyes back and forth between Tom and Philip.

Tom could see the little wheels turning in his head, "You know that Philip loves you, and that he wouldn't do anything to harm you, or your mom?"

Jimmy nodded, but remained pulled back in his chair.

"Your mom's not happy here," Tom said. "You know that?"

Jimmy stirred and sat up a little.

"I want you to know that I love you too. And I love your mom. I think that what Philip wants to do here is best for everyone."

Jimmy sat up, still looking a little unconvinced.

Philip leaned toward Jimmy. "Tom's worked things out so that it should all go very quickly, but it's going to be a bit scary at times, and you mustn't go unless you're prepared to see things through."

Jimmy turned to Tom.

"That's right, Jimmy. It will be a bit of an adventure — and scary at times."

The words "scary" and "adventure" seemed to capture Jimmy's imagination. Tom outlined the plan.

When he got to the part calling for Jimmy to dress up as a girl, Jimmy made a face. "A *girl?*"

"It's only for a couple of hours," Tom explained, glancing at Philip for some support.

"Yes, and Sarah and Sean will be waiting just over the border with your real clothes," Philip said.

"We're all dying to have you and your mom back," Tom said.

Jimmy smiled. "I miss Sarah; Claire never laughs."

ta ta ta

Meagan stood at the top of the stairway listening to the low murmur of voices — Claire giving Gregory a report. She strolled down the stairs. As she neared the bottom, Gregory came storming out of the kitchen.

She said, "Do you realize that I can't find a dictionary anywhere in this house?"

He looked at her as if she had just announced that the Queen of England was waiting in the garage.

"You know that I don't want Jimmy out of this house without myself, or Claire, going along."

She reached the bottom of the stairs, "Yes, and I understand your reasons, but this is just Jimmy showing Philip his new school."

Gregory winced. "How long are they gone? When will they be back?"

"They just left." She half-turned toward the stairs. "They should be back in a half hour, unless Jimmy talks Philip into an ice cream." She started up the stairs.

He shook his fist at her. "That brother of yours..."

She turned her head to gaze at him for a moment before continuing up the stairs.

A little later, she heard Gregory announce to Claire — more than loud enough for her to overhear, "I'm going out to find that clown."

🐾 🐾 🐾

Jimmy agreed to go with Tom; the two men shook hands and parted. Tom drove with great care, not wanting any kind of an incident, which might blow the whole plan. He spoke to Jimmy without looking over at him. "I've met Mrs. Foley; she's very nice. She has two boys, one younger and one older than you."

"Why aren't you going with me?"

"Well, Jimmy, there's the matter of the passports; they have to match. I don't have a ten year old daughter with the right kind of passport."

Jimmy thought about that for a moment and then asked, "I mean, why can't you come along with Mrs. Foley?"

Tom glanced over. "I might be arrested."

"*Arrested?*"

"It's nothing for you to worry about. If I don't have you with me, they can't do anything to me. And, besides, remember that Sarah and Sean will be waiting for you — *with boy's clothes* — just across the border."

"You might be arrested?"

"Jimmy, listen. Getting you and your mother home and together is the right thing to do. There won't be any problems, once it's over."

Tom pulled off the road onto a treeless, grassless plot featuring a sign for Callahan's Auto Repairs and one long wooden garage building. The building had been painted barn-red, but that was years ago. It appeared that Callahan was not doing much business these days. He stopped in front of the last bay, and the large overhead door rolled up. He drove in and found a smiling Dan O'Coyle waiting.

"I thought that you wanted to stay in the background?" Tom said, getting out of his car.

"Wouldn't want to miss the last act," O'Coyle said. "And this must be Jimmy."

He shook Jimmy's hand and led him over to a small office; Tom followed.

"This is Mrs. Foley," O'Coyle said.

A woman, who had been sitting in the corner, stood up and came forward, smiling at Jimmy. Tom noticed that she was holding a doll. She was younger than he expected, and trimmer. Her hair was dark and swept back to a barrette; she wore glasses with large lenses and steel rims. She reminded Tom of a slightly impoverished alumna from an eastern liberal arts college.

"These are your clothes, Jimmy." O'Coyle reached down for a grocery bag and handed it to Jimmy. "You can change in there." He pointed to the men's' room.

Jimmy took the bag and turned to Tom who nodded for him to go ahead.

A minute later, he stuck his head out. "Do I have to put on the underwear?"

"Yes, Jimmy, put on everything," Tom said, "but go pee before you do."

Jimmy emerged; Tom took one look and felt the blood leaving his face. Oh God, what have I done? Jimmy wore a blue dress with a small white floral print and a white collar. The collar hung loose — he had not buttoned it at the back; the dress was noticeably short, and the ties for a bow hung down behind his ankles. The embroidered white sox rumpled around his calves — one longer than the other. He still wore his own brown leather shoes and held black patent-leather shoes by their thin straps. "These are too tight," he said.

Tom glanced at O'Coyle.

Mrs. Foley stepped forward. "Come to me, Jimmy." She sat in a chair and went straight to work. She buttoned the dress, pulled it down and tied a large bow at the small of Jimmy's back. She folded the sox to even length. "Take off those shoes," she said.

She handed Jimmy's shoes to O'Coyle. "Girls often hold their shoes to avoid getting them scuffed," she said. She turned back to Jimmy. She brushed his hair and set a white hat on his head. The hat, which had a fancy fringe across the top, fit close and almost covered his ears. She brushed some hair down onto his forehead. Finally, she held him at arms length to examine her work.

Jimmy rolled his eyes and dropped his chin.

She tapped him under the chin to close his mouth and pulled him forward for a kiss. "You're a good boy," she said.

O'Coyle said that everyone should get on as quickly as possible. Mrs. Foley gave the doll to Jimmy and showed him how to hold it. Jimmy's eyes were on Tom.

"Okay, Jimmy," Tom got down on one knee, putting his arm around Jimmy. "You can do this just fine. Remember, your name is Irene until you're with Sarah." He hugged Jimmy with both arms.

Tom followed Mrs. Foley at a distance toward the border crossing at Middletown.

 ❧ ❧ ❧

From the window in the guestroom, Meagan watched as Gregory rushed through the gate and headed for the school. Perhaps, she should have gone with him for Philip's protection. But then, she thought it unlikely that Gregory would do anything to Philip with Jimmy there. How long would it be before they were back; Philip looking hurt and embarrassed? She strolled into Jimmy's room and passed the time slowly folding some of his clean clothes and tidying up his drawers.

She heard a sound and got to the window just in time to see Gregory running into the house — alone. She went downstairs.

"That dumb son of a bitch has disappeared," he yelled, to no one in particular. He spotted Meagan. "If you're up to something..." His finger jabbed the air in her direction.

She followed him into his office. Claire stood behind her in the doorway.

Gregory turned his back as he started talking into the phone. He turned back to her, slammed the phone down and said, "The RUC will find him. If he's headed for the border, I'll cut his nuts off."

Meagan said, "My god, Gregory, they've just stopped for an ice cream, or gone to the park."

Again, his finger jabbed at her, "I *looked* in the ice-cream shop, and they haven't had time to get to the park. And, I'm on to you, Meagan; I'm on to you."

She gave him a look and turned to stride out, forcing Claire to give ground. She went into the living room and sat down with a magazine, dimly aware of Claire passing the doorway with a cool expression on her face. She barely saw the pages on her lap. Where could they have gone? Philip should have known better. He should have been back by now. With the police involved, the whole thing will be very messy. She drifted on, turning pages, reading a few things, but mostly wondering how Philip could be so oblivious.

"They got him!" Gregory stood in the doorway.
She jumped up, "Is Jimmy all right?"
"*Jimmy's* not with him."
"What?"
"That's right. So guess who we're looking for now?"
Meagan stood in the middle of the room, gaping at him.

"That American fuck is going to rue the day he set foot in Northern Ireland."

Meagan moved forward to protest, "Gregory, this is all some silly mistake."

"It's a mistake all right. I'm going down to personally interview your brother."

She watched him turn and leave before she went back to sit down and stare off into space. She felt numb. What kind of craziness is this? Jimmy is *my* son. What right has anyone — anyone — even Philip to interfere? I'll get him back. I've got to. I've got to get him back.

❧ ❧ ❧

As they approached Middletown, Tom held back. He pulled off and watched as Mrs. Foley's car was stopped by the RUC — an unusual occurrence these days when the border was not even marked. He worried that someone might see him watching so he drove into a nearby parking lot. As he got out of the car, he saw Mrs. Foley drive across. Yahoo! Time to call Meagan. He drove to a phone. A woman answered — not Meagan.

He was ready. "This is Sergeant Durgin, of the RUC," he said, speaking gruffly. "I need to speak to Mrs. McDonald." He waited.

"Yes?" It was Meagan's voice, sounding anxious.

"Meagan, this is Tom. Listen carefully. I'm calling from Middletown. Jimmy's across the border with Sarah; I'm about to try to cross myself. You get out of there and get yourself home."

Silence.

"Meagan did you hear me?"

"Yes." Another pause, and then in a measured exaggerated tone, she said, "I can't believe you've done this. I cannot believe that you could be so stupid. Philip's in jail, and you have put Jimmy in danger with your wildness. I hope they catch you, and that you rot in jail."

"Meagan, please. It wasn't my idea; it was Philip's. I only helped to make it safer for Jimmy."

She hissed back at him, "Philip's idea! *Philip's* idea." She hung up.

He held the phone away from his face and stared at it. "Oh, my god!"

He waited a moment, struggling to regain control of his emotions, which hovered somewhere between anger and despair. Then, he placed two more phone calls: one to the American Embassy in Dublin, and one to Jerry Healey. He left messages at both and then drove to the border crossing.

CHAPTER EIGHTEEN

Meagan checked on Claire's whereabouts and then closed the door to make a call to Steven Mulligan, the solicitor in Belfast. She told him what had happened, "And I'm leaving to go home to Jimmy. I want you to look after Philip," she said.

"Is it wise for you to leave now?" he asked, "Jimmy's safe at home; Philip's the one that needs protection."

"There are some things I can do better from home to help Philip," she said, "I can't say what they are at present."

She hung up, opened the door and sat down to wait for Gregory.

ᐤ ᐤ ᐤ

The sergeant held onto Tom's passport and opened the door for him to get out of the car. Another officer drove his car off to the side as he followed the sergeant into a trailer-office. Inside, the linoleum floor was polished and the air smelled of cleaning solution. Tom entered what apparently was the main room; it took up most of the trailer's length. To his left, there was a closed door. To his front, there was a desk, and between that and the door on his left, a long table. Sitting at the end of the table was an RUC captain, a man in his late forties, rotund and wearing a well-trimmed full mustache. He looked every inch the typical British burgher — in uniform. Behind the desk, sat a younger

RUC lieutenant. Thin, clean, freshly pressed uniform, and an officious manner.

The lieutenant casually looked through his passport, and then gazed at him across the desk. "We love it when you Americans come here and tell us how to run the country, but snatching our children is going a bit over the top, wouldn't you agree?"

Tom looked him in the eye, but made no reply.

The lieutenant nodded at him, "Well, we don't have to deal with you here. I do hope that you haven't any plans for this evening." He motioned to the sergeant, who came over to handcuff Tom and lead him out to an armored van. The captain stood up and went through the other door.

ès ès ès

Gregory appeared in the living room doorway and did a little cha-cha dance. "We got him! We got your boyfriend. Now all we need is a witness to put them together with Jimmy. And, *that* shouldn't be too difficult."

Meagan coolly closed her magazine and got up to face him. "How nice for you. I'm going home to be with Jimmy. I only waited to tell you why you must see that no harm comes to Philip."

"You can't leave." He blocked the doorway.

"There's a copy of your little book in safe hands," she said, brushing past him. "I never would have expected some of those people to take dirty money."

He half stepped aside. "You're lying."

"Really? McFarland, Raferty, Smith. Need I go on?" She walked to the front door and picked up her suitcase.

"There's one more thing for you to think about," he said.

"And what might that be?"

"You accused me of using Jimmy. And after all, he is my own son. What about this Brogan guy? Look what *he's* doing with Jimmy. You're better off here, Meagan."

She stepped out.

❧ ❧ ❧

Tom sat on the simple hard bunk bed and scanned his small cell. It was surprisingly clean, including the toilet and sink, and modern with light gray walls and a window that looked almost ordinary. He smiled to think that he expected stone walls, dripping with moisture, heavily barred windows, and maybe a rat peering out from a little hole in the corner. He wasn't worried; how could they make a big case out of getting a kid back to his rightful home? But Meagan? That was another story. How could she be so pissed? Philip will tell her. My god, even if was my idea, how could she be so upset? She's probably home with Jimmy right now. Philip will be okay. God damn it, it *was* his idea.

He lay back and raised his forearm to shield his eyes. He must have dozed; the door opened with a clank, startling him, and he followed the guard to an office where his passport and personal articles were handed to him without a word.

"I expect transport back to my car," he said.

Another captain who had been sitting behind a desk observing, drummed the fingers of one hand on the side of his other fist and then got up to leave. Ten minutes later, a young officer came in to tell him that a car was waiting to take him to Middletown.

He drove through the night and stopped at his farm only long enough to shower and put on fresh clothes. It was still early; he knew that Meagan would be up; he drove over without calling ahead. Her car was parked near the barn. Getting out of the car, he realized that he had no clear idea of what he was going to say, only a jumble of thoughts in his head.

Sarah met him with a smile and let him into the vestibule. She went off as Jimmy appeared in the hallway. He came straight to Tom, grinning and holding up his arms as if to demonstrate that he was back to being his real self. Tom bent to hug and kiss him. Then he spotted Meagan coming down the hall.

There was no smile, no gesture of welcome or warmth. She stopped a few feet away, one hand folded over the other at her front, "Jimmy, get back and finish your breakfast," she said.

Jimmy looked sheepishly at Tom and turned to leave.

Tom stood his ground, feeling as if some kind of standoff was in the making.

He took a deep breath. "I uh — I wanted to talk about Philip — about how to help him."

She gave him one nod of her head.

"Do we have to do it here?" he asked.

Without a word, she turned and headed down the hall. He followed. When she reached the center of the living room, she turned around and faced him with her arms folded. He stood a few feet away, wondering what to do with his hands.

"Meagan, if only you'd believe me; I only got into this because Philip was going to do it anyway."

She cut him off, "Stop it, Tom. You know almost as well as I do that Philip is neither physically, nor psychologically capable of such an action. And, he would never take such a chance with Jimmy."

"Okay, okay," he said, "Why don't we just concentrate on getting him back?"

"And how do you propose to do that? He's in there without his medications. He'll be lucky to stay alive."

"I'll do that. I'll bring his medications to him."

She turned and took a few steps away from him, toward the fireplace. She turned back. "You can bring them to our solicitor in Belfast."

"Okay, I'll do it. I'll do it today."

She strode toward the living room door. "I'll bring them over to you."

He moved directly behind her. "You know Meagan, you and Jimmy might have rotted up there if we didn't do *something*."

She turned and stood glaring at him, her hands in fists at her sides, "I would have walked out of there *with Jimmy* in a matter of days, if you hadn't interfered. If you hadn't been so jealous, so deathly afraid that I would wind up sleeping with Gregory."

"Please, Meagan, please."

She turned and headed back down the hall.

He chased after her. "What makes you think that Gregory would let you go?"

She stopped to face him. "I have information to indicate that he, and some others, have been taking dirty money." She continued down the hall.

"Dirty money?" He followed her. "You mean graft?"

She stopped at the door with her arms folded, but did not look at him.

"This could help to get Philip out," he said.

"Do you think that I'm unaware of that?"

"I mean right away. If it's used in the right way."

She glanced at him to indicate that she was listening.

"I know David Taylor, the top Unionist leader; I bet he'll pull strings to keep this from coming out."

She looked away, arms crossed, drumming her fingers. After an eternity, she sighed and glared back at him. "Come back in half an hour. I'll have the medications and a list of names, dates, money."

In exactly one half-hour, they stood on the porch. She handed him a package with Mulligan's name and address. "Be sure to emphasize the importance of these getting to Philip immediately." She took a sheet of paper from an envelope and showed it to him. "This is a list that I made from memory. Gregory keeps a record — a book — in his desk. He's probably moved it, but there are people who can find these things." She folded the paper into the envelope and tapped it into his hand.

She was close to him — not touching — but close. He thought that he saw something in her eyes — a glisten. Was she on the verge of tears? What would happen if he took her in his arms? She stepped away; his interview was over.

He started down the stairs, turning to see her closing the door, "There's one other thing," he said.

The door stopped.

"You're right. I was jealous, but I would have waited."

He ran down the rest of the stairs.

❧ ❧ ❧

There were no preliminaries, no tea, no comments on the weather. David Taylor was a man of few words. "Mr. Brogan, you said that you had information of vital importance to the party. What is it?"

He smiled as he looked at Taylor, in his trim dark suit, sitting behind his desk under the halo of Queen Elizabeth's portrait. Was that the same tie he had on last time?

Tom told him about Gregory, and finished by saying, "And so, as soon as Philip is back over the border, I'll give you some information immediately." He tapped his chest to indicate that he was carrying it. "And the location of Gregory's little black book. You can confront him and keep everything from coming out."

Taylor listened without a twitch. When Tom finished, he got up and went over to look out the window. For minutes not a word was spoken. He then returned and sat back behind his desk. "Things are not done that way in this country. I have not the slightest interest in covering up for Gregory McDonald."

Tom felt his stomach begin to hurt. Philip wasn't going to get out.

After a pause, during which he gazed past Tom, he returned to the subject, "I have no interest in helping McDonald in any way at all. I would like to see him out of the party."

Tom nodded and waited for him to continue.

Taylor fixed him with his eyes. "I want you to trust me."

Tom waited.

"We need to move immediately," Taylor said. "To get the book."

Tom nodded.

"I give you my word that we'll do everything possible to secure Mr. Clark's release."

Tom paused to think, and then asked, "How long before we have him back?"

Taylor held out his hands, "A week. It might take a month."

Tom got up very slowly and took the envelope out of his pocket, "He's a sick man, Mr. Taylor. Jail could kill him."

Taylor took the envelope. "I understand."

Tom returned to the farm and called Meagan with a report on his actions. She thanked him but offered no opening for further contact. He immersed himself in activities: He called Professor Gleason at Cornell about the trees, and following his advice, he had a core sample of the soil taken and analyzed. He worked with Sean on fences and replacing some rotted boards in the barn. He slept less and less each night.

He called Jerry to talk about his report, but found himself ranting about Meagan instead, "How can she just accuse me of lying like that?"

"The woman's under enormous stress, Tom. Cut her a little slack."

"*Slack?* What about me? I came to this country for peace and quiet. I'm in a nut house. The whole island's one big nut house!"

"Listen to me, Tom. One thing I've learned in politics is never to burn your bridges. Don't do anything irreversible, okay?"

"I hear you, but she's just not being fair."

"You sound like me, complaining about Alice."

Tom laughed. "Thanks, I'll be back in touch."

Aimlessly, he wandered about the house and later onto the porch. It was getting late; he sat in a rocking chair trying to interest himself in what kind of sunset was shaping up. He heard Brid come through the door behind him.

"I went over to see Sarah today," she said.

"That's nice."

"She says that Jimmy's looking for you to take him fishing."

He nodded and put the fingers of his left hand up to rub his temple. "I did promise him. It should be simple, wouldn't you think?"

She moved in front of him and stood at the top step of the porch, her hands folded, gazing off at the darkening hills.

"Did you see his mother?" he asked.

She shook her head, without turning to him. "I could ask Sarah to bring him over?" She glanced at him. "It would be better if you spoke to his mother yourself."

"Sure."

He glanced at his watch, and she turned to go inside. He followed her in, turning into his office. He called Helene and unloaded the whole story while she tried to slow him down so that she could understand most of it.

"Dad, Dad, you're very upset, and that's understandable, but look at all Meagan's been through. And, it is *her brother* that's in jail and very sick."

"Right, she's upset too, but how can she call me a liar?"

"She had her own plan..."

"How was I supposed to know that? I came back here thinking that I'd like to marry her, but she can't be calling me a liar and possibly be in love with me."

"Dad, you're reading too much into this. It can all work out."

"Are you telling me that she can be doing all this and be in love with me at the same time? She's killing me. I'm dying here."

"Yes."

"*Yes?*"

"It makes perfect sense to me."

There was a long pause, and then she said, "Don't do, or say anything until Philip comes home."

"Great. What if he comes home in a box?"
"You better pray that he doesn't."

The next afternoon, Tom received a call from David Taylor. "You can pick up Mr. Clark at noon tomorrow at Queens Court in Belfast."

"How's his health?"

"I have no idea. I've done what I can, Mr. Brogan; it's been less than ten days."

"I appreciate that."

He packed a bag and left an hour later for Belfast.

ૐ ૐ ૐ

He waited in the large high-ceilinged room, listening to the varied clinking of heels as they resonated from the marble floor. He studied the tapestry and the ornate plaster molding along the edge of the ceiling until a door opened at the far end to reveal a uniformed guard assisting a frail and halting Philip.

He sped across the room. "Can I help?"

Philip smiled and let go of the guard to take Tom's arm. They moved slowly toward the exit.

"You look as if you could stand a good meal," Tom said.

"I doubt that I can eat much."

"Some good lamb stew. I have to fatten you up before Meagan sees you."

Philip managed a laugh and held up the small bag that he was carrying. "I've got my medicines; I'll be fine."

They ate and then drove to Armagh, where Philip wanted to stop at a friend's house. Mark, his friend, came out to the car and gave Philip a package. "I heard the news," he said. "Sounds like your ex-brother-in-law, Gregory McDonald, will be a guest of the Queen for a while."

Philip shook his hand. "Poetic," he said. "Pure poetry."

When they got to the farm, Tom wanted Philip to stay overnight before going home.

"You really do want to fatten me up, don't you?" Philip said, "I'll be better off in my own bed."

When Meagan opened the door, he could see her struggling to retain her composure. She welcomed Philip with great affection and thanked Tom, but did not invite him in.

"I'll call to see how he is." Tom said.

The door closed. He got into his car, "Damn, what a bitch!"

❧ ❧ ❧

"I'll fix you something to eat," Meagan said, "and then you can get straight to bed."

"Tom's been feeding me since I got out," Philip said.

"Trying to salve his conscience, no doubt."

She helped him to get up the stairs and into his room. She started to undo his shirt.

"I'll get that," he said, "You bring that package that I left on the side table."

She looked quizzical.

"Please," he said.

She was back a moment later. He got up to go toward the bathroom, "You open that; I'll be brushing my teeth."

When he returned she was sitting on his bed leafing through some papers. "Where did these come from?"

"I ordered them weeks ago. They were part of my plan."

"Passports, birth certificates, a drivers' license?"

"They're all forgeries, of course."

She sat staring down at the documents in her hands. She looked up at him.

"I wasn't going to die here alone, Meagan — without you and Jimmy. It was all perfectly safe, but Tom said it would take too long, and that things could go bad. He wanted to stop me."

He sat next to her on the bed with a sly grin. "Fooled everybody, didn't I?"

With her mouth half open, she put the papers on the night table, got up and moved toward the door. "You had better get some sleep."

When Philip came down for breakfast the next morning Jimmy was waiting. He ran to Philip and wrapped his arms around his waist, "I knew that you'd be home soon."

Philip patted him. "That's more than I knew myself."

He sat down and said, "Good morning" to Meagan who sat in her usual chair by the window at the other end of the table with a half-finished breakfast in front of her. She did not return his greeting.

Instead, she said, "Slept well, did you?"

He peered at her face, apparently trying to confirm something in spite of the light coming from the window at her back.

She said, "I suppose that you are noticing that I did not sleep well?"

"Well, there's nothing like a sleep in your own bed. And it's been a while for me, as you know." He reached for the teapot and poured himself a cup.

"One of the benefits of a clear conscience, no doubt?"

He reached out a long arm to pull Jimmy to his side. "We're all together. Isn't that a blessing?"

Sarah came in with Philip's breakfast and to remove Meagan's plate. Meagan set her jaw and waited for her to leave.

Then she glared at Philip. "You have no idea of what's happened, do you?"

He made a little movement with his hands and then picked up his fork and waited for her to continue.

She glanced at Jimmy who was back in his place, paying close attention. "Jimmy, I have something to discuss with Philip."

Jimmy nodded knowingly and slipped out of his chair. Philip shoved some eggs into his mouth.

She watched Jimmy leave and then turned back to Philip. "Never in my wildest dreams would I have guessed that you would be capable of such an incredibly irresponsible and outlandish scheme. You totally destroyed my own plan to threaten Gregory with the exposure of his dirty dealings. And — And you have completely ruined my chances with Tom." She bit her lip and tapped nervously on the table.

He listened to her with his eggs, unchewed, in his mouth. After a time, he chewed, swallowed his eggs and said, "Tom only did what he did out of love for you and Jimmy."

"A lot of good that does me now."

"You blamed *him?*"

"He must think me a mad woman — That it runs in the family."

"You can call him, tell him it was a mistake. Tell him that you love him."

"Ha, the expert. I'm sure that he'll believe me."

"Prove it to him; ask him to marry you."

She jumped up and almost ran out of the room. "You're a total lunatic!"

As she passed out of the room, she spotted Jimmy sitting close enough to overhear. She shriveled him with a look. When she'd stormed past, he got up, went back into the breakfast room, slid into his chair, and waited for Philip to say something.

After a pause, Philip said, "Don't I remember something about you and Tom going fishing?"

Philip made the phone call. When Tom came for Jimmy, Meagan was nowhere to be seen.

ᔧ ᔧ ᔧ

They were back a little after three that afternoon. Tom looked at the sky. "It's a good day, Jimmy, when you can catch a couple of nice fish and just beat the rain. We better get you inside." He got out of the car and ran around to the back to open the boot and get the fish out for Jimmy.

Jimmy was right there to help. Tom handed him the fish, his rod, and his tackle box. They moved toward the steps, and Tom stopped there.

"Aren't you coming in?" Jimmy asked.

Tom shook his head.

Jimmy glanced down at his fish.

"Sarah will clean them." Tom said, "But you should learn how."

Jimmy's face conveyed his disappointment. The wind picked up, and Tom cocked his head for a look at the skies, now just on the verge of giving out.

He turned back to Jimmy. "I'd like to come in and teach you how to do it, but your mother's not very happy with me these days."

"If you come in, she might ask you to marry her."

Tom really laughed at that. "And is that something you would like to see?"

Jimmy grinned and nodded. The rain started in earnest.

"Are you going to stand out in the rain, or come in and clean those fish?" It was Meagan, standing at the doorway.

Tom gauged the distance to his car and decided that he would look stupid, running for it as the rain now came roaring down. He put his hand on Jimmy's shoulder, and they both went inside.

"I'll just show him how to do it, and be on my way when it lets up," he said to her as they removed their boots, put on slippers and went into the kitchen where Sarah set them up with a knife and cutting board. Tom showed Jimmy how to clean the first fish, and then helped him with the second. They were almost finished when Jimmy's hand slipped, causing Tom to grab at the knife and cut his thumb. Frightened, Jimmy ran for Meagan. Tom rinsed the cut and accepted a clean towel from Sarah as Meagan appeared.

"Come into the bathroom," she said, "I'll put some iodine on it and a bandage."

He followed her, holding his thumb in the towel. In the bathroom, she took some things out of the cabinet and then asked to see the cut.

"It's not bad," she said. "A tight bandage should do." She picked up the bottle of iodine.

"I hate that stuff," he said, "It's going to hurt worse than the cut."

"That doesn't sound like the brave man I thought you were," she said, dabbing a generous amount of iodine on his thumb.

"Jeeeez!"

She wiped his thumb with gauze. "I've never told you that, have I?"

"Told me what?" he asked, still blinking and wincing.

"That you're a brave man. You came to Ireland, in your grief, to start a new life. You faced down the IRA. You took risks to help Philip with his cockamamie scheme." She said this while slowly wrapping his thumb with gauze and tape.

He watched her eyes and hands. "Humm." He paused. "Don't forget about being nearly foul hooked by Jimmy while we were fishing and then being stabbed."

She smiled, now just holding his hand. "I mean it, Tom. I don't know how I could have been so foolish."

"Hey, how could anyone blame you?"

She held his arm close against her chest. "I'm going to try to be like you. I'm going to take a big risk."

"A big risk?"

"Will you marry me?"

He stared at her for what seemed like a long time, and then said, "That little bugger!"

She waited, still holding onto his arm.

"Well," he said, "I'm not sure that I can accept a proposal made in a bathroom."

She began to pull away, but his arms pulled her in.

"I'm not saying 'no,'" he said. "I just need to think it over." His arms held her fast, and he pushed her head back with his own, pushing down to get his mouth on hers.

He kissed her long and hard and then said, "I suppose I could give a tentative 'yes.'"

"You had best not take too long, or there will be a *tentative* withdrawal of the offer."

He kissed her again.

"Let's go tell Philip and Jimmy," he said.

THE END